Come by Sunday

Come by Sunday

THE FABULOUS, RUINED LIFE OF
DIANA DORS

DAMON WISE

SIDGWICK & JACKSON

First published 1998 by Sidgwick & Jackson
an imprint of Macmillan Publishers Ltd
25 Eccleston Place, London SW1W 9NF
and Basingstoke

Associated companies throughout the world

ISBN 0 283 06305 X

Copyright © Damon Wise 1998

3 5 7 9 8 6 4 2

A CIP catalogue record for this book is available from
the British Library.

Typeset by SetSystems Ltd, Saffron Walden, Essex
Printed and bound in Great Britain by
Mackays of Chatham plc, Chatham, Kent

ACKNOWLEDGEMENTS

Special thanks to the following for sharing their time and correspondence: George Baker, Honor Blackman, Max Clifford, Olive Dodds, Terry Gardener, Lionel Jeffries, George Melly, Desmond Morris, Frederick Mullally, Pete Murray, Anthony Newley, James Pickles, Victor Spinetti. Thanks also to John Kelly, who introduced me to *Swingin' Dors*; Bob Monkhouse, for permission to draw on his excellent autobiography, *Crying With Laughter* (Arrow, 1994); John Waters, for his encouraging impatience; and Ian Woodward, for very generously giving me access to a most perceptive, unpublished interview transcript. The following I would like to thank for their advice, help or courtesy: Alan Brook, Mike Bailey, Mel Bradman, Valerie Braithwaite, Charlotte Burleigh, Roy Carr, Roma Court, Terri Chapman, Bal and Steph Croce, Max Décharné, Fred Dellar, Margaret Duerden, Kenneth Earle, Jim and Kate Eccleston, Alan Field, Harry Fowler, all at Gerry's Club (especially Belinda, Cathi, Michael, Alison, Pearl, Ken), Dennis Gilding, Jane Giles, Pat Hayley, Lee Hill, Geoff Holder, Margaret Hughes, Ian Johnston, James Johnston, Walter Lassally, Christopher Lee, Kate Lee, David McGillivray, Jim Masters, Mickie Meads, Stanley Meadows, Joe Mendoza, Miles, Gordon Pleasant, PJ Proby, Ann Scanlon, Paula Shutkever, Jeffrey Simmons, Sotheby's, Jill Squire, the *Stage*, Kate Suiter, David Sullivan, the *Swindon Advertiser*, Dennis Termer, the *Veteran*, Karen Walter, Michael Caborn Waterfield, Derek Whitehurst,

Acknowledgements

Jean Williams, Colin Wills, Rebekah Wood and Tommy Yeardye. Respect is also due to Geoff and Sandra Wise, Steve and Sarah Wise, Lesley Sim and Alex Sim-Wise. Finally, a standing ovation for David Godwin, whose enthusiasm is truly inspirational, and Susan Hill, who gave the best possible advice and support. This book is for Jennie and also Leo, who lived life so fast he actually overtook it.

CONTENTS

Prologue   Junk Shop Venus   1

Chapter One   Siren from Swindon   3
Chapter Two   All that Lovely Money   28
Chapter Three   The Power that Beauty Wields   52
Chapter Four   Make Yourself Expensive   73
Chapter Five   A Real Human Being   95
Chapter Six   Go Home, Diana   117
Chapter Seven   Two Tinselly Bores   138
Chapter Eight   The Former Lady Hamilton   156
Chapter Nine   Death of a Salesman   173
Chapter Ten   Come by Sunday   193
Chapter Eleven   Disappointing the Vultures   215
Chapter Twelve   Madam Tits and Lips Meets Lake the Rake   240
Chapter Thirteen   Twentieth-century Boadicea   261

Epilogue   More Trouble Than You'll Ever Know   283

Filmography   292
Selected Television Appearances   294
Discography   295
Bibliography   296

JUNK SHOP VENUS

WHEN DIANA DORS died on 4 May 1984, few really knew who they were losing. Even though her face was plastered on the front page of every tabloid and – in Britain at least – the news of her death was truly inescapable, to many people, Diana Dors meant nothing at all. She was simply *there*, and the way everybody spoke, she had *always* been there, which made her death at the tragically early age of fifty-two seem less shocking than it truly was. She was so at home with fame she made it seem positively banal, which, of course, made it seem all the more obvious and all the less remarkable that practically the entire show business aristocracy of the time should decamp to the tiny Berkshire town of Sunningdale for her funeral.

Although Diana Dors was a film star and, in her day, had them queuing round the block, at the time of her death she hadn't made a successful film for nearly thirty years. Paradoxically in the one film everybody did remember – *Yield To the Night*, a box-office flop on its release in 1956 – she had been portrayed without make-up and made shockingly plain. Somewhat insultingly, in the later years of her career she was regarded as a 'personality' and her name was used to spice up quiz and chat shows alongside the roll-call of usual mediocrities. But in her time she had been a real contender. Since the forties, in fact, when, as Diana Fluck, she announced her intention to break out of the small town of Swindon and take on Hollywood.

What dogged Diana Dors in her final years was that she never truly made it there. But she had been invited there and lived and worked in Hollywood, even after her future was ostensibly finished one overheated August night in 1956. This failure eventually brought Diana back to Britain and back down to earth, in the public's eyes. Within ten years, she was touting a half-hearted cabaret routine round the working men's clubs of Britain, within twenty she was charging money for opening hotels and village fêtes. Her moment had passed, her era gone, but Diana Dors carried on so single-mindedly that when she died, few did their mathematics. By 1984, Diana's only serious rivals from the glamour-conscious 1950s had been dead for years – Marilyn Monroe in 1964, Jayne Mansfield in 1967. Many of her peers from the British film industry were long-forgotten, if they even survived at all. Nowadays, her films rarely show up on television, even in the dutifully nostalgic Sunday afternoon slot.

Diana Dors wrote several books – five in all, including two autobiographies – but she was so close to her times that she couldn't see herself clearly enough to know exactly what she'd achieved. *Swingin' Dors*, her first collection of memoirs, was published in 1960, when she was just twenty-eight, and its appearance provoked a storm of outrage. The cover showed Diana pouting seductively over her left shoulder, showing a daring expanse of thigh; a banner quote screamed, 'I've been a naughty girl!', and it flew off the shelves. Today, few even know of its existence. As a life story, it's unfinished. Some of it, she freely admitted, wasn't true. If Diana had followed her peers to an early grave it would be a thousand times more collectable; as it is, *Swingin' Dors* turns up more regularly in second-hand shops, not book stores or collectors' fairs.

Our siren from Swindon became our junk shop Venus. What went wrong?

Chapter One

SIREN FROM SWINDON

ALBERT EDWARD SIDNEY FLUCK wasn't there the night his first and only daughter was born. In fact, he was out quite a lot in those days and his wife often worried. At thirty-eight, Bert was not a well man, but he didn't like a fuss and he hid his illness from anyone who didn't need to know about it – which was almost everyone. Bert suffered from a serious heart complaint, a souvenir of the First World War, which he discovered was potentially fatal when he tried to cash his disability pension to put aside money for his child. His request was refused on medical grounds, and Bert calculated that he had roughly less than twelve years to live. When he went to see his doctor, he was told to give up smoking, drinking, going to the theatre or concerts and playing the piano, in case it might 'stir his emotions'. Bert didn't change his routine – he changed his doctor.

He led a very full social life indeed – playing piano down at the Swindon Empire, helping out at the local Working Men's Club – and 23 October 1931, clashed heavily with his bookings. While his wife, Winifred Maud Mary, suffered terrible labour pains in the tiny Haven Nursing Home just a few hundred yards from their house in Marlborough Road, Bert was addressing a meeting of the area's Masonic Lodge, his first as Worshipful Master.

The birth was not easy; Mary was in labour for a week, and when Diana Mary finally made her appearance her infant body was almost black, leading doctors to believe her mother had miscarried. Mary was forty-two, a hazardous age for pregnancy, and her condition took priority. Diana was taken to another room and revived while nurses worked to prevent Mary dying.

Perhaps not surprisingly, Diana always felt closer to her mother. Her father, she always thought, seemed cold and resentful, and it was only in later life that she pieced together his background. Bert's heart complaint was a souvenir of the malaria he had contracted while stationed in India during the First World War. Until his illness he'd been even more active, playing football every Sunday for nearly ten years, and a popular fixture at dances. An officer with the Royal Warwickshire Regiment, Bert turned heads with his 'tache and wry smile and he was never without a partner. He especially loved waltzing – the 'dreamy' kind, as he called it – and though he played the piano himself Bert was never one for the clatter of 'boogie-woogie'.

He met Mary during the war, while she was working in Swindon as one of the country's first postwomen and enjoying the attention. She was originally from Wales and moved to the area with her husband William Padget and his family, looking to find work. When war broke out, William enlisted for service and was subsequently killed in action, leaving his young wife a widow. Bert first spotted her at the post office where she worked and, typically for Bert, he thought her beautiful and smartly dressed – even his compliments were regimental.

Courtship was hard under wartime conditions, but Bert and Mary finally married on 9 March 1918. They 'honeymooned' at an army convalescent home in the Isle of Wight, where Bert was sent to recover from his injuries, making the most of things by playing the piano while Mary sang. Soon after leaving the service, Bert went to work as a clerk for the railway, then the biggest employer in the area, rising to become, much later, Second-in-charge of the Statistical Section Regional Accounts Department.

Theirs was a solid, if unspectacular marriage, making it all the more surprising when, after thirteen years, Mary became pregnant. There was, however, a curious twist to the story. Before Diana was born, Bert and Mary had a great friendship with a Swindon man named Gerry Lack, a frequent visitor to Marlborough Road who, for a short while, went everywhere with the Flucks – dances, parties – they even bought a car between the three of them. Gerry's visits mysteriously stopped soon after Diana was born, although he was present at Diana's christening on 13 December 1931, when he and Diana's aunts, Gwen (from her father's side), and Kit (from her mother's) became her godparents. Diana became very close to Aunt Kit and, as she grew older, Kit would feed her scandalous tidbits which soon added up in her precocious mind. Gerry was her real father, Kit told Diana, and he'd dropped Mary almost as soon as she was born – certainly, he was never seen at Marlborough Road after the christening.

In her teenage years, Diana thought this was the missing piece of the jigsaw, the perfect explanation for her father's remoteness and, more importantly, a legitimate reason to reject him and his staid, conservative values. Seeing Gerry's picture certainly seemed like finding the smoking gun – his wide, artless smile next to Bert's military stiff upper lip.

She grew up thinking her father was a mug, that the subject was never mentioned because he simply didn't know. In her memoirs, Diana called him naive, but her puzzling psychology only suggests naivety on her own part – if she wasn't Bert's child, didn't that explain his apparent coldness? The case for Gerry Lack was clearly very strong, but Kit liked to gossip, and Bert's family thought it was simply jealousy – Kit was unmarried and had no children, and this, they believed, was simply a nasty device to ruin her sister's home life. More importantly, the very idea of a Gerry Lack fed Diana's boredom and resentment as a teenager, enabling her to transfer all her frustration onto the only man she thought could ever stop her doing what she wanted – after all, he wasn't even her real father.

But even as a little girl, Diana soon sorted out the differences between her parents through her grandparents. Bert's mother, Catherine Fluck, she hated from the outset. Born Catherine Carter to a Gloucestershire farmer, one of many children, for a short time she was a seamstress's model. Diana grew to hate her reminiscences: how elegant she was with her eighteen-inch waist. Her first husband died and she remarried when Bert was a young boy, this time to a widower with five children of his own.

Catherine's second husband, Albert, was a tartar and his values were Victorian in the extreme. Bert's sister, Gwen, was conceived just before an enormous row and, when Catherine broke the news, Albert refused to speak to her for the whole nine months. Gwen was never a happy child and went on to live a dour, Spartan lifestyle, joining the Salvation Army as an adult; Diana later thought Gwen's unhappiness was the reason why, although she was never an alcoholic, Catherine kept bottles of the stuff secreted around the house.

Diana called her Grandma With The Teapots, on account of her prim collection of chinaware and hated visiting on a Sunday afternoon. Catherine was part of the small-town conservatism Diana despised; in her autobiography, *Dors by Diana*, written in 1981, she described how 'those boring, dreary Sunday evening teas gave birth to my loathing of Sunday, with its closed shops and everyone sitting around doing nothing interesting within the sound of church bells. To this day, I cannot hear church bells on a Sunday without being reminded of that time in my life.'

Mary's mother was another story. Georgina Dors, another farmer's daughter, hailed from Somerset, one of eight children. She was married to an Elijah Payne at sixteen and together they had four children, although the youngest, Melinda, died of pneumonia when she was only two years old. Then, at the age of twenty, Georgina did something extraordinary – she eloped with her brother-in-law, James, and with no money or prospects took her family to live in Wales. Georgina and James were never married, but lived as man and wife. Georgina's family disowned her.

They muddled through for a while, living hand to mouth, and Georgina gave birth to another three children, all boys. As money grew tighter, she began taking in washing from the local manor; before long, Mary was sent there to work as a maid, and it was there she first met William Padget, then working as a groom. After they married, Mary moved with him to Swindon. William enlisted and so, too, did one of Mary's brothers from her mother's first marriage, trusting Georgina and James to look after his young fiancée while he was gone. Within weeks, James and the girl had disappeared together, leaving Georgina alone in her cottage in Llanthry-thidd. Although she cursed him in his absence, Georgina still loved the old bounder, and when he died she marshalled his sons to the funeral. 'Whatever he did, he was still your father,' she insisted.

Georgina lived alone in her small cottage, with a little hen-run out the back and a near-feral cat whose affections were not easy to buy. Diana loved visiting the old woman – Grandma With The Chick-Chicks – and thought her stories incredibly romantic. Georgina loved life, and she certainly loved men, and it seemed to Diana there was nothing wrong in that.

If Bert Fluck wasn't a doting father in the way Diana wanted, he tried hard to be a good parent, even though it was established early on that he and Diana would never see eye to eye. Mary, on the other hand, adored Diana, perhaps a little too much. Diana correctly judged both parents' weaknesses – Bert's was Mary, Mary's was Diana – and moved quickly to exploit them. More often than not, she got what she wanted and, with Mary on her side, it seemed inconceivable that her father could stand in her way.

All things considered, Diana's was a very comfortable childhood, and Swindon fared surprisingly well throughout the thirties. For some areas of the country these were very difficult times, especially for industrial centres in the northwest and north-east – the calamitous run on Wall Street which had begun on 24 October 1929, sent shockwaves through every major world economy. Britain's manufacturing industries were underfunded and overstretched as it was, but the sudden worldwide slump hit its coal mines, steelworks and shipyards hard, leading to mass unemployment which reached a figure of over two million, where it hovered for most of the decade. Early in 1931, the prime minister Ramsay MacDonald had presented a package of radical cuts to his Labour party cabinet, but their hesitance forced drastic measures and MacDonald resigned on 23 August. The following day, after discussions with King George V, he announced the formation of a new, all-party National Government, working closely with his rivals the Conservatives, led by Stanley Baldwin, and the Liberals. Baldwin succeeded MacDonald as prime minister when the Conservatives took the lead in the election of 1935, but it was Neville Chamberlain – who took over from Baldwin two years later – who had the biggest effect on the face of society in the thirties.

Pioneering what perhaps may be described as a domestic revolution, Chamberlain advocated investment in housing, transport and consumer goods, which was good news for middle- and lower middle-class lifestyles – and good for Swindon. Prior to 1835, Swindon had primarily been a low-population, agricultural-based town and although there had been attempts before that time to connect the merchants of Bristol with the city of London, they had failed. A canal linking the river Avon with the Thames, for example, was not successful. So the arrival of the Great Western Railway, under the supervision of Isambard Kingdom Brunel, which provided a vital link in Britain's transport and shipping system, made Swindon a pivotal junction in the fast-growing rail system. By 1842, it was a fully operative railway town, with a whole village for the workers – the New Town – which wasn't fully integrated with Swindon Old Town until 1900.

The Flucks lived in the Old Town, in a smart modern semi which was built under the new drive to encourage private housing and was considered very posh indeed. The joke ran that on Marlborough Road they came out in fur coats to scrub their doorsteps.

Mary spent a lot of time with Diana, and that time was often spent at the cinema – from the age of three, Diana was taken regularly, up to four times a week. Sound had not long been introduced and, as the studio system became established, Hollywood was entering its baroque period, which Diana found captivating – it soon became the most important thing in her life. Aunt Kit would find Diana in her mother's room, parading around in Mary's dresses and shoes, and the child would frown when she entered the room. She hated to be disturbed.

School was just a distraction, and during her time at Selwood House in Bath Road she was never a star pupil. Miss Ruth and Miss Daisy Cockey, the two prim, grey-haired sisters who ran the school, found Diana exasperating, doodling film stars' names in the margins of her exercise books, looking determinedly into thin air with the arrogant manner of a child who knows her time is being wasted. The Cockeys came from a terribly decent family – three rear

9

admirals and a long-dead uncle who had served with Nelson – and schooling was the family business, handed down by their mother, who used to run a very exclusive school in Frome. The Cockeys moved to Swindon in 1890, taking up residence at the three-storey house in Bath Road where up to forty private pupils paid for tuition in French, algebra and tennis, with extra lessons available for a fee. Bath Road's young ladies were expected to be tidy and demure and were at best, if the Cockeys were being honest with themselves, being educated to become intelligent housewives. The Second World War was still some way in the distance and, among the middle classes, working women were something of a novelty, if not a total vulgarity. The school's young men, meanwhile, could probably look forward to a white-collar post with the Great Western Railway, which perhaps explains why the Cockey sisters held Diana's father in such high regard and why the very thought of her bullish, defensive mother was enough to make their bone-china teacups rattle in their matching saucers.

Diana's troubles began when she developed a lazy eye and was prescribed glasses with a little black pad over the right lens. The pad was an insult and a hindrance to her budding life of glamour. Even as a child, Diana knew the value of flirting, a fact that first struck her when she went to a friend's birthday party at the age of five and the boys paid her a lot of attention. She knew she held some form of power over them, even if she didn't know quite what it was. She felt humiliated by the pad and tore it off as soon as she was out of school. Diana played it up to her mother, and to restore her flagging confidence Mary took her to the hairdresser's, where her hair was curled into a fashionable Shirley Temple perm. Bert was furious. It reminded him of the time, just a few years previously, when Mary had had her own waist-length, almost pre-Raphaelite tresses trimmed to a mannish twenties bob. 'You ruined your own hair,' he stormed, 'now you're going to do the same with hers.'

Bert sensed he was losing his grip on his daughter, and he was right. Mary became her co-conspirator and was easy to lead astray – she didn't take much persuading to keep Diana off school and take her to the movies instead. The only part of her education Diana seemed to enjoy were the elocution lessons she took after hours at school. Mary had really only wanted her daughter to lose the Swindon dialect, a soft West Country burr that reflected the counties around it, but Diana seized on the chance to perform, winning first prize two years running, in 1943 and 1944, for her recitals at the Cheltenham Arts Festival, which made news in the local paper.

It was with some horror that she discovered her father's plans for her. Bert's idea of 'a good job' was being a secretary, and he seemed inordinately keen to see her married off, preferably to 'some decent sort of chap.' She was only seven years old, but she could feel herself being measured up for a life she didn't want; a life at odds with the life she saw in the movies, which was what she *did* want for herself. The following year, Diana raised eyebrows during an English class at Selwood House with an essay entitled 'What I would like to be when I grow up'. What she would have liked didn't come into it; Diana was going to be a film star, with a big house, a swimming pool and a cream telephone. Why on earth she should want a cream telephone even Diana couldn't say. It was just the movies. It was just glamorous. It was her birthright.

Unsurprisingly, Diana was quite excited about the prospect of war. For one thing, she thought, it might break the boredom and, God, she hated to be bored. Bert entertained the troops down at the local army base and he often took Diana with him. If an act dropped out, or if there was time, Diana would take the stage, tap-dancing wildly and singing 'Ma, I Miss Your Apple Pie' in a warbled homage to Shirley Temple. Bert took her down to the Working Men's Club, too, where she danced on the tables and Bert's cheerfully indulgent friends applauded.

In her innocence, Diana immediately assumed she was on her way to stardom – after all, Shirley Temple had made her first feature film at the age of four. She became obsessed with the story that sixteen-year-old Lana Turner was discovered in a drug store, drinking an ice-cream soda. This set the clock ticking. She had to be discovered, but how? Would she be in McIlroy's department store, drinking tea with her mother? She doubted it. Her first ever attempt to break into show business hadn't been too inspired – as a little girl she'd laid a little note inside the top of the dustbin saying who she was, where she lived, that she could sing, dance and act, and could anyone out there help her break into the film business?

The most immediate repercussion of the war was that it threatened to put a temporary end to the Flucks' annual holiday at Weston-super-Mare, where they took a couple of rooms every July at Meadow Villas in Orchard Street, a rooming house run by Bessie Hacker, a woman in her mid-sixties. Diana called her Auntie Bessie and danced on her little front lawn; the landlady thought the Flucks a charming and respectable family. They'd stayed there every year since Diana was two, and their regularity was a measure of Bert's attitude to life. 'I like to do the same things,' he told a reporter in a rare interview some ten years later. Small wonder that Diana began to crave excitement, never thinking of the consequences.

Bert was a staid, reliable and popular man – a perfect gentleman. Always smart, the word in those days was dapper, and his height — he was very tall — gave him an air of authority. Good-looking, too — everyone who didn't believe the rumours about Gerry Lack thought that was where Diana's looks came from. Throughout her life, Diana consistently chose the men her friends and family warned her away from — the men who showed her the most exciting time, made her life complicated and exhilarating. Maybe Diana's problems began here, and her difficulties with her marriages and love affairs come down to the first man in her life, her father. Diana made it her aim in life to escape from Swindon which she did soon enough, but she could never quite escape the shadow of her father, a man whose stern, responsible memory she tried to erase with a string of some of the most unsuitable lovers.

Diana's first real brush with sex came at an early age. In the first years of the war, the Flucks finally abandoned Weston-super-Mare after their annual visit found the place sandbagged and unwelcoming in the face of a possible attack. Grandma Dors had died in 1937, so in 1942 the family decided to visit Diana's great-uncle Joe, Georgina's brother, at his farm in the Mendips. Another of Georgina's brothers, Arthur, was also there, a scruffy little character, always swigging at a cider bottle and showing an unseemly interest in his niece's ten-year-old daughter. One afternoon Arthur followed Diana into the stables, slipped a drunken arm around her and tried to kiss her. Diana pushed him away, startled and repulsed by the alcoholic fumes from his stale breath, and Arthur fell to the floor in an inebriated heap. She ran inside, scared and confused — there was clearly something wrong, but she had no idea what. She never told her parents.

Back in Swindon, the war seemed at a comfortably safe remove although German bombers were beginning to strike further and further inland blitzing Coventry and London in the spring of 1941. As a vital connection in Britain's railway network, Swindon was certainly a strategic target, but evacuation was never deemed necessary and the town emerged relatively unscathed. Diana was more concerned with the economic impact of the war and the effect of rationing, which began in January 1940 as a measure to conserve supplies of such basic provisions as sugar and butter and which grew to include most everyday items. Some rationing, of clothes, for example, continued for several years after the war ended and was not formally abandoned until 1949. To join the war effort, families were encouraged to dig over their gardens and plant vegetables, which the Flucks did willingly, leaving Diana to play in the street outside.

If there was any danger, Diana didn't feel it, and 1941 passed like any fondly remembered childhood year. That summer she developed a crush on Michael Wheeler, a young boy of her age, whose house backed onto the Flucks'.

Michael was a choirboy at the local church and, much to Bert's pleasure, Diana started going every week. Diana had never liked dolls, in fact it was almost a mild phobia – she thought them lifeless and fragile and she hated the ease with which they came apart. Instead, she pushed Michael's little sister Roma round in a doll's pram. 'My baby!' she'd beam as they thundered up and down Marlborough Road.

Bert had always wanted Diana to learn the piano, which she did – though never very well, since she lied to her tutor about the amount of practice she was doing and tried everything she could to avoid going to classes. Nevertheless, she enjoyed playing for an audience and when Michael and Roma came round they played families, Diana sitting at the piano stool, hammering out 'The Merry, Merry Pipes of Pan' and bellowing along with more gusto than talent.

Sadly, Michael fell victim to Diana's first brush with sophistication. For her twelfth birthday, she had a party, and all her friends came. Michael wore short trousers – the only boy to do so – and Diana was mortified. Not only did her crush fade but she gave him the cold shoulder for many weeks after. It was, she decided much, much later, the most shallow thing she'd ever done in her life, and despite the events of the next two decades, this one silly, almost insignificant, childhood affair grew to haunt her. Ironically, it also became one of her few publicized regrets.

After Michael, Diana really began to develop as a woman. She became impatient with childhood and began to wear make-up and dress much older than her age, tossing her golden hair and strutting like a movie queen.

In the spring of 1944, in anticipation of D-Day, when the Allied Forces landed in Normandy, Swindon planned to play host to a stream of incoming GIs, a prospect which thrilled Diana, especially when she heard that Bert and Mary planned to take in a lodger. As luck would have it, the Flucks' GI was from California, but when Diana pumped him for information about the latest news from Hollywood she was terribly disappointed – he came from a little farming town, miles out of state.

Diana enjoyed the attention from GI Joe. 'Veronica Lake!' they'd call out as she clattered down the street in the highest heels that rationing would allow and, though she pretended to be annoyed by the comparison, she was secretly flattered that they recognized her as Swindon's little piece of Hollywood. One afternoon she was walking through the town centre with her mother when a military service van drove past, with a crowd of GIs in the back. They called out to Mary and her daughter with the details of an upcoming dance at the Army camp, and begged them to go. Mary wasn't exactly keen, but Diana kept plugging away until she got what she wanted. The dance was, to her at least, a very glamorous affair. Wearing her best red dress, prized nylon stockings and heels, with her hair curled into the most adult style, Diana told everyone she was seventeen and, give or take a few years, they seemed to believe her. After that night, Mary took her every week, although her agenda was somewhat different. She didn't seem at all concerned that her newly teenaged daughter was dressed up far beyond her years, flirting with much older men whose thoughts were far from Bert's idea of decent. While Diana danced, Mary buttered up the camp cook, taking home a bagful of all-important provisions.

At just thirteen, Diana's life became an exaggerated teenage limbo. On her way to school, she kept her head down in case any of her Saturday night dancing partners found out their seventeen-year-old sweetheart was an under-age schoolgirl. At the same time, she was becoming far too adult for her friends, as she realized when her attempts to teach them to jive at dancing class proved dismally beyond their comprehension.

But her visits to the GI camp had not gone unnoticed at school, especially by one of the teachers who was dating a GI herself but was seldom invited to their parties and was especially hurt to hear that one of her pupils had a much higher social profile than herself. The end came when Diana was whisked away to a small gathering by a Military Policeman, whom Bert knew and approved of, and returned home the worse for wear after a night drinking pineapple juice – also rationed and therefore exotic – laced with gin. Mary guessed and carefully manoeuvred Bert out of Diana's path until the following day. The teacher in question was less forgiving – not for any moral reasons, thought Diana – simply out of jealousy.

Diana had several classroom confrontations with this teacher who finally reached the end of her tether and swore at her – 'Oh, hell!'. Diana promptly went home and told her mother. The next day, Mary stormed down to Selwood House and complained about this shocking language. It wasn't such a bad thing to say, Miss Daisy thought, and the teacher denied it, but Mary put up a fearsome fight. Whatever was said that day was never made clear by anyone concerned, but obviously the issue was Diana herself, not a loose-tongued mistress. The Cockeys kept a professional attitude to Diana's achievements – they thought she was a talented and intelligent young girl, but clearly they disapproved of her lifestyle and were somewhat aghast to see that Mary was actively encouraging it. The end result was that Diana was summarily dismissed and Mary fetched her from class immediately. The Cockeys never said publicly that Diana was expelled. In their rather quaint, genteel way, they preferred to say that Mary Fluck was asked to withdraw her daughter but, either way, Diana didn't really care.

She was sent to a less respectable school, which closed down not long after. Bert was mortified to find that scripture was not on the curriculum. He made a dignified appeal to the Cockeys to take Diana back, but they regretfully turned down his request, and Diana stayed where she was. Miss Ruth and Miss Daisy never talked about the affair and reluctantly faced the *Daily Sketch* in 1956 with a plea for no publicity. 'We want the children to be proud of the school,' said Miss Daisy. 'We try to give them a nice background. We are not eager that they should boast, "Ours is the school Diana Dors went to."'

At her new school, Diana met a boy from the school over the road – seventeen-year-old Desmond Morris, future writer and anthropologist, whose mother ran a tobacconist's in Victoria Road. Desmond's family owned a small plot of land with its own lake and a little island, which he paddled Diana over to in a rowing boat. His island encampment consisted of a tent, a gramophone and a pile of swing records, and Diana taught him to jitterbug. Later, when Desmond got his first car they took long trips into the Wiltshire countryside.

Towards the end of the war, Desmond was conscripted and, through a devious chain of subterfuge, mailed her a Valentine card via a friend in Devizes. Diana went to enormous trouble to track down the culprit and within the week had sent off a letter on notepaper headed with her address and phone number.

February 20th 1945

Dear Desmond,

Thank you so much for your letter, I hope you don't think I'm too previous in writing but I expect you like getting letters as much as I do.

My last letter was rather small, but writing for the first time I didn't know quite what to write about, anyway I'll make up for it in this (I hope).

I was only wondering the other day if there were any 'school bands' about . . . I should love to hear that band of yours, what do you play by the way Mr Morrison [sic]? I imagine you with a trumpet — crazy isn't it, I probably shot a long way out then, what does your friend Mike play? Or isn't he in it? Oh & by the way I don't suppose you do, but if you ever wanted some-one to do a bit of vocal work, I'd love to — that is, if you'd have me, true I got up and sang 'You Are My Sunshine' at the party but that wasn't much, & please don't judge me by it, I used to do a lot of troop shows though at the beginning of the war.

I would very much like you to introduce me to your friend Mike, that card was beautifully done, & anyway I'm sure if you had done it you would have done it just as well, thank Mike very much and tell him I like the sound of his name, it sounds rather sweet — don't forget now, at all costs if he is like you he'll be very charming. Now I'll tell you something you've probably been trying to fathom out, how I got to know your address — think once more — ten minute pause — what! You still haven't guessed, O.K. here goes. Whoever posted that letter

*did a very silly thing, you see even if he did post it in Devizes so as
to try & cleverly conceal the fact that it was Dourtsea he forgot one
thing, & that was using an economy label, now by carefully tearing it
off I discovered the address, & I did think of writing an anonymous
letter to the headmaster calling him all the sweetest names I could
think of, you know darling, sweetheart, honey, sugar, angel pie etc
but I thought twice, & I thought writing to you would be quite
sufficient, besides he might worry his head off about [it], and sit
daydreaming in class — now don't you tell him all that, will you!*

*Well! Desmond I've kind of run out of words[.] I hope sincerely
this hasn't bored you, but I tried my best, at the letter I mean, (not
the writing), I know its terrible, perhaps when I get to know you
better I'll be able to write in clearer words. Cheerio for now, & please
write if you can, soon.*
Love, Diana

PS Keep up that band, it must be really *good.*

Though they kept in touch, Diana was distracted from
Desmond by the events of that summer. Holidaying again in
Weston-super-Mare, Mary contrived to lose Bert for the
afternoon while Diana prepared for a Modern Venus beauty
contest organized for the Forces by *Soldier* magazine. On her
entry form Diana claimed she was seventeen, and there were
few to doubt her as she sashayed along the catwalk, like a
teenage Betty Grable, in a red and white bathing suit with
matching red heels. Mary watched proudly as Diana took
third place and went into the final, where she came third
again. Comedian Jack Watson was on both panels and voted
for her on both occasions. 'This girl's got something,' he
decided. 'I'm damned if I know what it is, but she certainly
has it.'

Part of Diana's prize was a photo shoot for *Soldier*, and
since her picture had already been taken by the local press,
Bert had to be told. He wasn't happy, but by that time it
seemed his opinion ceased to count in the Fluck household,

so Bert let it go. If he put his foot down, he reasoned, it would only get worse. He really, truly believed she'd grow out of it.

Diana, for her part, was most pleased when her bathing suit snap appeared in the *Advertiser*, and it was spotted almost immediately by a professor of art at a nearby college – Shrivenham American University, SAU for short – which had been set up specially for the GI population. The professor offered her a couple of life-modelling slots, which became more and more regular and paid her a guinea an hour. When she mentioned her show business aspirations, they found a place for her on the college drama course, and Diana made several campus appearances in plays like *Death Takes a Holiday* and *One Week In Paris*. She even performed with the camp band, singing 'It Had to Be You' for a local radio broadcast.

Soon, Diana had a GI boyfriend, an eighteen–year-old Texan, whose mother sent over parcels of clothing and make-up that couldn't be bought in dowdy wartime Britain. She thought herself quite the modern miss, walking in her thick wedge heels and, she told herself, with her star qualities being recognized on campus, discovery could not be far away. But deep down, despite her surface sophistication, Diana was still the little girl who thought that a note in the dustbin could get her into the movies, and still believed movie stars really were just 'found', ready made, in drug stores and cafés. It was this naivety that kept her going, and it was this naivety which made her almost immune to failure – it simply wasn't possible.

Diana finally lost her patience with her father and began investigating drama schools with a view to persuading her parents to allow her to attend the London Academy of Music and Dramatic Art (LAMDA) for one day a week. Again, Mary backed her in what was really quite an unreasonable demand for a fourteen-year-old – but Mary always backed her daughter in her battle to conquer childhood, to the extent that many thought the way she supported Diana's tarting and primping was quite unseemly. But with Mary behind her, half the battle was won, and Bert gracefully gave way on condition that Diana take a teaching course and that some day she would return to teach elocution in Swindon. Diana quickly agreed, although she had no intention of honouring the promise.

Diana's quest for stardom was accelerated when a GI photographer she sometimes modelled for said he knew a man who could get her into the movies. He wrote out a letter of introduction, and that November Mary escorted Diana down to a west London studio, where they met up with a man by the name of Keating on the set of a film called *This Man is Mine*, starring Glynis Johns. It transpired that Keating was merely an assistant director on the film, but he was helpful enough and he arranged a meeting with a casting director by the name of Weston-Drury. Diana turned up for the interview in her finest imported clothing, and the poor man suffered palpitations when she announced that she was only fourteen. Time was running out, she barked, and what was he going to do about it?

Weston-Drury took Diana's details, promising to let her know. Bert relented to Diana's constant nagging and allowed her to move to London full-time. She travelled down on the 5 a.m. train with Wrens and workmen, and the heavy pall of high-tar smoke in the carriages put her off the habit for life, no matter how appealing Bette Davis made it seem. Alighting at Paddington on her way to the YWCA at Kensington, where she would live for the next three years, she couldn't miss the huge hoarding advertising Drene shampoo, one of the few products involved in a pioneering drive by Gains-borough Studios to create a British star system. Gainsborough had established a repertory cast of players and encouraged them to advertise in a bid to create a Hollywood-style glamour and sweep away the music-hall image of thirties

British film. Diana didn't yet know it, but she was soon to advertise Drene herself.

College was a challenge which Diana took surprisingly seriously. She enjoyed the life, dashing between classes with a volume of Shakespeare in one hand, taking bites at a sardine sandwich, then heading off to student get-togethers, swapping notes and getting pleasantly drunk on cooking sherry. Her favourite class was self-expression, held every Friday by a woman called Frieda; not surprisingly, these periods became known as 'Frieda's Fridays'. During a role-play exercise in one of her classes, they needed someone to play a vamp and Diana was immediately put forward. She'd never thought about it before but she tried out for the role and acquitted herself so well that Frieda affectionately called her The Vamp forever after. 'Some girls are born vamps,' Diana mused later. 'I studied to be one.'

At the end of the first year she passed her end of term examinations with little difficulty. One of the examiners that year was casting director Eric L'Epine Smith, and he talked to Diana about a role in a film he was working on, a George King production of a West End stage play, *The Shop at Sly Corner*. The story concerned a crooked antiques dealer, Heiss, who pays off a young blackmailer, Arch, to protect his innocent daughter. Diana was to play, as she put it in her own words, 'the spiv's tarty girlfriend.'

The Academy baulked when L'Epine Smith made the suggestion, but he wasn't daunted by her age and arranged a meeting with King. Diana told him she was seventeen, which suited him, and she tested well, so she got the part, for the then massive sum of £8 a day. Diana had a lot of fun, relishing the part of Archie's slack-jawed, flighty mistress. As Archie prepared to put £1,000 down on a new sports car, she whined, 'But Archie, I want some new earrings!' He snapped back, 'Shaddap! You 'ad a bracelet last month, di'n'yer?' More telling was a scene in which Heiss visited Archie's flat and stared forlornly at a treasured painting, of sentimental value only, that Archie had taken from him. Diana, lounging about, waiting for her man to return – if he would ever return – said blankly, 'Well, I can't see anything in it, myself. No glamour.' She paused. 'I love glamour – don't you?'

Mid-way through shooting, L'Epine Smith's conscience got the better of him and he tried to tell King her real age. King wouldn't hear of it, and neither would the crew. By this time, Diana's cleavage was taking on its legendary proportions, and a rumour swept the technical crew that she was keeping it up with gaffer tape.

During Diana's time at LAMDA she also acquired an agent. Unbeknownst to her, Keating had also forwarded her details to an agency, run by a man named Gordon Harbord who was looking for talent to send to a film then in casting. He put her forward for Powell and Pressburger's *Black Narcissus*, offending Diana's glamorous sensibility when he revealed that the part – in Diana's words 'a coloured girl' – would require heavy make-up. She lost the part to Jean Simmons anyway, and the Swindon prima donna was swiftly cut down to size. After *The Shop at Sly Corner*, however, this was forgotten and Diana signed a contract with Harbord.

The first thing to do was change her name; any fool could see that Fluck had to go. Diana Carroll and Diana Scarlett were suggested, but finally they settled for her grandmother's family name, Dors. Much later, stories circulated that her new name had caused a lot of consternation in Swindon, and that a local parson, or some such minor dignitary, had made a stir when he welcomed her to a local fête. Remembering she'd changed her name and suddenly realizing he'd forgotten its replacement, he haplessly introduced her as 'Diana Fl . . . oh, fuck!' In other versions of the story, equally unverifiable, she materialized as 'Diana Clunt' . . .

Her first engagement as Diana Dors was, ironically, a small, uncredited part in the now-dated, patronizing Sydney Box/Gainsborough production *Holiday Camp* (1947) with Jack Warner. Diana wasn't exactly screen tested, Harbord simply asked if she could jitterbug and she said she could, so that was it − £10 a day. The finished product suggests he should have asked whether she was any good at it.

The next film was a much bigger deal. It was called *Dancing with Crime* (1947) and featured Richard Attenborough in one of his first starring roles. The story involved a murder enquiry at a dance hall, where Diana's character, Annette, worked as a hostess. Diana's lines were few but classic. One was, 'Look out, Fi, here they come,' when the doors were opened. Then there was the scene in which she first encountered the detective (Gary Marsh) on a deserted dance floor. 'Are you dancing?' she had to ask. 'No,' he replied, 'It's just the way I walk.'

Filming took place at Southall Studios in February 1947, but this was not the dream factory of Hollywood myth. London had suffered terribly in the war, and as well as a general mood of gloom − briefly dispelled in November with the state wedding of the future Queen Elizabeth II and Philip Mountbatten − there were still acute shortages. Bread had been rationed in 1946, and the workforce had been so unimpressed with prime minister Winston Churchill's home affairs policy that they had voted him out of office, with a humiliating majority, in July 1945. One of the aftershocks was a series of power strikes, which meant that heating was not provided at Southall Studios and that the streets were in near total darkness as Diana made her way to the studio, getting up at 5 a.m. for a 7 a.m. start.

Stationed at a barracks far from home, Desmond Morris

had kept an eye on Diana's progress and wrote to her at Southall, asking for some pin-up shots. She sent back an array of signed black and white prints, which made Morris extremely popular at camp, and a hand-written, four-page letter. 'It's too cold!' she complained. 'We are busy on the dance hall sequences and I have to wear an off the shoulder and backless evening gown that they have so sweetly provided – why couldn't they have got something with sleeves this weather? Don't answer that . . .' The letter was signed 'Diana – DORS, if you don't mind!'

Because of the film's theme, there were a lot of extras on *Dancing with Crime*. The casting director in particular was deeply unpopular, always throwing people off the set and getting new dancers in to replace them; the turnover was terrific. Somehow Terry Gardener stayed the course. He was in his twenties, an Ilford born song and dance man, and much more worldly than Diana. Terry was also gay, and she found that fascinating, eavesdropping on him and his dancing partner, a very chic nightclub hostess. 'Look at this kid!' he'd tease. 'She's listening to everything we're saying, trying to find out what life's all about!'

The sheltered Swindon girl didn't know what to make of Terry's sexuality, but she wasn't really sure about anything in those days. She just knew he was different and found him great fun, as did most of the women that worked in films. Gays were generally accepted by sophisticated people, and there were plenty in the film world. Although Diana wasn't sophisticated, she wasn't dumb either, and she and Terry forged a friendship that lasted through to the sixties. She wasn't what you'd call a beautiful kid, he thought, but with that personality, that beautiful, thick head of hair and those lovely eyes, the star quality was there without any doubt at all. When she went home between shoots, Diana would drive her mother wild with his outrageous stories: 'That Terry said . . .'

Mary rose to the bait. 'I'd love to get my hands on him,' she'd wail. 'How dare that fairy talk like that in front of you!'

A few months later, Diana was summoned to Gainsborough for a Sydney Box production, *Streets Paved with Water*, a drama starring Maxwell Reed and set on the Grand Union Canal. Box had hired two screenwriters fresh from the forces, Joe Mendoza and Anthony Skene, and to get round the union he hired them as trainee directors. Joe and Tony handled the screen tests, and Diana tested very well for the second female lead. She was to play Jane Hylton's bad sister, inevitably trying to break up her sister's romance with co-star Andrew Crawford, and she was looking forward to it. 'Give me the tough roles,' she told the press, 'something I can get my teeth into.'

The weekend after the audition, Diana went home to visit her parents, who Sydney Box had contacted with a tempting offer. Now working for Gainsborough, and hence under contract to the Rank Organisation, Box had brought with him a project he'd begun at Riverside Studios in December 1945. He called it The Company of Youth, though it later became known disparagingly as the Rank Charm School, a title that still causes its former alumni to shudder. Originally, the aim was to build up a simple retinue of talent and keep them busy in ever-changing roles, but under Rank the scheme became a more ambitious attempt to build a British Hollywood.

But Diana wasn't thinking about that when she accepted Box's invitation to join. She was still thinking about money. She'd start with Rank at £10 a week, on a sliding scale that would take her to a projected £300 a week after ten years. She was elated, although the fine print – which of course she thought didn't apply to her – pointed out that Rank could renegotiate the contract every year. And in her naivety, she didn't realize that more established actresses, particularly those with more stage experience, like Honor Blackman, were already earning £100 a week. But none of this mattered. Diana was on her way, and *Streets Paved with Water* was her passport.

Unfortunately, the film fell through at the last minute. Box had recently had a critical success with *The Brothers*, a striking film about a Skye orphan, shot in a distinctive semi-documentary style, and he wanted that film's cameraman to be the cinematographer on *Streets*. The film's backers wanted their own man, and an almighty political battle broke out as the film went into production. Mendoza and Skene were directing, and shot at least two weeks of footage around Paddington, but each day's footage was coming back out of focus and underexposed. Box suspected sabotage and closed down the production; it was never completed.

Diana, however, was in no mood for looking back. She'd always wanted to be a movie star, and this was where it started.

Chapter Two

ALL THAT LOVELY MONEY

J. ARTHUR RANK was considered something of a joke when he first started dabbling in the film industry. The unassuming son of Yorkshire flour millionaire Joe Rank, he inherited two of his father's most striking features – his money and his religion. Joe Rank was a devout Methodist and ran his flour mills accordingly, closing them for twenty-four hours every weekend to observe the sabbath. He believed in the work ethic and ran his business with a curiously un-Christian sensibility, finally making his fortune when cheap American wheat flooded the market by importing wheat even more cheaply from the British colonies, and ruthlessly putting his competitors out of work.

Joe Rank developed his spiritual life in tandem with his work and ploughed his profits into Methodism, building chapels for his workforce in a bid to convert them. J. Arthur Rank did not share his father's bullishness but he shared his evangelism, and it was this that brought him, in 1933, to the Religious Film Society, a moral watchdog movement set up to counteract what they saw as the decadent and dangerous mainstream. Rank soon moved on from such humble beginnings, with deals and mergers that by 1946 made him the biggest film producer in Britain and a definite match for the American studios. Not only did Rank own the means to produce, distribute and exhibit his own British-made movies, he also benefited from a surge in cinema admissions that reached an all-time high – 1,635 million that year – with

British films proving more popular than their American rivals.

Rank was in a very strong position, conducting high-profile talks with the major American studios which looked set to put British film-making on the map, until the Labour government stepped in the following year. Trying to gather together a workable budget to offset the huge debts brought on by the war, the Chancellor of the Exchequer, Hugh Dalton, slapped hefty taxes on American imports, with a staggering 75 per cent levy on American films which horrified American distributors. Rank was mortified, 'All my work was thrown away,' he moaned. 'My two months in America went for nowt.' But, with unexpected help from the government, he made plans the following year to turn the situation round. Since he owned vital shares in the Odeon cinema chain, he could, with the board's consent, bring its programming in line with his own needs. In his mind, an American freeze meant a boom-time for British films, with reissued classics like *Brief Encounter* and Alexander Korda's bank-busting epics – his 1939 imperial war drama *The Four Feathers*, or the quirky Arabian Nights adventure *The Thief of Baghdad* (1940) – sharing screenspace with new productions. Rank sincerely believed Britain had the talent, and his producers went out looking for it.

The Company of Youth was housed at Highbury Studios, one of Rank's minor properties in Islington. By the time Diana arrived there in 1947, aged fifteen, the operation had ceased to be Sydney Box's training operation and had taken on an altogether more cosmetic purpose under the aegis of Rank's new production advisor, Earl St John.

St John was an American from Baton Rouge, Louisiana; a bit showy – half façade – but well-liked by the people he worked with. Then in his mid-fifties, St John was passionate about film and very much wanted Britain to compete on an equal footing with the Americans. As he saw it, the Company of Youth was an opportunity to build a British Hollywood, a chance to scrub away the drab realism of the war years and replace it with a new and glamorous star system.

The Company of Youth was nominally headed up by David Henley, although the day-to-day running was more closely overseen by his assistant, Olive Dodds, who was thirty-five and former secretary to John Davis – 'JD' – Rank's chief accountant and right-hand man. JD wasn't particularly old but he seemed that way because he held the purse strings. Olive thought him a tartar, but she got on all right with him. Then again, it was her job to get on with him. You had to – or else. You had to do things his way, then turn it around so you got what *you* really wanted.

JD also wanted a British Hollywood, but for a more practical reason – films made so much money there. They were extremely popular even in Britain at that time and JD saw the potential. For one thing, you could take entertainment to the people. Of course, there were provincial theatres, but the country's biggest acting talent was seldom seen outside the West End. With cinema, however, the biggest international stars could be made accessible to the smallest hick towns.

The Rank Organisation saw the cinema largely as an offshoot of the stage – Olive combed the West End theatres on expenses looking for good, presentable players – and this thinking shaped their output. The late forties and early fifties saw a lot of stage adaptations go into production. Those commissioned for the screen tended to be wooden, over-scripted three-act melodramas built on the most clumsy moral lessons, warning against the dangers of crime, drink, gambling, loose women or, if in doubt, the lot.

Rank had plenty of established and respected actors on its books, like Alec Guinness and Flora Robson, and was well stocked with character actors, but it began a search to find what it thought would be more cinematic talent — beautiful girls and matinée-idol leading men. If the face was right, hair, clothing and even teeth could be worked on, and a full-time wardrobe mistress, Julie Harris, was employed — although the clothes remained strictly the property of Rank.

In an overhang from the class-conscious war years, the Rank Organisation was still a little embarrassed and awkward about its product. Films, in the immediate post-war period, were still quite vulgar and their audiences were different. Personality was more important than talent in those days, and certainly it was no good being talented without any personality if you wanted to become a star. A good example of Rank's methodology was Anthony Steel, who left the army a major before signing with the company. Steel was in his twenties, distinguished and good-looking, and thanks to army training, had an excellent speaking voice, but he was by no means a great actor. That was no problem, thought Olive. He was all right for films.

Highbury Studios, in reality, were nothing so grand; Rank used them as glorified schoolrooms, where future stars were given acting, elocution and, most famously, deportment classes. Although some of the School's charges were inexperienced — Constance Smith came via a beauty pageant, and Susan Shaw, when she was plain Patsy Sloots, was previously a clerical trainee at the Ministry of Information, earning £5 a week — others, like Diana, Pete Murray and Belinda Lee, spotted after a year at RADA, felt their time was being wasted. And with much of the raw, untutored talent that came its way, it was the Company that was really wasting its time.

Singing classes were held by Helen Goss, acting classes by Molly Terraine, a former silent movie actress whose pupils feared and, in some cases, actively disliked her. Molly didn't give much leeway, and Olive frequently found herself having to mediate. Kay Kendall, who once climbed out of a window to avoid a photo session with Rank photographer Cornell Lucas, always saw Olive as a sort of agony aunt, and Anthony Steel went to see her when Molly's lessons were becoming too much. 'Olive, I can't stand it,' he'd say, 'I *cannot* go back.' 'Tony, it isn't for long,' she'd remind him. 'Just stick it out a bit.'

Although Olive and Molly did their best, Rank's producers were under no obligation to use in-house talent, and actors like Christopher Lee quickly became bored. The Company wasn't being used in a constructive way at all – and it's potential stars weren't getting any film-making experience either in small roles or even as extras – and just as actors resented not being used, so Rank's producers resented having their stars 'discovered' for them.

If the Company's players weren't being kept busy at Highbury, they were often being sent out to any one of a number of personal appearances organized by Rank's PR chief, Theo Cowan. These could be anything from village fêtes, to fashion shows and premieres, and sometimes a hall would be booked simply on the understanding that some of Rank's stars would be attending – a sort of fan-club event based on the belief that, if the people there really were stars, they must deserve fans. The public was surprisingly deferential to people in show business, and anyone in film or theatre was treated with a certain amount of awe.

One of Diana's first bookings was a *Sunday Pictorial* garden party down at Morden Hall. The paper had one every year, for the film industry, and thousands were invited, including the stars. Political editor Frederick Mullally was obliged to go, even though there was nothing in it for him, but he did meet Dors. She hadn't made a picture for Rank then but she was striking – the first thing he noticed was that luscious lower lip. Her breasts, of course, went without saying, but her brashness and her openness were striking, too. A lot of these

Charm School girls just stood there pouting, he thought, putting on little sultry acts that didn't fool anybody, but not Diana. She handled that kind of event very well indeed.

Pete Murray was scouted for Rank while still at RADA, although his acting ambitions were swiftly forgotten in 1950 when he went abroad to join Radio Luxembourg, at that time the only serious competitor to the BBC, as an announcer and DJ. On Theo Cowan's instruction, Murray found himself doing some of the most 'damn stupid' things. Murray's own view was that they were all far too young – stars were generally more mature, not young nineteen- or twenty-year-olds plucked straight out of college or off the street. He thought about it sometimes, but not that much. He didn't really care – he was being paid – but he couldn't help thinking the whole thing a total waste of time. It was what they all thought, on the few occasions that it was talked about, but everyone was too wrapped up in their own careers to really be bothered.

Like many others, Murray began to look at his training another way – if this wasn't helping him break into film, it could help him in other professions, and he realized this the night he compèred his first fashion show in Exeter, after a film premiere. It was the first time he'd ever done anything like it, he'd only ever been an actor before. He enjoyed all that, it was good fun, but this time he was working without a script, without direction, and he was getting a lot of laughs. These things were probably a waste of time from everybody else's point of view, he thought, but they were far more useful than acting, what little there was of it.

The Company was a shock to Diana – especially Molly. Diana considered herself very modern, and so she was, for the times. Molly, on the other hand, was very old-fashioned indeed. Again, Olive found herself in the middle. 'Oh, darling!' Diana would beg, looking up from under the bang of hair that tumbled over her right eye.

When she started with Rank, Diana's hair wasn't quite the full platinum it subsequently became, but she was still decidedly and positively blonde. Her hair was almost solid from the amount of lacquer she used on it, and Olive recognized the style as Veronica Lake's, which was very outré as far as she was concerned.

One occasion always stood out in Olive's mind – the day she took a cab through Knightsbridge and saw Diana walking along in the high heat of summer, wearing the shortest of shorts, shirt tied at the waist, everything showing. That, in itself, wasn't really done, not by Mr Rank's young ladies anyway, but Diana was carrying a brown paper bag, eating cherries and spitting the stones into the gutter. Anyone could have photographed her. It would have been a scandal! It was so, well . . . common was the word they used in those days. She stopped the cab and whisked Diana inside. The girl was a doll, thought Olive, but she had to learn to behave in public. 'Diana, you can't *do* that,' she said and, not for the last time came the inevitable reply, 'Oh, darling.'

Like many at Rank, Olive looked down a little at Diana, but she admired her honesty. Diana liked the money and made no bones about it; she was an open book. 'I want what I want, what I want I can get' seemed to be her motto, with the best good humour in the world. Olive saw her as the opposite side of the scale to Virginia McKenna, Rank's classic English rose. Virginia was a lady, as it were. Diana wasn't a lady, didn't intend to be a lady and wouldn't have *wanted* to be a lady in the first place.

During her time with Rank, Diana was still living at the YWCA but often went home at weekends to visit her parents. The local press had made a big fuss about *The Shop at Sly Corner* early in the summer, and she'd already become a Swindon legend. Mary enjoyed the attention, probably more than her daughter, when she swanned into McIlroy's every morning, up the wide staircase to the coffee shop, with her friend, Mrs Butler. She was something of a local celebrity herself, and the girls on the shopfloor couldn't resist making comments out of earshot. After all, Mary Fluck was a *big* woman. 'You know the old saying, "You should look at the mother before you marry the daughter."' They'd fall about. 'She looks like she's smiling at you over the top of a pile of crumpets!'

Jean Williams was working in the fabric department the day Mary brought Diana in to buy material for her first trouser suit. She couldn't have blue because Susan Shaw's was blue, so they settled for pale green. Diana was with her friend Christine, who always wanted to be a model, but she didn't have the same spark of life. Charisma was an overused word in those days, thought Jean – very few people had what Diana had. She wasn't absolutely what you'd call beautiful, but her skin was perfect, her lips were as full as you could get in days before collagen, and her hair was truly golden – naturally golden. She had very small eyes, Jean noticed, but they twinkled with mischief. Christine was a more classic beauty, but next to Diana she was a mannequin. She never said a word, and no one was holding their breath waiting.

When the Flucks left and the salesgirls broke for tea, the claws came out. There was a lot of bitchiness about Diana, but it was the breathless, silly kind that came with a bit of excitement. 'You lot are all just jealous,' Jean said. And they were. Diana was in the movies and the fan magazines and she was starting to make the newspapers, but in every other respect she was exactly the same as them. They weren't jealous of her looks or her talent, they were jealous of that intense force that was driving her.

★

When filming began on *Oliver Twist*, Diana's first film for Rank, rumours that she had started 'fooling around' with boys quickly went round the production. Diana felt uneasy and couldn't help thinking the crew would leeringly discuss her when she wasn't there, imagining a sex life far beyond her fifteen years. It even reached the top: director David Lean asked to see her privately, on the pretext of running through her lines, and she was shocked when the great man of British cinema made what was surely a clumsy pass at her. Diana's veneer of sophistication suddenly dropped at moments like this; she was truly flustered. Lean cut short their 'rehearsal' and it was never mentioned again.

Diana played the part of Charlotte, the frumpy, shrewish maid who makes Oliver's life a misery while he stays with the undertaker, Sowerberry. It was the first of her celebrated non-glamour roles, and she was glad of the chance to actually act for a change — after all, she'd been to LAMDA. Rank was very pleased with her performance, and issued a cheerfully unflattering press biography to that effect.

> With nothing but her considerable dramatic powers to help her, Diana endows Charlotte with all the baseness which Dickens wrote into the character. Whereas in her previous parts she always played glamorous girls of today, for this part she has to shed all her glamour and adopt the dowdy costumes and make-up that coincide with the drawings Cruickshank made to the specifications of Charles Dickens.

Other young actresses might have drawn the line at playing such a part so early in their career, but to Diana it was all the same thing. Ugly, beautiful — either way she was only playing a part, and she really didn't connect with the nymphette image that was being constructed for her. 'Diana Dors' was fast becoming a part like any other, and the gap between truth and reality became clear that summer when Rank's publicity department introduced Diana to the press with a fake news story claiming that she'd already had eight offers of marriage. From whom, it declined to specify.

For the rest of 1947 Diana ran through a string of undistinguished films – with titles like *Goodtime Girl*, *My Sister and I*, including *Penny and the Pownall Case*, a cheap little mystery for which they made her cut her hair. Diana complained, but Molly Terraine wasn't having it. 'You don't see Olivier complaining,' she snapped. Lord Olivier was at that time filming *Hamlet*, for Rank and Two Cities, at Denham Studios and wore his hair in a bizarre blond pageboy cut. No, thought Diana, but there's a bit of a difference.

While screen-testing with director Robert Siodmak for a film that subsequently never went into production, Diana met a man who changed her life. Guy Rolfe was an actor, much older than her, in his early thirties, who immediately saw the contradictions in this busty, sexy teenager. They dated for a while, Rolfe wining and dining her then delivering her, on time, to the YWCA. Diana thought he was quite the gentleman. In reality, Rolfe was married. His wife was an actress, too, and after dropping Diana off he drove to pick her up from the stage door. Even when she realized this it didn't stop her seeing him, but there was a sadness about their relationship, such as it was, that she couldn't define. Eventually, it deteriorated to such an extent that Diana sat alone on her sixteenth birthday waiting for him to call. They later made up, to a degree, but it all finished a few weeks later when Diana walked into a restaurant where Rolfe was seated with his wife. He blanked her. She left immediately, and that was the end of it.

Diana's misery was compounded soon after when a producer asked to see her in private. She thought it was her big break when in actual fact it was a tasteless ploy to persuade her to remove her clothes – the producer said he had heard she was putting on weight, and he wanted to see for himself whether Rank's investment would be causing them trouble. Luckily for Diana, a suspicious secretary interrupted the 'meeting' and the subject of her 'puppy fat' was dropped.

Early the following year, Diana went back to Swindon where she met up with Desmond Morris again, who was back on leave. He took her to a lavish party on the outskirts of town. She stayed over, and in the small hours of the morning one of the guests crawled into her bed. He pawed at her unsuccessfully for a few minutes before they both fell fast asleep. The following day, she raised the subject with Mary. 'Do you think it's possible to spend a night in bed with a man,' she asked carefully, 'and not have sex with him?' Mary was emphatic. 'Of course not!'

She returned to London as confused about sex as she was when she left. She was in this strange limbo, with the body of a mature woman and the bewildered mind of an unworldly sixteen-year-old girl. Before her sixteenth birthday, Sydney Box had placed a strict embargo on her and warned that anyone taking advantage would be in serious danger – now that security had gone. She was alone with the wolves, but was that a good thing or a bad thing? She didn't know.

Diana's next film was *Here Come the Huggetts*, which saw Jack Warner and Kathleen Harrison reprising their two-dimensional, cor-blimey-mum roles from *Holiday Camp*, as Joe and Ethel Huggett. The Huggetts weren't too popular with the critics, but audiences liked them and Rank produced two more spin-offs over the next few years, adding Jane Hylton, Susan Shaw and Petula Clark as their three daughters. Diana played their flighty cousin who led them astray, borrowing the car without permission and crashing it, but always learning her lesson in the final reel. One day on the set, director Ken Annakin nudged Diana and pointed to Shaw who was rehearsing a scene. 'Susan's going to be an enormous star,' he whispered. 'She's got the lot – talent, looks and common sense. She'll go a long way.' Diana nodded, but deep down she was crushed. What about me? she thought. It was a typical starlet reaction.

Shortly after, however, an interesting role came up for Diana on a new Gainsborough film being shot in Halifax, *A Boy, a Girl and a Bike*. Honor Blackman and John McCallum were taking the leads, but Diana had a good role and it finally gave her a chance to meet her co-star, Anthony Newley. Of course, they had both been in *Oliver Twist* – Newley played the Artful Dodger – but all Diana's scenes were set in a dingy coffin shop and she had hardly met anyone during her few days' work. That was the trouble with making movies; when she thought about it, it was actually quite a dull and lonely occupation.

Diana and Newley travelled up to Halifax by train, with the film's producer, Ralph Keene chaperoning them. Although Tony had a lot of rough edges, Diana found him good company. They were the same age, for a start, but Newley's background was drastically different. He was illegitimate, for one thing, and had been raised single-handedly by his mother, when his father left them, in a tiny house in Hackney, in London's East End. At fourteen Newley turned up at a Fleet Street newspaper, hoping to find work. While he was waiting for an interview, he saw an advert in that day's paper advertising for child actors and decided he'd have a go at that instead. Surprisingly, he passed the audition. Here he was, only fourteen being paid twelve quid a week to pull faces – it was a fortune! When he was later put under contract, Newley found the whole Rank thing extraordinary. He was a kid out of the gutter, a working-class boy with absolutely no social manners at all, but Diana, he thought, already had a social veneer. She seemed much older than her years, and her LAMDA training made him feel something of a fraud. Newley was raw, undisciplined, and his memory was famously terrible, sometimes needing over twenty takes to get a scene right. Directors seethed, but what could they do? They were paying adult wages to teenage kids, a fatal combination.

Newley fell head over heels for Dors. In lust, that is. After all, he was sixteen and a virgin. But Diana, he thought, never really seemed to know he was there. She was electric, magnetic, and other women couldn't compete in the same room, but he was just an awkward, tongue-tied teenage boy. For her part, Diana had noticed Newley, but she'd been distracted by a slightly older boy, Gil, who was working with the technicians. Diana had been talking to some of the cast and crew, voicing her fears and misapprehensions about sex, and she was secretly pleased with the advice she was getting. There was none of her mother's Victorian doom-mongering and even less of Bert's fatherly get-yourself-a-decent-chap advice. It wasn't a big deal at all, it seemed. Which was all the encouragement she needed.

Gil was her first target. They'd been flirting for weeks, but finally they made love in her hotel room, one night during filming. Gil wasn't a virgin and seemed disappointed that Diana was. Diana was disappointed full stop, but they tried again over the next couple of weeks until she finally convinced herself that sex was as good as it was cracked up to be. When filming finished, she knew it would be the end – there'd be no more creeping into the YWCA at night, much less with a man – so on her return to London, Diana set about looking for a flat. She found one, taking a six-month lease on a tiny service flat just off the King's Road, Chelsea, not far from World's End. Her parents were furious, but what could they do? Diana talked them round and they grudgingly accepted.

In the meantime, Diana's hopes of converting her little

flat into a love nest were dashed that summer. She dated Gil, on and off, but she knew he wasn't interested any more and found herself spending more and more time with Newley. She hadn't noticed how much he'd fallen for her, in fact, he had to spell it out. She was surprised and flattered. When she thought about it, she was interested, too. They met frequently, drinking in fashionable private drinking clubs and turning heads at Rank's occasional cocktail parties. One in particular found them sitting under the grand piano with their drinks, French-kissing furiously. It was a very formal occasion, and some of Rank's most prestigious names were present – Alec Guinness was there, sitting by the door – so it was hardly the time or the place. They knew they were behaving badly and they knew it had been noted. But they were young – just kids – and didn't really care.

Newley finally lost his virginity to Diana one night in a small Chelsea bedsit, lent to them for the occasion by a French-Oriental gentleman of their acquaintance. They kept the lights low, and Charles Trenier's 'La Mer' played endlessly on the radiogram – French music was considered very chic at that time. It was the perfect setting for seduction, but Newley was disappointed and he was sure Diana was disappointed, too – in him. If she was, she didn't mention it.

Newley became a regular visitor at the flat, and for his seventeenth birthday Diana even let him host a party there while she was out filming. He immediately drew up a motley guest list, some successful actors, some unsuccessful actors and some friends from his other, less glamorous life. Of course, the party went straight out of control, making enough noise to provoke neighbours into calling the police. The guests scattered and even Newley was so terrified he ran away from his own party.

★

Christmas 1947 was very strange for Diana. She was invited to her Aunt Kit's in Cardiff, and couldn't help feeling like some kind of circus act laid on for curious relatives. She was back in Chelsea before the year was out, spending New Year's Eve with friends in the Cross Keys pub. That night she met a man who made a big impression on her; his name was Michael Caborn-Waterfield – Kim to his friends.

Kim was a year older than Diana. He came originally from Bedfordshire and his was a happy childhood, he said, tainted only by the fact that his parents divorced when he was nine. His father, Vivian, was a company director, but when war broke out he was posted abroad with the air force, and Kim and his brother John went with him. In 1943, they returned to England and moved to Surrey with their mother, Yvonne. Kim soon tired of school and, two years later, ran away to work at a racing stables near Winchester. He hoped to become a professional jockey, but a broken wrist put paid to that idea and at sixteen he moved to London, living a hand-to-mouth existence as an actor before snaring a job as an office boy to producer-director Alexander Korda, then a legend in the British film industry. He supplemented his earnings with acting roles, and had a small part in Peter Ustinov's *Vice Versa*, although he was never serious about his craft and the parts he was offered were usually dependent on his horse-riding ability. By the time he met Diana he was earning up to £75 a week and she was fascinated by what he later called 'my careless attitude to life'.

Kim was a big wheel with the Chelsea set, which was rather racy in those days. Chelsea had yet to become the fashion centre it was in the sixties. There were no boutiques at that time and the area was epitomized by well-heeled young men of indeterminate means who vroomed up and down the main street in open-top Bentleys, usually with women of indeterminate virtue.

Diana and Kim circled for a while, each trying to impress

the other, until finally the ice broke. Much later, Kim told the *Pictorial*: 'Once I asked Diana which car she would like to go out in with me. She laughed and said, "Is there a choice?" I led her up to the window of my flat and pointed to five cars parked below. They were: an old Rolls, a Hudson Terraplane, an Isotta Fraschini, a Delahaye and a Railton. None had cost me more than £300. Diana's reaction was typical. "Let's drive in the lot," she said. So I tied all five cars together with ropes. We got in the first one and drove off, towing the others. But we didn't get far. The police stopped me and ordered me to untie the cars.'

They saw a lot of each other after that. In the meantime, she was still wondering what to do about Newley and went to see him at his flat in South Kensington. Newley knew something was up and, although he had company, he behaved quite badly towards her. Diana didn't stay long. That night Newley woke with a start. It was 3 a.m. and suddenly his bedside light flicked on. A man stood over him – was it Kim? – and picked up his alarm clock. He snorted to himself, 'Even his clock is wrong' – and punched Newley in the face. They fought all over Newley's apartment, neither really wanting to fight but neither wanting to back down, and it degenerated into a slanging match, both of them sweating and panting, 'You be careful', 'No, you be careful', 'And you'd better . . .'

But when he thought about it, Newley realized he hadn't been anything more than a distraction to her. Diana had a predilection for men who were . . . exciting, to put it mildly, and if it was between him and Kim, he knew who'd win. As it was, Diana did choose Kim, and they started dating.

Kim lived with his friend Patrick Beresford in a big flat in St John's Wood and Diana would take her studio double, Oona, along for double dates. Kim really knew how to live well, despite his age, and Diana marvelled at his sophistication when they toured the bars and clubs of the West End – he seemed to know every licensee in town. Kim, likewise, marvelled at her stamina: even when she began work in December 1948 on her next film, *Diamond City*, they'd fall into bed at 4 a.m. or later, and at 6 a.m. she'd be up and waiting for the studio car. He didn't know how she did it. But Diana was cutting it very fine.

The film itself was something of an oddity, a British-made western set in South Africa. She played a saloon girl alongside Honor Blackman, whom she'd enjoyed working with on *A Boy, a Girl and a Bike*. Diana took the role after Jean Kent refused, which was, thought Honor, typical Rank. Actresses like herself were put under contract, and then if a big star like Phyllis Calvert or Valerie Hobson said they wouldn't play a certain part, Rank would take a name at random and throw one of the others into it. This was why they played unlikely characters on occasion; it wasn't a question of trying to build up a career, they were just being used. There was no planning at all.

Even though Diana was being driven to Denham studio for a 6.30 a.m. call, dozing all the way after just a couple of hours' sleep, only the make-up artist really knew the worst of it, smoothing out the dark circles under her eyes with a layer of foundation. For the cast, though, Diana was maddening at that time of the morning, singing, dancing and cracking risqué jokes. Honor liked Diana, she was very direct. Too direct sometimes, especially where sex was concerned, because even though she was slightly older, Honor felt positively innocent by comparison. She thought some of Diana's friends were quite alarming, too – loud and flashy, not her line of country. They didn't meet socially at all.

Filming went without a hitch, and Diana even weathered a barrage of ribald teasing from director David MacDonald. The fight scenes, however, didn't go so well. Honor was brought up with a brother and knew how to box and fight clean. Diana had no such compunction and started pulling at

Honor's hair – they both had wigs on but it still hurt like hell. Honor fought back angrily and the two women tussled around the set in their ridiculous saloon-girl corsets, bosoms falling out of their dresses.

When filming wrapped, Diana collapsed in her dressing room. The producers were told it was flu, and she was sent home to her parents' house in Swindon, where they heard for the first time about her new friend Kim and his particular lifestyle. Bert couldn't understand it – the man had to be a crook. It simply wasn't possible to live, and live so well, without a trade. Mary was similarly outraged, but for different reasons, seeing Kim as the louche London scoundrel they hoped Diana would never meet.

She returned to London with their complaints ringing in her ears. Worse than that, she had to find somewhere new to live, since her Chelsea landlord refused to renew her lease after countless late-night drinking parties. She took a flat in Jermyn Street, a tight, airless place with no natural lighting, and pretty soon Kim had moved in with her, having been unable to keep up the rent on his own place. They didn't have much money – most of it was Diana's, from her Rank contract – but they managed to get by, eating potatoes and onions and spending what little they had on going out.

In the afternoons, they usually went to S&F Grill on Denman Street near Piccadilly. The S&F was a coffee bar – in the years following the war, coffee was still something of a luxury. It was a popular haunt for actors, producers and young hopefuls, and at that time Kim was something of a hopeful himself, in show business at least. He imagined, very grandly, that the 'S&F' stood for 'Stage and Film' and was amused many years later to find out they were actually the manager's initials: Stan Freeman.

They were very good to their customers there; people would stay for four or five hours at a stretch with the same empty cup in front of them, and whenever a big name came in – like Robert Morley – a hush would fall over the room. The waitresses were pretty and surprisingly tolerant of what could be a boisterous crowd, especially when Digby Wolfe and Harry Fowler were around. Pete Murray went nearly every day, even though he was living at home in Osterley, and often stayed over at Diana's place. But as for Newley, it wasn't really on his circuit and he thought it a bit too posh for the likes of him. He was still somewhat confused by his schizophrenic lifestyle, running with his actor friends and the Chelsea pack-rats one minute then jumping on the bus to visit his old mum the next.

When the S&F closed at 6 p.m. they'd adjourn to The White Room, a little drinking club across the road, or a friend's place, where they'd drink till late. Harry Fowler would entertain them with wisecracks, stories and pranks that were far beyond the pale. He'd pick up the phone, dial a number at random and say he was calling from Radio Luxembourg, which was then the only alternative to the BBC. Fowler would pretend to be a game-show host, and his victims always fell for it.

'For five pounds, can you tell me . . .'

Everyone else in the room pissed themselves with laughter, too afraid to laugh out loud in case they ruined it.

'Do you want to gamble or stick with what you've got?'

How far would he dare to take it?

'Now . . . for a free holiday – yes, that's right a free holiday – can you tell me . . . who . . . fucked . . . Henry The Eighth?'

Click.

Fowler hated pomposity and took any opportunity to deflate egos. Diana was the same, and she loved to hear his stories. A few years later, he made a film with Sir Donald Wolfit, a bombastic British actor who was knighted in 1957 for his lurid Shakespearean turns. On one occasion when Wolfit's dresser came into the room and asked, 'Anything I can do for you, Don?' Wolfit fixed him with an imperious glare. 'If you wish to address me, you address me as *Sir Donald.*' The dresser backed out, kowtowing. 'I'm very sorry, Sir Donald, if there's anything I can do for you . . .' In the meantime, Fowler had heard the whole thing. 'Morning, Don,' he'd yell, sauntering onto the set. 'How's it going, Don?' It was relentless. 'Ere, Don.' 'Got the time, Don?' 'Do me a favour, Don . . .'

Diana had found the fast crowd, and she loved it. She hated to be bored, more than anything, and so her immediate court – and she did tend to attract acolytes – was the one that could keep her most amused. Every night it was 'Who shall we put on?' 'Who shall we make fun of?' There was definitely an element of spite, but Diana was not interested in cruelty. She was a woman who craved – as did her immediate circle – something to happen all the time. The drinking, the smoking . . . 'Let's pull his trousers down!' . . . It was a very fast life and you had to be tough to hang onto it.

Diana's parents were still not impressed by Kim so when they came to visit, she arranged for them to meet his mother, Yvonne. Yvonne was young, in her late thirties, urbane, sophisticated and a great socialite. It was the worst approach Diana could have taken; Yvonne was clearly part of what Bert called Diana's 'rackety' lifestyle, and now he knew where Kim got it from. How did these people make a living? He steadfastly refused to meet him.

The flat was getting on Diana's nerves and Kim hated it, too, so they moved to Earl's Court, where they took a flat not far from the YWCA. The rent was still tight but they managed. Diana received a crate of Drene every month for modelling their shampoo, which they sold on to a local Polish chemist for half the price. Diana's salary was up to

£20 a week by now, but she wasn't doing anything for it, so Rank decided to send her out with a touring company. She wasn't looking forward to it anyway, but when she found she was pregnant, shortly after her eighteenth birthday, she was terrified. Fortunately, the play was a flop and didn't last the haul to the West End, as the producer had hoped. Back in London, Diana's friends made enquiries, and the pregnancy was terminated, after a lot of pain and a great deal of torment, on a kitchen table in Battersea. The decision was not taken lightly. Even if the child hadn't threatened Diana's career, illegitimacy was still a social stigma in Britain and the route she chose, abortion, was equally risky if the news was ever leaked. Even the procurement of an abortion by a third party was forbidden by law, and the practice would not be legalized until an act of Parliament was passed in October 1967. The state-sanctioned alternative – in which the young mother 'disappeared' to a nursing home and was obliged to give up the baby for adoption – was clearly just as traumatic.

Diana was very shaken by the experience, and Christmas 1949 was especially bleak, not to mention broke. Her fortunes picked up early the following year with *Dance Hall*, in which she appeared alongside Bonar Colleano and Petula Clark. Born Bonar William Sullivan in New York, 1924, Colleano was not a retiring, simpering star. He came from a circus background – Colleano's All-Star Circus – and the new family tradename was derived from an anagram of Bonar's great-grandfather's children. At five he was dancing, at six he was walking the tightrope in Madison Square Garden, and at twelve his family moved to London, where he was educated in Streatham and Eltham. Colleano made his film debut in 1945 in Anthony Asquith's *The Way to the Stars*, and four years later Laurence Olivier cast him opposite his wife, Vivien Leigh, as Stanley Kowalski in *A Streetcar Named Desire*. After getting quite a reputation as a radio comedian, Colleano became well-known for his snappy, mordant wit, which caused red faces when he compèred the diamond jubilee dinner held by the National Association of Theatrical and Kine Employees in December 1950. As Rank's losses hit an all-time record, Colleano noted that its founder had a new signature tune: 'There's no business like no business!' He was a funny, physical comedian, and weirdly good-looking, but his recklessness was becoming a problem. Although he was still married to actress Tamara Lees, Colleano's womanizing was well known and their relationship was rocky. In fact, two years after they were married Lees went with a British film unit to Italy in 1948 and never returned; the suit he later filed for divorce in the winter of 1951 on the grounds of 'abandonment', went uncontested.

Petula Clark, meanwhile, was just a year younger than Diana but the age difference seemed much greater. She'd been discovered at the age of ten and quickly became a child star, singing for the troops on the BBC broadcasts to the Forces. Rank signed her as a contract artist when she was twelve, and she spent most of her teenage years playing children much younger than herself. People in Swindon thought Mary was a pushy stage mother, but Clark's father, Leslie, was notorious in the industry, mostly for refusing to break the news that her mother had died until she'd finished rehearsing for a BBC TV show. Peter Ustinov thought Petula gave the impression of being someone who was wound up in the morning and put back in her box at night. Partly at her father's insistence, partly because there were few roles for teenagers and mostly because she was only five feet tall, Clark continued to take much younger roles, wearing ankle socks, flat shoes, and binding her breasts to keep them flat. She felt she was looking through a window at life without really taking part in it. Secretly, she bought jeans and loafers and wore them round the house. Secretly, she envied Diana Dors.

Diana hated *Dance Hall* and in fact – ever since *Diamond*

City – was starting to tire of the whole film-making process. That spring, she took a role in a play being put together by Kenneth Tynan, called *Man of the World*, starring Roger Livesey and Ursula Jean. It opened at the Hammersmith Lyric, where she first met fellow cast member Lionel Jeffries, who was to remain a close friend throughout her life. Jeffries was immediately struck by her professionalism. She got on with it, he thought – there was none of the preening that came with some of the usual Charm School bimbos. She was never one for saying, 'I'll make it one day!' 'I'm going to be a big star!' She worked surprisingly hard.

Man of the World brought good reviews, and Diana was feeling pretty pleased with herself that summer of 1950, so she bought a Ford V8 on hire purchase to celebrate. She and Kim drove down to Cornwall for a week's holiday; the weather was beautiful but when they returned, a storm set in. First the car was repossessed on account of lapsed payments, then, out of the blue, Diana was summoned to the Rank offices in Soho. Olive had to break the news that the company was in trouble: they were closing studios, shedding staff and dropping contract players. More to the point, they were dropping her. It happened every year – contracts were brought up at meetings for the board to decide on – if the actor or actress got the thumbs down they were given a bit of notice and Rank would help them out with clothes and board, so they weren't thrown out onto the street. Diana couldn't take it in. 'All that lovely money,' she sighed.

Rank's troubles had been going on for the last year. His plan to stand firm against the Americans had backfired – they fought back with subtlety and intelligence against his plans to re-promote British classics, not least by refusing to lease their films as second features, which was effectively what Rank had wanted. In the meantime, the statistics of 1946 were not holding up and British films were no longer prevailing at the box office. In a remarkable comedown, Rank made a public statement: 'Unfortunately, many of the films we produced were not of the quality to ensure reasonable returns. It can now be seen that our plans to meet an unexpected and critical situation were too ambitious, that we made demands on the creative talent in the industry that were beyond its resources and that as a result, we spread our production capacity, in which I still have unshaken faith, too thinly over the films we made.'

As Diana made her way home, she thought back to a poem she used to recite at Highbury to amuse the others. The irony did not escape her.

> *I signed a contract with my friend J. Arthur Rank,*
> *My dressing room was lousy and the films all stank,*
> *He handled his films like a flour mill, brother,*
> *With corn in one hand and the sack in the other.*

Chapter Three

THE POWER THAT
BEAUTY WIELDS

DIANA WAS NOT the only one to be disappointed. On New Year's Day, 1951, Kim finally received the inheritance he'd been waiting for. It was a cheque from his mother for £50. To make matters worse, the estate agents were terminating their lease, and as Diana and Kim packed up to leave there was a knock at the door. It was Kim's brother, John, who was in a pretty bad way, financially, himself. He asked if he could borrow the radio to pawn it and found out very quickly that this was not the best time to be asking. Diana blew up. There was an almighty row about it, and although Kim tried to calm things down, John stormed out and down the stairs, to the car where a friend was waiting for him. The car was unusual for its time, though not for Diana's set – a long, powder-blue American car. Diana looked out of the window as John jumped into the car and caught sight of the driver's face. He was good-looking, and familiar, too – one of the faces from the S&F, she thought – so she asked Kim who it was. Dennis Hamilton, he told her. The name rang a bell.

Their next flat was a step down, found in a hurry and costing as much as they were prepared to afford, which wasn't a lot. It was a bedsit in Collingham Road, South Kensington, run by a retired major who gave them a good rate because he thought their show business connections could bring him some film work. Unlikely, they thought, and shook on it. Diana's next film bailed them out considerably, and she pocketed what was then a massive £800 for British Lion's *Beauty Queen*, later retitled *Lady Godiva Rides Again*. The story, about a girl who inadvertently wins a beauty contest even though it's supposed to be rigged, was intended as a satire on the glamour trade but fell rather short of its target. Diana played an experienced old hand on the circuit.

While on location, she spent some time in Folkestone with one of the cast, a small-time actress called Jane. Jane offered her a lift back up to London when filming finished and her boyfriend drove down to collect her. He was an osteopath, Dr Stephen Ward, and from the way Jane spoke he was very well connected indeed. When he finally arrived, in a flashy new sports car, Diana thought him arrogant and aloof. He took Diana out for a spin and she found his driving matched his personality. Ward at that time was carving out his reputation as a ladies' man, juggling a respectable life at his West End practice with extra-curricular activities as a surprisingly good portrait artist and, less salubriously, as a patron of clandestine sex parties, of the kind Diana would come to know very well indeed.

Born in October 1912 in Lemsford, near Hatfield, Hertfordshire, Ward came from a highly respectable middle-class family. His father was Canon Arthur Evelyn Ward, and when Stephen was ten the whole family moved to Torquay, where his father took over the parish of the village of Ilsham. He had a good, private education, but between the ages of nineteen and twenty-one Stephen didn't do much with his life, zipping round in his green MG, always out with the local smart set. Then he heard of some ground-breaking research being carried out at the Kirksville College of Osteopathy and Surgery, Missouri, USA. It caught his interest, so a family friend gave him the money to enrol.

Ward left Kirksville in 1938 with a good degree and in January 1941 he joined the army, being stationed at the local

Bovington Camp in Dorset. After demob in 1946, he worked at an inauspicious clinic until one day the American Embassy telephoned on behalf of Ambassador Averil Harriman. They needed an osteopath, and Ward was thinking on his feet. 'I'd recommend Dr Stephen Ward,' he told them gruffly, 'he's really first-class. If you'd like to hold, I'll put you through.'

Harriman was his first blue-chip client and more came his way: foreign dignitaries, cabinet ministers, movie stars and royalty. Ward was very taken with appearances, and if his clients were agreeable he'd execute a little pastel sketch.

When Diana first met Ward in 1951, his notoriety lay waiting, many years ahead. Then in his early forties, Ward had a singular talent for finding young ladies and shaping them for society. His most notable success was Vicky Martin, a girl from the East End of London whom Ward transformed into a sophisticated and presentable – in terms of etiquette, that is, since it went without saying that she was beautiful – young woman. This was the scene in the square mile that was Mayfair, an oddly formal courtship where men were introduced to younger women dressed impeccably, made-up perfectly, hair held up in the formal evening style. They were often penniless, but Ward was not, as was later charged, running a call-girl racket, he was merely trying, somewhat high-mindedly, to play Pygmalion. Ward had his own theories of beauty, and in his own strange, snobbish way was something of a democrat. In 1963 he wrote an extraordinary piece for *Today* magazine entitled 'The Power That Beauty Wields':

Beauty is a fashion and, like all fashions, must gain acceptance or look out of place. What was beautiful yesterday may look ugly today, and vice-versa. Beauty, like fashion, is created in men's minds. It is a point of view. Only one thing is certain, that beauty knows no barriers of birth or environment, and like the word 'love' is different in each mind.

Whatever happened or was said in that car on their first meeting clearly created no spark. Although she was about the right age for his unique private treatment, Diana came ready-made and had her own agenda. She wasn't flattered or impressed by the trappings of the fast set – maybe a few years ago, but not now – and she didn't want to be a consort, batting her eyelashes at diplomats and millionaires. Ward's circle positively preyed on starlets, a nebulous category which served as the female equivalent of 'resting' actors, but Dors was too far up the ladder for that.

When they returned to the hotel, Ward announced that the car was too small and they drove off without her. Diana was furious and had to wait hours for a through train. She never liked him after that, no matter what she read or whatever people told her.

Dennis Hamilton was a lot like Stephen Ward himself, but with very different motives. He enjoyed the company of women, usually in bed, and was quite the charmer, too, with the kind of average good looks that look better with money. Of course he didn't have any, but Dennis had the confidence of a man with twice, three times his income and was not afraid of a bounced cheque. To Dennis, image was everything, and from an early age he dropped his full name – Hamilton Gittins, betraying his working-class Welsh roots – to affect a more refined air.

Diana had first met him at the S&F; one of his friends made the introduction and they'd struck up a conversation. She'd heard a few things about Dennis and the word wasn't good, but there was something about him, she couldn't deny that. He had tickets reserved to see Danny Kaye at the Palladium that night and was on his way to collect them. He gave her a look.

'What are you doing tonight?'

'I'm busy.'

'Come with me.'

'I'm sorry . . .'

'Let's get the tickets.'

'No, really.'

'Why not?'

'It's raining.'

'My car's outside.'

'Thanks, but . . . No. I'm busy.'

'Oh, come on.'

He just wouldn't take no. As she thought about it, Dennis put some money down on the table, enough to pay her tab, even though she was with friends. A few minutes later she was on her way.

After the show, Dennis took her to The White Room where they talked for hours. Dennis was twenty-six. He came from Luton in Bedfordshire where his father, Stanley Gittins, ran a pub called The Parrot in New Town Street. They discovered they had a lot in common, mostly superficial details like the fact that they shared the same birthday and that Dennis lived in the same road as the flat she shared with Kim. Like Kim, Dennis had dabbled in acting, mostly as a stand-in, although he boasted a fleeting appearance in Lord Olivier's *Hamlet* (1948), but he had given it up. He was now selling water-softeners, or trying to, since the product was not of the highest standard.

Kim, in the meantime, was involved in an ill-advised business deal of his own, which went horribly wrong in the summer of 1951 when he was imprisoned for two weeks by a judge who warned him sternly about the dangers of 'easy money'. While Kim was inside, Dennis moved quickly, bombarding Diana with notes and flowers then finally – and suddenly – asking her to marry him. Diana was surprised and confused. Her three-year relationship with Kim was foundering, and she was finding his jealousy hard to deal with. Kim looked quite young, and it infuriated him when other men made passes at her thinking they were safe to do so. He was quick-tempered in those days, and he couldn't let these people go unchallenged. There was also the matter of Diana's parents, who still refused to meet him, which was a headache for both of them. When a starlet came out of the woodwork claiming to be seeing Kim on the side, the circumstances made Diana's mind up for her. She accepted, and Dennis borrowed the money for a ring.

Although Bert and Mary were bemused, they approved of Dennis because he had, to their mind, what seemed to be a proper job. The wedding was set for 4 p.m. on 3 July 1951, at Caxton Hall, and because Diana was still only nineteen (the legal age was twenty-one) she needed her parents' consent for the marriage application. They were away at the time, and Diana claimed they'd agreed in principle over the phone, but it seems strange that a father as old-fashioned as Bert would not wish to meet his future son-in-law and that a mother as devoted as Mary would miss her only daughter's wedding. Whatever the case, their signatures were duly forged.

The day of the ceremony was nothing if not exciting. Dennis had been having an affair with a married woman and was going to be cited in her husband's divorce papers. The woman had heard about his impending marriage and threatened to turn up with a pistol and shoot herself on the steps of the registry office. Diana only found this out on the day, and wondered if the smattering of fans, press and paparazzi might see a little more than they'd bargained for. When they got inside, the registrar took them into an adjoining room and said he'd received a phone call telling him that the application was forged. He refused to carry out the service.

Dennis was riled. He grabbed the registrar by the collar and pushed him against the wall. 'You'll marry us, all right, or I'll knock your fucking teeth down your throat.' Dennis often claimed to have been a boxer, or a prize-fighter, in his youth, and frequently threw his weight about. Usually, this was aimed at a strategic target – if he complained in a restaurant, he'd find the most puny, elderly, emphysemic waiter and push him around while his cronies laughed. Diana hadn't seen this side of him before and, although she was shocked, she found it strangely impressive. In those days there was a certain criminal glamour that was considered exciting – before rock'n'roll, that is, which took over in another kind of dangerous way.

There was no honeymoon after the wedding, just a meal with friends at a little restaurant called Olivelli's, and Diana spent the next few days at the studio working on *Lady Godiva*. Occasionally she'd pick up a newspaper and read about the honeymoon she and Dennis were having. It sounded marvellous.

Moving out of Collingham Road they found a place in Beauchamp Place, Knightsbridge, which they paid for with the £450 Diana received for her latest film, *The Last Page*, a thriller she was making at Bray studios. Diana had been lightening her hair for a couple of years, but in the months prior to the wedding she finally managed the full peroxide platinum – she was now officially a blonde and, since Roman times, blondes had always had more fun.

She was still in touch with Kim, who told her he was planning to go to the continent, and she gave him the money for the fare. When Dennis found out he was furious and, given his predilection for the least resistant targets, hit her. This was to become the pattern with Dennis. He was charming all right, and hilariously funny, especially in the face of financial ruin. When a group of debt collectors called on him later with regard to one of many unpaid debts, Dennis ushered them inside and poured them a drink. 'Well, Mr Hamilton,' asked one. 'What do you intend to do?' 'My dear fellow, there's nothing I *can* do,' said Dennis. 'I'm broke!'

But when the laughter stopped, things turned very ugly indeed and his temper was most intimidating. Diana wanted to have fun, but at what price? To her friends she was a mystery; Hamilton was unacceptable to a lot of people, but she didn't seem to see that. Or if she did, she wasn't willing to drop him. She was so in thrall to the excitement of life – and partly blinkered by naivety, despite her experience – that any compromise which would enable her to reach the heights had to be worthwhile. She married Dennis on the rebound, but the part of her that really loved him kept them together. For his part, Dennis wanted her, or seemed to. It was a challenge, and maybe on some level it fed into Diana's need to perform, to have some form of control or magnetize an audience. Or maybe, and most likely, it was a rebellion against her father, a way of rejecting his small-town conservatism and his paternal caution. And, certainly, there were very few men in her life that her father would have approved of.

As the Hamiltons settled into married life, money became increasingly tight. Dennis wasn't selling any water softeners and Diana wasn't getting any work, so she was thrilled when an American producer, Robert Lippert, who'd worked on *The Last Page*, offered her a contract in the States. It was what she had always wanted: a chance to go to Hollywood. But there was one small drawback: she had to divorce Dennis. Diana's agent held his ground, but Lippert was emphatic – they couldn't market her as a sexy movie blonde unless she was single and available. He even suggested they remarry later – 'It'll be great for publicity!'

While Diana agonized about the outcome, it was time to move again. Creditors were closing in, Dennis's car was repossessed and the rent was months overdue, so they decamped to a cottage in Dunsfold, Surrey, for which they paid six guineas a week. Diana was a city girl and, initially, hated the change but she soon warmed to it and was amused to see how different Dennis seemed in such a relaxed setting. He even tried to make a go of the water softener business and invested in a flash American car, a red Cord, which broke down so often they traded it for a slow but reliable Opel that rarely moved faster than 25 m.p.h.

Together they went up to Luton to visit Dennis's parents and stopped off on the way back, in Harpenden, to see if there was any trade there. Dennis spent three days going from door to door, but water softeners were not in demand. They spent the evenings at the Toll Gate hotel, with Dennis buying rounds at the bar and running up a tab, and it soon became clear that there wasn't enough money for petrol, let alone the hotel bill. On the third night, Dennis backed up the Opel close to the hotel, Diana threw their cases out of the window and climbed out after them. They made their getaway in total darkness.

To compound her depression, Diana's American contract fell through. She was distraught, but Dennis had an idea. He was going to announce to the press that she had turned it down.

'Dennis, you can't.'

'Watch me.'

He picked up the phone and called all the newspaper contacts he knew, saying that Diana had turned down a salary of £400 a week in Hollywood because the roles weren't good enough. Amazingly, they took the story without checking, and soon Diana was being very blasé about the deception. 'I was very tempted by the salary,' she told the press, 'but I've played too many dumb blondes. I didn't want to be typed in the same kind of part, so I decided to wait for a contract that would give me greater scope as an actress.'

The flurry of press interest gave her hope, but very little came her way over the next few weeks, except a part in comedian Terry-Thomas's BBC series, *How Do You View?*. Local tradesmen were starting to ask about their money, the rent was already in arrears, and even Dennis could see there was a limit to how long he could go around writing rubber cheques on the strength of his wife's failing career. Late one night, early in 1952, Dennis backed up the Opel once again and the Hamiltons removed to a new home in Esher, where their credit was, at least for the moment, still good.

When they moved, Diana was pregnant again, and this time she considered keeping the baby. Dennis wouldn't hear of it and contacted a doctor who specialized in discreet abortion services. He quoted a high price, and they fretted about finding the money, but at the last minute Diana received an offer of modelling for which she would be paid fifty guineas. The abortion was taken care of privately, and although the circumstances were comparatively more humane, Diana was no less distressed by the operation. She wanted children.

When the modelling assignment finally arrived, Dennis drove her up in the Opel. They passed a garage where a black, second-hand Rolls sat parked on the forecourt. 'We'll have that,' snapped Dennis, turning the car. He pulled into the garage and jumped out. 'Won't be a minute.'

Diana watched as he disappeared into the owner's office. The man is insane, she thought. Within twenty minutes, Dennis emerged smiling, with a sheaf of papers, and motioned her out of the car. He'd bought the Rolls for £350, approximately £350 more than they had to spend. Diana couldn't believe it, but Dennis's reasoning was impeccable – if their creditors saw they had a Rolls, they wouldn't pester them, and anyone who hired Diana would immediately pay over the odds when they saw what she was used to. 'Have I ever let you down?' he asked. Until then, she was forced to admit, he hadn't.

Within a few days she had an offer to do repertory work in a travelling revue show called *Rendezvous*, a play-within-a-play sketch show about a theatre group trying to persuade a wealthy financier to back their play. Dennis drove her to the audition in the Rolls and gave her a knowing, told-you-so smirk when she got the booking for £40 a week, twice her last Rank salary.

Rendezvous opened in Brighton and soon transferred to the Comedy Theatre in London, where it ran for just a month. She had two routines in the play: in one, she wore pigtails and a gymslip as a St Trinian's schoolgirl and danced around the stage singing 'I Want To Be A Gangster's Moll' before pulling a gun from her knickers and shooting the pianist; in the other, she sat dressed as Little Miss Muffett and recited the poem in eight different accents, including Welsh, Scottish, Cockney and American.

The play was an old-fashioned thing, once a big hit in Scandinavia in the thirties, and reviewers gave it crushing notices – 'amateurish', 'dull', 'naive' – with scant regard for its apparent star, Walter Chrisham. For Diana, however, it was a different story, and she was singled out for praise by almost everyone. 'The blonde is the success of the evening,' noted one reviewer, 'when she ceases to be merely decoration and becomes an amusing mimic and comedienne. This pleasant transformation is too long delayed. What the show needs is early Dors.'

Writing in the *Evening Standard*, Kenneth Tynan eclipsed them all:

> Beneath her robust and open-hearted physical allure, Miss Dors conceals the soul of an ugly duckling, a boisterous and jolly child, eager to be liked. She is an unabashed parodist of desire; as someone said of Mae West, she is pre-Freudian . . . I cannot guess whether Miss Dors has any real talent, and I do not violently care. What is clear is that her personality is a blessing to our theatre and could easily develop into a legend.

The review ended with these prescient words:

> Miss Dors is a landmark rather than a performer, and I expect the National Trust already have their eyes on her.

Diana read the newspapers avidly and she was most intrigued by the news reports about a recent robbery she'd suffered. During the run, while the Rolls was parked on Archer Street, someone had broken a window and stolen her radio. In the paper it said she'd lost £250 worth of jewellery, including an engagement ring worth £175. She asked Dennis how they could have got it so wrong. 'You should always exaggerate things for the newspapers,' he replied. 'It looks so much better in print.'

That was one of Dennis's favourite sayings. 'Always give numbers a nice, round sound,' was another. He was especially fond of 'hundreds' and, wherever possible, 'thousands'.

Rendezvous brought a lot of attention and a lot of offers. Olivier wanted her to do *The Beggars Opera*, which he and Peter Brook were then casting; she was offered a summer season in Blackpool with the play *Life with the Lyons*; and

Burt Lancaster called her to test for his new film, *His Majesty O'Keefe*. Diana was thrilled, but less so when she realized that the part was that of a Fijian native. It was *Black Narcissus* all over again, but nevertheless she wore a black wig, a sarong and stained her skin an olive brown. The results weren't bad, either, but she didn't get the part. Actually, she was relieved; when she made her first appearance on American screens, she didn't want to be seen as the poor man's Dorothy Lamour.

She took the Blackpool season, and once there received an intriguing proposition from an agent working for the Bernard Delfont Agency. He complimented Diana on the show, but quickly got down to business. He told her she could make up to £135 a week for a twenty-minute variety act – a few songs, a few sketches – and there would always be work when the film offers thinned out. 'You can't live on press cuttings,' he told her. 'You've got to make up your mind whether you're in this business for the money or the glory.' She decided she was in it for the money.

Diana had already signed for her next film, *My Wife's Lodger*, and Dennis drove her to the studio every day in the Rolls. Viking Studio was tiny, a little building in a cul-de-sac just off Kensington Church Street – there were studios everywhere in those days. Maurice Elvey was the director, not brilliantly creative but very capable, having cut his teeth during the silent years, and David Dent was the producer. One afternoon the first assistant director was checking the call sheet; they'd broken for lunch at 1 p.m. and it was already two minutes to 2 p.m. with no sign of Diana. He sent the third assistant director out to look. She wasn't in the dressing room, she wasn't in make-up, she wasn't in wardrobe ... he looked outside and ran back out of breath.

'I've found her.'

'Where is she?'

'She's in the Rolls.'

'Well, what's she doing?'

'She's . . . She's . . . having it off with her husband.'

'It's two o'clock in the afternoon, man. Tap on the bloody window!'

'I can't.'

'Oh bloody hell.'

The first assistant director marched out into the square, surrounded on all sides by residential houses. It was hardly private. He rapped on the window and shouted, 'Come on, Diana, let's get cracking.' Ten minutes later she'd gathered herself together and was back on the studio floor, as if nothing had happened.

Elvey was very pleased with her performance, especially the way she handled difficulties. There was one scene in particular that he wasn't happy with — in the script, Diana's screen father picked up some phenobarbitone sedative tablets by accident and was warned by police that he was in possession of a very dangerous drug. The scene ended there, with a fade-out, and Elvey thought it didn't work. Diana improvised a solution: 'Ee, Dad, yer might 'ave blown us all oop!' It was exactly what the scene needed.

Diana was very professional that way, so it came as a shock one afternoon when she suddenly stopped halfway through a take. 'I'm sorry,' she announced, 'but I'm not filming any more. I want to see the producer.' Dent was summoned and they went into a private room. 'Look, David, I've decided I can't go on unless I get more money.' It was a tense meeting, but they reached a compromise and the film finished shooting without another hitch. Diana even attended the film's premiere in Southport later that year, and Dennis planted a story in the press in October that Diana owned her own private plane and had flown there herself.

Like most men of his generation, Dennis actually seemed to believe he owned his wife. It was an overhang from the domesticity of pre-war society, a way of continuing to assert a husband's authority, but Diana was clearly no housewife and therefore outside the usual rules of oppression. Technically, she was financially independent, so Dennis had to find a way to undermine her confidence, which he did by appointing himself her manager and taking control of her business affairs. He also took charge in more subtle ways, as a kind of professional Svengali, by moulding her image and shaping the way she presented herself. Dennis was determined – and he said this often – that Diana should be the female equivalent of Errol Flynn, always in trouble, always in the news; which was ironic, since Errol Flynn at that time often said that he felt himself becoming a caricature of his old self – the male Mae West.

Diana's next appearance in the press certainly had a Flynn-like ring to it, and it was her first brush with unwelcome publicity. While she was working up in Blackpool, earning £100 a week on the twice-nightly show *Life with the Lyons* she was being sued at Westminster County Court by Euston Trust Ltd of Euston Road, Camden, for £38 14s 3d in unpaid rent. Diana's solicitors moved to have the hearing put back, saying that her attendance would mean breaking her contract. The prosecution's counsel opposed the application, saying, 'I should think she could afford to hire a plane and fly to London for the hearing. Blackpool, after all, is not Moscow.'

Judge Dale, who was presiding, adjourned the case on condition that the amount owing was paid that day. It was with a degree of bewilderment that he summed up the case, saying, 'It is the duty of the court to protect infants, although nowadays it seems infants earn over £100 a week.' The judge's remark was too good for the newspapers to pass over. 'This week's frightening query,' ran one such story. 'What is blonde, seductive Diana Dors, described in court this week as 'an infant', going to be like when she grows up?'

Diana returned from Blackpool with a contract for a West End play, *Remains to be Seen*, being staged by producer Jack Hylton later that year. The signing was dramatic – Diana was literally about to put pen to paper and sign with a London casino for a musical season when Dennis stopped her. The deal was good, very good, although Hylton would soon regret it.

Diana was pleased with her role. 'I'm a dance band cutie who gets mixed up in murder – dramatic stuff,' she told a reporter. 'A sort of dumb blonde with plenty of grey matter.' Even so, she couldn't resist a tease. 'My lines are so good, the censor cut some of them out,' she revealed.

During rehearsals for the play, Diana celebrated her twenty-first birthday. After seven years of behaving like one, she was officially an adult. Dennis hosted a party at their Chelsea flat and decorated the place especially for the occasion – he was quite enterprising, in that respect. Give him some plaster of Paris and a pot of paint and he could really make something of a room. The party was a success and Diana was touched by the efforts he'd gone to, but she went to bed early because she was due at the theatre next morning. Not long after, she was woken by the sound of a fight downstairs. A coat with important plane tickets in the pocket had gone missing, and one of the guests had drunkenly abused the man who was looking for it. She ran to the top of the stairs in time to see Dennis scuffling with the troublemaker, a friend of his so drunk he could barely stand. 'I'll tell Dors about you,' the man kept yelling. 'I'll spoil your fucking meal ticket. I'll tell her what you're like.' Diana went back to her room. She didn't know what he was talking about, but because she didn't want to know, she chose not to think about it. Which was hard.

At that time, Dennis was making quite a name for himself as a host, but the kind of party he preferred had nothing to do with birthdays – although many of his guests might have thought it was theirs. Comedian Bob Monkhouse, then twenty-four and making great headway as a scriptwriter for radio, was invited by Diana to a party the following month, after the two had worked together on the BBC's Forces broadcasts. The scene that greeted him was dingy in the extreme, with a low-lit ambience broken only by the smoke-hazy beam of a 16 m.m. projector that threw grainy images of backroom pornography – or 'stag films' as they were known – onto a vinyl screen. Alcohol was available, but few really drank to inebriation and sometimes a light chemical breeze of amyl nitrate – a prescription heart stimulant kept in ampoules and broken under the nose, usually during sex – wafted through the air. Couples were getting very intimate in the anonymity afforded them, and single men were helped out by any number of professional women or overly willing starlets brought in by Hamilton to liven up proceedings.

One especially eager young woman collared Monkhouse, and while the two were getting physically acquainted, Dennis tapped them on the shoulder and motioned them over. All night, Dennis had been spiriting couples away, but few seemed to return to the party. He took them to a sparsely furnished bedroom and closed the door, whispering, 'You've got about a quarter of an hour, so make the most of it.' The scene that unfolded was typical of the seductions that happened in that particular room: Monkhouse fumbled for the bed clothes (there were none) and looked for the light switch (he was discouraged). Looking up, there was a large mirror on the ceiling – which in itself was kinky, if not exactly sinister. As his partner grew visibly more and more frantic, Monkhouse began to feel that something was not quite right. She kept looking up, as if she were performing, and a stifled squeal of laughter from upstairs caused the penny to drop. It was a two-way mirror.

Monkhouse grabbed his clothes, shouting up at the mirror, 'You creepy bastard, Hamilton!' His new friend simply shrugged. 'He's a homo,' she told her audience – which was somewhat implausible, given the circumstances. Diana met Monkhouse in the hall, and he was taken upstairs to an even darker room, lit only by the glow from the room he'd just vacated. She seemed amused but genuinely upset that the whole situation had backfired. 'Some people absolutely adore putting on a show,' she explained. 'They come back to my parties just to do that.' Diana genuinely thought it was all a bit of a laugh; after all, no harm was really being done. For Diana, sex was fun, and it was well known in acting circles, about that kind of living. It was intensely exciting, and glamorous, and dangerous, and Dors pushed it to the limit. But then again, was it the men in her life who dragged that element into it? The hole-in-the-ceiling thing simply flashed round certain circles, but there were two ways it could be read. On the one hand, Diana was an earthy, guilt-free, modern hostess; on the other, Dennis was a scheming, sadistic manipulator of his friends' most predictable weaknesses. Both readings were true enough.

It was rumoured that Diana had been 'on the game' while living at the YMCA, and jokes were made when her name first appeared in studio publicity. But these were just rumours and where partygoers were concerned, she was strictly off-limits. Dennis was jealously possessive of his wife, as Monkhouse found the following year when he and Diana worked together on a Sunday evening radio show in central London. Diana came on strong and Monkhouse responded, booking a furnished apartment off Oxford Street where they subsequently spent a pleasant afternoon in bed together. Diana told Monkhouse that Dennis was in New York, but it transpired that this was just a ruse to lower his guard. Monkhouse was mortified and his paranoia intensified when Dennis later found out about the affair. In fact, he claimed to have spent the next six years of his life looking over his shoulder, especially when, in the summer of 1956, Hamilton approached him on the way into a party and pulled him aside. Dennis ranted and raved, then pulled out a cutthroat razor and waved it in front of his face. 'I'm going to slit your eyeballs,' he hissed, prompting Monkhouse to raise his knee and violently connect with Hamilton's groin. The next three years were intimidating; Monkhouse even heard that Dennis had a contract out on his life. Dennis's reputation really was fierce and, while they were together, Diana's other liaisons were surely few and far between.

Remains to be Seen opened in Oxford on 10 November 1952. Set in New York, the play was as feeble as its pun, centring on the police investigation into the murder of a local gangster. 'Among the 19 characters floating about the stage,' wrote the *Daily Telegraph*, 'are several policemen (with fingerprints as the one idea in their heads), the "cutie" of a dance band who is apparently the dead man's niece, a presentable solicitor (played by Newton Wayne), a Chinese houseboy and Dick Henderson Jnr as the janitor of the flat, whose hobby is swing music.'

The Star reported that the only encouraging thing to say about it was that ' . . . with all its bad points, it shows the verve and saucy charm of Diana Dors.' The *News of the World* described her as a 'golden asset' to this 'jumble of jazz and murder'; while the *Daily Mirror*'s review was headlined simply: DIANA DORS DESERVES A BETTER PLAY.

Diana, wrote the *Evening Standard*:

> . . . adds to the chaos by playing it all wrong. As written, the character is that of a nice, good-hearted, uninhibited girl: Miss Dors seizes on the last adjective and wields it like a battle-axe . . . I admire her skill at diving in and out of bathrobes – a more resolute kimonophobe I have

rarely seen. But Miss Dors can perform more charmingly, less stridently than this.

It was billed as a distant cousin to *Arsenic and Old Lace*, which was perhaps a discreet way of telling the audience it was meant to be funny, and if it was, it didn't work. When the play finally transferred to the West End it closed on Saturday 20 December after five nights and seven performances, posting losses of £5,000. 'When will Diana Dors be a success in a flop?' quipped Bonar Colleano.

Dennis, in the meantime, had been working on Diana's profile. In a little over a year, her image had changed considerably, and her Rank image now seemed positively demure – pearls and cocktail dresses, ankle-length patterned dresses, button-sleeved sweaters and wedge-heel shoes. Her look had been very forties, like a young, flighty Andrews sister. Now, with an end to rationing in sight, clothing was about to become much more extravagant and far less practical. The war effort had seen women drafted into service, into munitions and landwork, and the fashions of the day reflected this in the masculine cut of women's skirts and suits. The government also had a major influence, issuing sewing patterns and guidelines that dictated the lengths of cuffs and hems, discouraging pockets as wasteful.

In Europe, women's style had changed forever in 1947, when fashion designer Christian Dior unveiled his latest collection – which the media hailed as 'The New Look' – in Paris. It was a haute-couture concept, beyond the reach of ordinary women, but it marked a return to revealing necklines, pinched waists and hour-glass figures. Dior was inspired by Edwardian fashions and his dresses required yards of fabric, causing a sensation when he held a show at London's Savoy Hotel in April 1950. Femininity was coming back into vogue, and with her bust and hips, Diana was almost uniquely placed in the British film industry to take advantage. And although the Dior look was ultra-chic, Diana borrowed it, adapted it and used it to her advantage – she wasn't one of Dior's ice maidens, she was earthy and accessible. To women, she seemed like one of the girls – someone like themselves, proof that dreams really could come true. To men, she seemed available, and the twinkle in her eyes suggested she was perhaps a little dangerous. There was a certain vicarious pleasure to be had from a fashion plate that didn't follow the rules.

To capitalize on her success, Dennis announced at the end of November that Diana was to become a limited company; the capital was set at £100 in £1 shares and the objects of the company were quoted as being 'to carry on the business of cinematograph film producers, film renters and directors of film productions.' This they never actually got around to, but, as Diana pointed out, 'The company has other interests – in property. My husband is a co-director and we are buying houses, renovating them and selling – at a profit. We've already invested in seven houses. It's a safer business than filming.'

By the end of 1952, Diana was a fixture in the daily press, so much so that the *News of the World*'s letters page printed a poem sent in by Ray Anzarat of Westbourne Court, London W2:

> *Unless she can curb*
> *Publicity blurb*
> *We'll end up slamming Dors*
> *Cos now Diana bores.*

But Dennis Hamilton was only just getting started.

Chapter Four

MAKE YOURSELF EXPENSIVE

1953 BEGAN WITH a spat that set a new precedent, having more to do with something Diana wasn't doing than anything she was. She'd been in talks the previous month to appear on BBC radio's Light Programme from 6 January in a revamped version of *All-Star Bill*, which would alternate with the regular Forces show. Two days before the show was due to start, however, Diana pulled out, and the papers carried rumours of a row she'd had with the show's producer, Dennis Main Wilson, about taking second billing to Tony Hancock. Diana wondered how she could have walked out of the show before she'd even had a chance to walk *in*. The problem, she said, was that she'd asked to see a script and when the BBC refused to send one she declined to appear. 'I'm not conceited,' she protested, 'just hard worked.'

And the offers were certainly coming in. She'd been asked to do cabaret in the West End, a production of *Guys and Dolls* was coming to London, and Sam Wanamaker was hoping to persuade her to take part in a Sean O'Casey play he was directing. Instead, she returned to more familiar territory and began a four-week variety tour on 16 February, taking in Brighton, Birmingham and Portsmouth. Diana dreamed of headlining at the London Palladium; instead, she opened her tour at the Glasgow Empire, a venue notorious in the trade for its demanding and difficult audiences. She arrived with a sketchy eighteen-minute act worked out, and during rehearsals Diana stunned the lighting director with a blank look when he asked what 'lighting plot' she used. She hadn't the faintest idea. That night, as she blundered through her act, eighteen minutes became twenty-eight and the manager stood furiously at the side of the stage threatening to bring down the curtain. By the end of the week it was down to just seven minutes, and when Diana collected her money – £266 in cash – it almost seemed worth it. 'This is the game, Dors,' said Dennis. 'To hell with all that acting rubbish!'

Even so, Diana's film work could still pay well. Her first film of 1953, *Is Your Honeymoon Really Necessary?*, another tepid sex farce in which she co-starred with Bonar Colleano, brought £1,000 for three weeks' work. She was offered the same amount to appear that summer in *It's a Grand Life*, starring Frank Randle, a once-famous but fast-fading northern comedian. Diana winced at the prospect of five weeks in the north.

One afternoon as they headed back to their Chelsea flat Dennis nudged her with his elbow and pointed to the car beside them. She looked across and saw Sir Carol Reed sitting in the passenger seat. After a string of critical and commercial successes in the forties, most notably with *The Third Man*, Reed was then one of the most respected directors working in Britain, and roles in his films were sought after and fought over. 'That'll be the day,' said Dennis. 'When you make a picture for *him*.'

It's a Grand Life was produced by Mancunian Films, a small but successful company that made films exclusively for the northern market, using names like Sandy Powell, 'Two-Ton' Tessie O'Shea and Josef Locke. Randle, then in his early fifties, was one of their draws, but by 1953 his life was anything but grand. Born Arthur McEvoy in 1901, his claim to fame was a boyhood friendship with George Formby – the two would play together on street corners – but Randle started his show business career as a comic gymnast and juggler, earning £7 a week. By the time his career in music hall, and later films, took hold in the forties, his fee had risen to the £1,000 mark. He was most famous for his travelling revue, *Randle's Scandals*, which often ran into trouble with the censor for using unacceptable material. But Randle fought his corner. 'My act is vulgar not filthy,' he protested, and he believed in the difference. Randle's act was character based, with little set pieces like 'The Vulgar Boatman' and 'The Hiker' – a beer-swilling, womanizing, geriatric rambler – but his charisma seemed to evaporate south of Birmingham. The comedian's only attempt to win over London audiences failed in 1951 when his show at the Alhambra theatre was pulled after two weeks.

Diana didn't know this would be Randle's last ever film but she could have guessed. She shuddered at his alcoholism, the way he treated the women in his life, and his predilection for firing guns in his dressing room, which was truly frightening. She wasn't surprised when he died four years later but, personally she felt rather sorry for him.

There were frequent pauses in production, and finally, when Randle disappeared on a bender and filming halted altogether, Diana and Dennis went off to Blackpool to visit friends they'd made while Diana was appearing in *Life with the Lyons*. It was a Saturday night, 18 July, when they checked into the Mayfair Hotel, and they called a few people, inviting them over for a party. One, Frank Rogers, was out, so Dennis, Diana and a fifty-two-year-old jeweller by the name of Freddie Markell went round to his ground-floor flat in Park Road. Rogers was still out when they got there, so Dennis manoeuvred the window open and they all climbed in, giggling. They waited half an hour, playing records on his gramophone, until boredom began to set in. 'Come on,' said Dennis. He grabbed half a bottle of whisky, half a bottle of wine, half a bottle of gin and a bottle of vermouth, then handed them to Diana and Markell. Before leaving by the front door, Dennis stopped to scrawl a note for their host: 'We shall be drinking and getting pissed at your expense tonight. Waited over an hour for you. We thought we would leave you some wine.' To bait him further, Dennis added a hasty sketch of Rogers having badly drawn sex with a naked woman.

Rogers came home at midnight but he didn't notice anything strange until 2 a.m., when he opened his drinks cabinet. Dennis called shortly after, inviting him to the Mayfair, but Rogers refused, and when he finally found the note he became furious. Rogers made a formal complaint to the police, and the three were arrested the following day on charges of breaking and entering and theft. Diana was taken to the police station, where the staff seemed more interested in her autograph than her fingerprints and she was finally released on a surety of £10. 'I thought I was worth more than that,' she told them.

When the story broke in the media, Rogers became very embarrassed. Markell was an old friend – they'd once shared a flat together – and Rogers hadn't known he was involved. He tried to withdraw the charges, claiming Markell had 'full permission to enter my flat under any circumstances and with whom he chooses', but Chief Constable Harry Barnes insisted on proceeding. 'This is a serious matter,' he announced. 'It's burglary!'

Diana arrived at court the following week in a cream Rolls Royce – 'They give me so much confidence,' she explained – lent by a Manchester promoter who wanted her to appear at the Hulme Hippodrome. She was wearing tight black cocktail trousers, a white wrap-over sweater, gold sandals and big gypsy earrings, a fact that was noted by every reporter in attendance.

The trial was absurd and hinged on a strange technicality – since no one had actually seen them enter, they were accused of breaking out of the building because of an eyewitness who had noticed them leaving. Dennis's excuse was that this was a prank that backfired – they were going to invite Rogers to the Mayfair, pour him drinks all night, then reveal that he was, in fact, drinking his own liquor. It squared with Dennis and Diana's idea of fun, but if this really was the case, why did Dennis leave Rogers a note that would more or less tell him this? The judge was not impressed and found all three guilty of larceny of goods valued at £4 7s 6d; Diana was given an absolute discharge and Dennis and Markell were each fined £10.

Dennis called a meeting of Diana Dors Ltd, with a view to suing the police for false arrest and loss of prestige, but within a few weeks he had cooled down. Besides, the story generated a lot of press, which, in turn, brought a deluge of variety offers. 'It's surprising what a thing like that can do for an actress,' said Diana.

Her next film was already being discussed. Coincidentally, it was a women-in-prison drama based on the true story of Joan Henry, who herself had spent eight months in jail, with technical advice from Mary Size, former governor of Askham Grange, an open prison in Yorkshire. The film was called *The Weak and the Wicked*, and though Diana already knew which of two she would be playing, it was a more challenging role than the usual fluff she was offered. A lot of her peers were moving into television, but since appearing as sexy seductress Cuddles in the Terry-Thomas show – which provoked the inevitable stream of complaints from 'outraged' viewers – she'd had few invitations. 'I don't see why I should be kept off TV just because of a few letters from jealous women, do you?' she asked Dennis.

Diana was certainly becoming too hot to handle for many people, and in August she was dropped as honorary vice-president of the Swindon Town Hockey Club on the grounds that she was not a resident of the area and could not therefore take 'an active interest'. Diana, who hadn't been a local resident when they asked her in the first place, knew exactly what they really meant, and her riposte was made in the pages of the daily press. 'May I suggest that if the club hasn't already got a badge, it should get a new one. It might consider having a hockey stick surmounted by a halo, with the motto: "Smug",' she said.

In the meantime, her old friend Kim Waterfield was up to his neck in legal trouble that made Diana's 'crime' look like possession of an overdue library book. Kim had mostly been living abroad since his split with Diana and moved in very exclusive circles. This was how he came to be at a party given by Barbara Warner, daughter of Warner Brothers mogul Jack Warner, at her father's Cap d'Antibes villa on the French Riviera on 26 August 1953. Kim had known eighteen-year-old Barbara for several years, and they'd even been unofficially engaged, but her father had disapproved. Jack Warner was a gambling man and a regular fixture at the casinos of Monte Carlo, betting heavy stakes until the early hours, so there was always quite a lot of money on the premises. On the night of the party Kim was with his friend Bobby McKew, and by the time it had ended, Warner's safe was £25,000 lighter. Kim and Bobby were suspected but not − for the moment at least − arrested, although the case was far from closed.

Kim was in the papers a lot over the next few years and it certainly wasn't for acting.

By September 1953, when filming began on *The Weak and the Wicked*, Diana was already tired of making movies. But the money was certainly good and it kept her in a lifestyle that was starting to attract attention in the press. These were still austere times; the country faced massive post-war debts and the devaluation of the pound in 1949 had signposted the economic crisis. For the average Briton, rationing was still an everyday reality (continuing until 1954) and news stories boasting of Diana's fabulous income upset quite a few people. When *Picturegoer* magazine confronted her with claims that some of its readers were already beginning to 'shoot at' her over the amount she was making, she retorted: 'I could shoot *myself* sometimes for playing in a film. I make more [money] in variety. And I loathe getting up at the crack of dawn for the studio.' The same people would also criticize her for her love of 'town and nightlife', the magazine suggested. 'And who doesn't?' she shot back. 'At any rate, I don't put on the sweet homegirl act.'

Although still only twenty-one, Diana was already aware of a time limit on her earning power and she'd already begun to think of retiring at around the age of thirty, when she figured she'd be past her prime, and starting a family with Dennis somewhere outside London. Diana Dors Ltd existed purely as a money-making venture to realize this plan, and at around this time the company had apparently dealt with over a dozen houses in London and the Home Counties. Dennis would scout for houses, have them surveyed, renovate them and, having raised a mortgage with a soft-touch lender, some of whom, before the days of strict regulation, were happy with an application on headed notepaper, he would then sell them on for what he called 'modern' prices. As well as their home in Chelsea, Dennis claimed to have had property in Harpenden, Wareham and even both their home towns, Swindon and Luton.

Diana wasn't precious about her home and could be incredibly generous when the need arose. At a party one night she met a young actor, Victor Spinetti, who'd not long arrived in London from his native Wales. Diana gave him a key to the house in Chelsea and, remembering the days spent eating potatoes and onions in Earls Court, begged him to look after himself. 'Don't ever go without food,' she warned. 'Come round to the house and have a meal. If there's no one in, help yourself from the kitchen.' He felt an immediate warmth, and her concern came in soothing mantras: 'Look after yourself', 'Let me know what you're doing', 'Don't go without anything to eat'. In other words, she offered a basic, proper, mothering kind of help, which he very much appreciated. One day he found a ring in the street that had been run over by a car. It was a cheap old thing, nothing posh, but it had a beautiful blue stone which was the colour of her eyes. He took it to her as a present and she made such a fuss about it, he was quite embarrassed. She actually had it made into a proper ring – it was the perfect colour, she said.

Spinetti often dropped in; sometimes Diana was there, sometimes the housekeeper fixed him a meal. He was struggling back then and the first time he ever saw a big-screen television – hanging on the wall, with a tiger-skin covered magnifying 'projector' – was at Diana's place. He'd lie on the tiger-skin rug on the floor and look up. It seemed idyllic, and if there were any problems between Dennis and Diana, Spinetti only saw the sunny side. Sometimes they went for drives together and Dennis would pull up outside Peter Jones' department store in Sloane Square, in his powder-blue Cadillac, and beckon the commissionaire.

'Can I help you, sir?'

'Yes. I want to buy a ribbon . . . to match the colour of your eyes!' Then he'd pull away – tyres screaming, everyone laughing. He was outrageous that way. Things were going well for Dennis, and it was possibly their happiest time together. Although she soon came to resent the way he pimped her talent, Diana never denied that he was the architect of her initial breakthrough and was quite in awe of his sense of fun and talent for hyperbole.

Although she pretended otherwise to the press, the property business was mostly Dennis's concern, if it ever really existed as a serious proposition. It brought in a bit of money, but Diana was much more fixated on stardom, and there was plenty to keep her busy. When *The Weak and the Wicked* finished shooting, Dennis arranged a whistle-stop tour of London cinemas to promote *Is Your Honeymoon Really Necessary?* Diana was bored with the usual, formal kind of personal appearance, which she had suffered at the Charm School, so audiences were treated instead to a reprise of her Little Miss Muffet routine from the ill-fated *Rendezvous* – it was, she thought, 'a nice change'. Her enthusiasm waned when the tour grew to incorporate 'last-minute' extra dates. The first stop was a shop where a few curious customers had gathered and even the manager seemed surprised to see her. 'What do I do?' she asked. 'Well, nothing, really,' he replied, handing her a box of chocolates. 'You're here, like we said in the advertisement. That's all.' With his hustler's mindset, Dennis correctly surmised that someone was pocketing money on the side and quickly put a stop to any further appointments. 'Eye witnesses' – perhaps on behalf of the people who had organized these ad hoc appearances – claimed it was because she had a drink problem.

Diana extended her repertoire in November with the release of her first ever single, 'I Feel So Mmm'/'A Kiss and a Cuddle', and finished the year with her first venture into pantomime at the Boscombe Hippodrome, Bournemouth, playing the lead in *Aladdin*. Dennis joined her onstage, playing one of a gaggle of Chinese policemen, but his usual bravado dissolved when it came to delivering his one and only line: 'Here comes Widow Twankey with her laundry basket.' Typical Dennis, thought Diana. Cocky and confident when someone else's neck was on the line, usually hers.

The Weak and the Wicked premiered in February 1954, and the reviews were good. In an article headlined 'Dors Deglamorised', *Picturegoer* praised her decision to take on a role so at odds with her public image: 'Like Mae West, Diana has a good, honest earthiness about her performances – off and on stage – that makes a sharp contrast to the milk and water personalities of many young players. She gives the impression of having lived . . . Call her blatant, call her tough, call her anything you like. But can you *ignore* a character like Diana?'

Actually, many directors thought they could, and Diana spent the first six months of 1954 on tour with her variety act. When a film did come along, it was a silly whodunnit called *Miss Tulip Stays the Night*, a flat, stagey murder mystery that climaxed with the creakiest of fallback devices – the deadly identical twin. Needless to say, it did little to raise her artistic credibility.

But then, Diana's financial demands sometimes caused just as many problems, like the time she walked out of *The Frankie Howerd Show* when the BBC cut her twenty-five-guinea fee to twenty. Her stock rose dramatically, however, when her new agent, Al Parker, called and said that Carol Reed was casting for a film starting in the late summer. It was to be a light drama, set in London's Petticoat Lane area, about a boy who owns a one-horned kid goat. Believing it to have a unicorn's magic powers, he makes a series of wishes he thinks his pet can grant. No one really knew it then, but Reed's own magic powers were beginning to falter, and the film Parker wanted Diana to sign for, *A Kid for Two Farthings* – her first in colour – was further evidence of his creative decline. But even so, it was still a big deal. She had to wait ten days before being confirmed for the part, but she was blasé about it in public. 'I've been in the business too long, darling, and I've had too many disappointments,' she said. 'I was thrilled that he should want me, but after that I just forgot about it.'

Reed finally gave her the female lead – the part of a luckless boxer's girlfriend, which, he said at the time, provided 'the romance' – and did not make that decision lightly. 'I had seen a lot of her films and thought she was right for the part,' he said. 'I ran them through again – and I was *sure*. I think she has a fine sense of comedy – and I also wanted a girl who could act. Diana is a nice little actress.'

She was delighted that someone had finally acknowledged her capabilities. 'This is some league I'm in,' she told the press. 'Oh, I know certain people look down their noses at me because I have worked in variety and I can wiggle when I walk and I like living a full life. But let them laugh now.'

Diana noticed the Reed effect immediately; first, her salary was fixed at £1,700, enabling her to give up variety for a few months, and secondly, it brought a flood of other lucrative offers, including £200 for a cameo in J. Lee-Thompson's *As Long as They're Happy*. Most bizarre was a plan by millionaire George Dawson to have Diana promote a batch of rejected welfare orange juice he'd bought from the government. It was to be called 'Diana Juice' – 'The juice that Dors adores' – but she backed out of talks when Dawson failed to meet her asking price.

Dennis immediately put the money from her film fee to use, buying the house next door and renovating it for resale, and by the time *A Kid for Two Farthings* went into production in August, he'd persuaded Diana to move again, this time to a huge Thameside house in Bray. The house was their most lavish yet, costing between £7,000 and £8,000, depending on who Dennis was talking to, and Diana spoke wearily of a need for 'fresh air and open spaces. We feel cramped in London – and the time has come for a change.' Bray was also very much part of the River Scene, a more refined and upmarket extension of the major scenes – Mayfair and Chelsea – that dominated London society. Lord Astor lived nearby, at Cliveden, as did society hairdresser Raymond 'Mr Teasy-Weasy' Bessone, and its proximity to all the major film studios – Pinewood, Bray, Shepperton and, in those days, Nettlefold – attracted quite a lot of show business people.

The house had five bedrooms, two and a half acres of lawn, a tennis court and a boathouse. It was decorated in a Tudor style, which Diana loved – 'All thick beams and low ceilings and warmth and darkness!' – so they set about making the house even more Tudor, with extra beams. Was it hard to match them up, a journalist asked? 'Oh no, the house is quite new,' said Diana. 'It was built just before the war. We had no trouble matching beams.' The Tudor effect was accentuated by a tree-house telephone box in the garden and Dennis's plans to convert the boathouse into a bar.

The Reed film did wonders for Diana's social life, but she remained somewhat gauche, despite their standard of living. When film director John Huston came to dinner, Diana was stunned when the legendary drinker and man's man asked for a pink gin. 'I'm afraid we only have the ordinary kind,' she told him. 'Do you have any bitters?' he replied. 'We certainly have – there's plenty of cold beer in the cellar.'

Workwise, Diana's plans to lever herself out of B-features forever came unstuck in September, when a year-old port-folio of 3D glamour photographs, taken by the exotically named Roye-Vala, made the news. The book, which was called *Diana Dors in 3-D*, sold at 2s 6d (including glasses) and was billed as 'Stereo-Glamour Series 3' (another in the series featured starlet Carole Lesley, born Maureen Rippingdale). The pictures showed an under-dressed Diana, posed with wisps of strategically placed chiffon; this was tame stuff, and Diana had already forgotten about it.

Nevertheless, on 7 September, Halifax magistrates announced its intention to prosecute fifty-three-year-old shopkeeper John Gray for possession of sixteen 'obscene' titles, including *Diana Dors in 3-D*, *Windows in Paris*, *Awful Disclosures of Maria Monk*, *Eve* and *More Eves Without Leaves*. Mr John Bastian, prosecuting, was emphatic about the charge. 'How,' he asked, 'can a picture publication of a British film star scantily clad – a detective said she was practically nude! – be described as anything other than obscene? Coming into the hands of any person, it can have nothing but a corrupt and depraving influence!'

Diana was not upset by the attention but she angrily rejected allegations that she had actually posed for them nude: 'What, me, darling? In this stage of my career? Not me, darling!' A month later, Halifax borough magistrates reconvened, having spent the past few weeks reading sixty-one copies of the offending magazines, just to be sure. Barrister James Pickles, later to become Judge Pickles, represented the book's publishers, Trans-Atlantic Authors of Lamb's Conduit Street in Holborn, London. He wasn't a fan of Dors by any means – if he thought about her at all it was as a shallow copy of Marilyn Monroe, who was about to take tenure as Hollywood's biggest female star – but the book clearly showed Diana in various costumes. In one picture she was fully dressed (albeit wearing 17th-century *Wicked Lady* garb), in another she was wearing an ample bathing costume, and even with the most meagre coverage – a magazine, a fur wrap – her breasts were covered. Pickles asked the magistrates not to destroy the books on grounds of artistic merit, and the chairman extended the reprieve to all sixteen titles, even though he said, gravely, that some of them came 'very close' to obscenity.

Diana just about weathered the criticism. It had been a close thing – Sir Carol wasn't exactly thrilled by the publicity – but *A Kid for Two Farthings* had just about wrapped by that time anyway, and when the fuss died down Dennis took Diana to Paris for her twenty-third birthday. They came back to a potentially more damaging controversy. Dennis had, for some time, been inflating Diana's value through the pages of the press, and his little trick of adding extra noughts here and there had begun to be noticed. In the House of Commons on 28 October 1954, there was a debate about film stars and their tax allowances, in particular the case of actor Robert Newton, who reputedly had arrears of £46,000. Conservative MP, Henry Price, asked Henry Brooke, financial secretary to the Treasury, if he knew ' . . . of the case of an actress who was allowed to charge a mink coat as 'expenses', and also the case of Diana Dors, who draws £60 a week, £50 of which is tax free.' Brooke replied that he was not at liberty to discuss individual cases but promised to 'look into it'.

The press were straight on the phone to Diana, who had a suitably haughty dismissal prepared. 'I am employed by my company, Diana Dors Ltd,' she explained. 'Obviously, I earn far more than £60 per week – during the film which I have finished I was paid £200 a day. All the money I earn goes into the company, from which I draw an expense account, which can be anything – £40, £60 or £100 a week.'

To make things clearer, she helpfully tabulated her weekly expenses:

Entertaining	£40
Fan mail secretary	£10
Stationery, stamps, photos	£15
Hairdresser (twice)	£5
Running new Cadillac	£14
Tips	£10
Personal and household	£60

Then there was the small matter of clothes. 'Over a period of one year they can cost me a few thousand,' she told *Picturegoer*. 'A girl has to be impeccably turned out or some critic will say, 'Tatty Miss So-and-so looks like a dog's dinner . . .' You can never be photographed in the same thing twice. Well, you can . . . but you just don't.'

Britain's tax laws were already ill-equipped to deal with irregular earnings and irregular employment, and since the Rank fiasco there had been few credible attempts to create tax incentives that would help the British film industry compete internationally. But there was also a bitter subtext of snobbery. Victor Spinetti was appalled – how very English, he thought, to denounce someone to the taxman. That petty fascination with other people's belongings: 'How could she afford it? She's no better than anyone else!' Years later, he met an MP who boasted of earning an extra £80,000 a year just for asking questions about betting shops. Just the kind of hard-faced bastard who asked questions about Diana Dors. 'How could she live like this . . . ?' She just lived well, that was all.

Diana was indignant. Talking to the *Mirror*, she said, 'As far as looking into my company is concerned, I would like to get up in the Commons and ask MPs, "How can one compete with American stars when 19s 6d in the pound has to be paid in income tax?" It is beyond me. What the MPs overlook is the fact that an actor or actress has only seven or ten years at the outside in which to make money.'

Almost immediately, Dennis set up another company, this one called Diador Ltd, which was to deal exclusively with film production. Diana was said to be developing a film called *The Rough and the Smooth*, based on a novel by Robin Maugham, to co-star Edward G. Robinson and be directed by Ida Lupino, although it never went ahead. In fact, Diador never made anything at all, so perhaps it was just a fit of pique, a bid to break away from her stereotype. 'I'm tired of always being the bad girl, the floosie, the sexy dame,' she said. 'I want to try to extend the range and try something a bit different . . . But not *too* different,' she hastily added. 'I don't see myself as Juliet in *Romeo and Juliet*.' Strangely, when *The Rough and the Smooth* was actually made in 1959, it was criticized for being old-fashioned, the story of an archaeologist who is distracted from his marriage to the daughter of a wealthy newspaper owner by a beautiful, enigmatic woman. In other words, a floosie. A sexy dame.

In November, after a spread in the *Daily Mirror* repeated Dennis's outrageous claims about their earning power, the tax man pounced on the Hamiltons. It even made the one o'clock news that Dennis and Diana had to sign an affidavit swearing that they had left nothing out of their previous income tax return. 'Having got that for evidence,' said Diana, 'they are now going through our accounts again with a magnifying glass. But they won't find anything wrong.'

Indeed, despite some obvious ruses – including the lion-skin rug that Diana insisted cost £3 10s from a junk shop – the Revenue did not proceed with its enquiries. The Hamiltons made a lot of the fact that their tax affairs were in order, which technically they were, but this was only because their actual income was so much lower than Dennis's homespun PR boasted. His accountants begged him to calm down, but Dennis manipulated this misleading state of affairs to his advantage when the Rank Organisation wrote to offer a new, seven-year contract, which Diana claimed to be worth a projected £100,000, to make two films a year. 'Not bad, eh?' said Diana, remembering the early days. 'I'm grateful for the offer – but I think I can do better on my own.'

She thought about it for three weeks, in particular the options in Rank's favour and, remembering Dennis's handling of the American contract, declined the offer in a most public fashion. 'I don't like not being free to turn down scripts,' she said. 'I see no reason to be under contract – I can ask for my own terms now. I got a kick out of being offered that contract and turning it down. The way they let

Above left The former Diana Fluck steps out as one of Mr Rank's young ladies (1950). © PICTORIAL

Above A pre-blonde Diana poses for an early Rank publicity shot (circa 1950). © PICTORIAL

Left Modelling swimwear and showing off her rather too ample curves in a publicity shot for *Lady Godiva Rides Again* (May 1951). © UPI/CORBIS

Left Outside Caxton Hall after marrying her first husband, Dennis Hamilton (3 May, 1951). © HULTON-DEUTSCH COLLECTION/CORBIS

Below left Catering for her co–star in Carol Reed's *A Kid for Two Farthings* (1955), Diana's first film in colour. © PICTORIAL

Left A typical glamourpuss shot from the mid 50s, complete with the cream telephone she always seemed so keen on.
© CORBIS/EVERETT

Below Diana causes a stir at the Venice film festival a few days after punting down the canal in a mink bikini made to her own design (August 1955). © PICTORIAL

Opposite centre Diana admirably maintains her dignity while putting a labour-saving robot through its paces (February 1952). Happily, this was not the kitchen of the future. © UPI/CORBIS

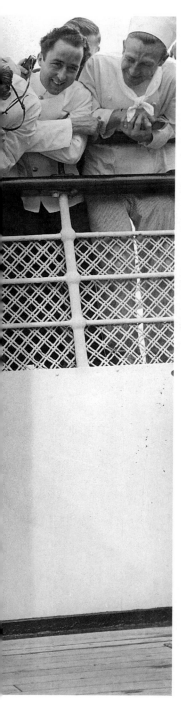

Left Diana gives British readers an insight into her lavish Hollywood lifestyle as filming starts on *I Married a Woman* (summer 1956). © PICTORIAL

Above The sophisticate siren look that RKO hoped would whet American audience's appetite for Britain's own Marilyn Monroe (circa 1956).
© PICTORIAL

Centre Diana and Teasy-Weasy entertaining Howard Keel at her home in Coldwater Canyon, Beverly Hills, shortly before the infamous pool party went horribly wrong on 19 August 1956.
© UPI/CORBIS-BETTMANN

Diana poses with the mariachi band who played at the party. Photographer Stewart Sawyer, alleged to have pushed Diana and her friends into the pool, later claimed that Diana kicked him in the head. Her footwear suggests otherwise (circa 1956).

© PICTORIAL

me loose when I was just a starlet – £20 a week they were paying me, with my co-star getting £25,000 or something. Still, what the hell? It's all experience.'

With Dennis's guidance, Diana began to get a handle on the publicity machine, which irked the studios enormously. One of her publicists found it difficult to get her pin-up shots into the papers because, he complained, 'news editors said she'd soon be in the news anyway.' As 1954 came to a close, even her driving lessons were considered newsworthy. Taking a mock test in December, she was failed by her instructor, who described her as being 'apt to take risks' at turns, 'inconsistent' with the mirror and unable to 'position correctly' in the road. For courtesy to other vehicles and road users, she was marked 'inconsiderate'. 'The candidate has sound vehicle control but is unreliable in road procedure,' he concluded. 'She is below the required standard.'

Diana suspected prejudice on the examiner's part. 'They don't expect blondes to drive straight,' she fumed.

Diana's disappointment was quickly dispelled in the new year with the offer of a role in Ken Annakin's *Value for Money*. It was another morality play, in which a Yorkshire businessman has to choose between his childhood sweetheart and gold-digging girlfriend, but Diana's dismay at being offered another 'floosie' role took a back seat when money was discussed – £5,000 – a career high. Nevertheless, she played the part reluctantly. 'It's funny how people always associate blondes with that sort of thing,' she said. 'When I started in films I was pushed into one little vamp part after the other, with nothing to do but make eyes and wiggle my hips – so everybody thinks I've got to where I've got to on setbacks. It prevents me playing a nun, for one thing. And I'd like to play a nun.'

Diana was already feeling hemmed in by her sexy image

and she began to downplay it – through the press, for example by letting it slip that she was working on a book of children's stories, to be titled *Tales Tweetie-Pie Told Me*, in honour of her budgerigar. 'People seem to forget that I've got another side to me,' she protested. 'I suppose I'm a bit crazy, but I don't drink or smoke and I like animals more than people. I have a houseful of pets, and a husband, and I love them all. And I like oil paintings and music and all of that sort of thing. People forget that. Still,' she said, brightening, 'I might as well cash in on sex now, while I've got it. It can't last forever, can it?'

These attempts to foreground her sensitive side were greeted with scepticism, prompting the *Sunday Express* to run a gossip item noting caustically that 'a whole week has passed without Diana Dors announcing she wants to play a nun in films.'

When *Value for Money* began shooting at Pinewood in January, Diana was bemused to find an imported rival sex symbol installed in the dressing room next to hers. Almost three years younger than Diana, Brigitte Bardot had first come to fame as a model when she posed as a cover girl for *Elle* magazine at the age of fifteen. At eighteen, she married twenty-four-year-old Roger Vadim, then learning his trade as an assistant director and working as a journalist for *Paris Match*, and the same year she made her film debut in one of the prolific Jean Boyer's lightweight, unpretentious entertainments, *Un Trou Normand*, also known as *Crazy for Love*. In fact, she made a lot of films in that vein until her husband made his directorial debut some years later, in 1956, with the scandalous *Et dieu créa la femme* (*And God Created Woman*). Only then was 'BB' the legend, truly born.

When she and Diana met, Bardot was in Pinewood to make her British debut in *Doctor at Sea*, the second in a popular line of whimsical medical comedies starring Dirk Bogarde, and she had already begun to invade Diana's precious media territory. Diana was doubly dismayed to find that Bardot sang a musical number in the film and had made a demonstration disc to rehearse with, which she played over and over as her famously eccentric vocal struggled to find the melody. Finally, Dennis had enough, and when Bardot was called into the set he broke into her dressing room and used a nail to scratch a crude locked groove into the vinyl. When Bardot returned, she quickly got the message.

It was also while filming *Value for Money* that Diana met another rival, although this one had neither the looks nor the figure to offer the same kind of competition. She'd been invited to judge a fancy dress competition at Poole Harbour Yacht Club, and arrived to find that her fellow judge was to be Lady Norah Docker, wife of millionaire industrialist Bernard.

Born Norah Turner in Derby, June 1906, she had been dogged by controversy ever since her car salesman father committed suicide when she was sixteen – a drastic measure to avoid bad business complications. Norah and her three brothers and sisters were not provided for, and although her mother took over a pub to make ends meet, Norah moved to London to become a dancing instructor at the Café De Paris. It was here that she met her first husband, Clement Callingham, a wealthy executive with wine merchant Henekey's, and when he died in 1945, Norah wasted little time grieving. The following year she married Sir William Collins, a director of Fortnum and Mason and nearly thirty years her senior. This particular union was dissolved the same way as the first, when Collins died in 1947 leaving Norah a quarter of a million pounds richer.

Bernard was her third husband – at only ten years her senior, her safest bet so far – and a director of BSA, which produced motorcycles and, through its Daimler subsidiary, motor cars. Norah liked money and would go to great lengths to announce the fact. Where other girls were satisfied with fur, she demanded mink. Where they were satisfied with zircon, she insisted on diamonds. When she drank, it was always champagne – and it had to be pink, because she loved the colour. 'Make yourself expensive,' was her manifesto. In 1951, to help her husband's company, Norah had an idea that made her name and began her fifteen-year residency in the pages of the national press.

At a cost of £8,500, she commissioned a gold Daimler, and although some corners were cut – using gold leaf and chrome, or even brass – she claimed it sent shockwaves through the grey conformism of struggling Britain. She wanted to raise Daimler's profile internationally, she said, and when her plan seemed to work, she took it on herself to interfere more and more in Bernard's work, thinking that a little glamour and reckless spending would cheer everything up. As a publicity stunt, the gold Daimler was unmatched – but while Norah saw herself as Britannia, the people of Britain saw only Marie Antoinette, at odds with society and out of touch with the problems left behind by the war. Norah's movements were keenly tracked by the press as she moved across Europe, infuriating the working class and upper class alike with her crusading vulgarity. While they were amused, and even impressed, by her outspokenness, Norah had crossed far beyond the fine line that Diana Dors and some of her free-spending show business friends were approaching. In fact, her slow downfall began soon after she and Diana met, when BSA shareholders tried to oust Bernard from the board.

In amongst the damning evidence – some of it exaggerated, to make Bernard a scapegoat for the company's terrible losses – was an expense sheet charging the company over £7,000 for clothes bought by Norah to wear to the Paris motor show. To foil the bid, Norah sent out letters, each containing a little picture of herself, and bought air-time on commercial television to plead their case. When Bernard was finally sacked in 1956, Norah didn't understand it. In truth, many of the company's troubles weren't entirely his fault and everyone at BSA could easily have lived with Bernard Docker.

They just couldn't bear his wife.

The sudden windfall that *Value for Money* brought Diana was quickly made use of, and Dennis felt little compunction about spending it. When the *Daily Sketch* asked him what he actually did for his share of Diana's income, he replied, somewhat tersely, 'I keep her in the role of a fabulous star who is always doing something different from any body else.' In a nutshell, he decided, 'I promoted her and taught her how to act big.'

Meanwhile, he was spending big, buying first a yacht then an outrageous new car, a twenty-two-foot, two-seater Delahaye. Costing £2,750 second hand – it was custom-built for a French industrial millionaire – it boasted gold-trim handles, twenty-seven gold-plated knobs on the dashboard, a sixty-horse-power engine and was capable of speeds up to 180 m.p.h. Diana had still not passed her driving test by the time it went into the garage with the Cadillac and the Rolls.

But while the Hamiltons' recent excesses were dominating the tabloids, Diana's work did not go unnoticed, and when *A Kid for Two Farthings* was released that spring, Kenneth Tynan contributed a glowing two-page eulogy for *Picturegoer* magazine. 'In the new Carol Reed picture,' he wrote, 'she has a chance of playing an ingénue who is neither a doll nor a slut, and it is already her favourite film, as Reed is her favourite director. But even if it has failed to turn her into a great actress, I, for one, shall not mind. To expect her to act as well is like expecting [the] Boulder Dam to play chess.'

Diana, in the meantime, was still anxious to get her production company started, although she only had the title for its first film. And a good one, too — the story would write itself, she thought. It was to be called *Mink and Millions*.

Chapter Five

A REAL HUMAN BEING

IN APRIL 1955 Mary was rushed into the Masonic Hospital for a hernia operation. It was a success, but Mary came out in a seriously weakened condition. Both Bert and Diana were extremely worried. They'd talked about Mary's illness when they spent Christmas together at Diana's house in Bray, but neither really knew how serious it would be. They were heartened when Mary showed signs of improving and, as the days passed, Diana really thought the worst was over, but three weeks later, at the age of sixty-five, Mary suffered a relapse and died.

Diana was devastated. Since her affair with Kim, she'd never been as close to her mother as she once had been and she regretted that particular period of warfare. To compound the tragedy, there was the irony of the situation – Mary, who had spent nearly forty precarious years living with a man who had a dangerous heart condition, had suffered a fatal heart attack herself.

Diana called Rank and arranged to reschedule a shoot she was about to start, a slapstick reptile romp, to be directed by her old friend J. Lee-Thompson, called *An Alligator Named Daisy*. Mary's death seemed unreal and Diana attended the funeral in a daze, unable to comprehend that the coffin being lowered into the ground really contained her mother's body. Bert's wreath, and its simple message, brought it home.

If Mary had held on for only a few weeks longer she'd have seen some very important developments in her daughter's career. First, the Rank Organisation came back to Diana for further talks. The previous year had been very good for them, and after John Davis's radical cutbacks – which had released Diana, among others, from her original contract – the company was beginning to get on top of its debts. Profits even seemed possible, although Rank's lucrative venture into the manufacture and distribution of photocopying machines, through subsidiary company Rank Xerox, was still a year in the offing.

Over lunch with Earl St John himself, Dennis negotiated an incredible five-year, non-exclusive contract, with no options, which required Diana to make just one film a year for the studio, or give them ten weeks of her time. At £7,000 per film – which Dennis managed to raise from an initial offer of £6,000 – Diana announced that it would make her the highest paid film actress in the country after Vivien Leigh. She was amused that Rank wanted her back so badly but she was gracious about it. 'I don't think I was much of an asset in those early days,' she conceded. 'Too plump and not much of an actress.'

Secondly, Mary missed the chance of seeing her daughter mixing with royalty when *A Kid for Two Farthings* followed its screening at the Cannes film festival with a charity premiere in the West End of London, attended by the Queen and Prince Phillip.

Predictably, Diana's sudden respectability was somewhat short-lived, and the wisdom of presenting Diana to HRH was publicly questioned after a newspaper report by John Balfour asked 'Are British films going too far?' The article, which concerned a scene in *Value for Money* where Diana removes her clothes to entice her boyfriend (played by John Gregson), was accompanied by a near full-page publicity still that showed her peering round a bathroom door, her right leg, thigh and shoulder visible and clearly naked. 'The shot, it's true, shows only a portion of the Rank star,' wrote Balfour, 'but this kind of pose has turned France's film industry into a nightmare of banned reels and X certificates. We don't want that here.'

Diana acknowledged that she was, indeed, nude, adding that the shot, which required her to show 'as much as I could – and as little', had been tricky. Balfour asked if she expected censor trouble. 'That's not my baby,' she told him, so he approached Rank directly. The company replied that the censor had seen the script and looked likely to approve it, saying 'a Diana Dors film is always bound to be spicy – within limits.' Arthur Watkins – secretary to the British Board of Film Censors, as it was then known – was asked to qualify the Board's position. Watkins, himself a playwright, was a liberal voice, and he downplayed any attempts to sensationalize the issue. 'Our rule is quite simple: nudity is barred. So is the suggestion of nudity if it becomes too blatant. Still, we haven't seen this film yet, not even a photograph. Until we do, you'll have to be your own censor.'

Balfour's article concluded with a grumpy broadside at both Diana and the company: 'Even as an advance publicity "still" the pose is cheap, and it is not the kind of cheapness Mr Rank's studios can afford to indulge. Nor, for that matter, Miss Dors herself – just at a time when her genuine talent as an actress is being recognized. I look to Mr Watkins, a fair and far from prudish censor, to save Diana and her employers from themselves.'

Such criticism hit home strongly at the Rank Organisation. Rank considered the medium to be family entertainment and its cinema chain discriminated heavily against films with an adult theme – between 1951 and 1957, its cinemas showed only six X-rated films. Having paid extravagantly for Diana's services, members of the Rank board were already beginning to wonder if she wasn't a bit strong for their traditionally conservative tastes. When *Value for Money* was eventually released, Diana's 'nude' scene was nowhere in evidence.

With so much money at her disposal, Diana was able to take time off that summer and kept a comparatively low profile. Dennis bought a property in Maidenhead and made plans to turn it into an espresso bar. Coffee was still exotic in the post-war lifestyle, and Dennis planned to reflect this with his usual flair for decor. Originally it was to be called The Jungle, staffed by women in sarongs and featuring marmosets in bamboo cages, but he settled instead for El Toucan, in honour of the two South American birds he'd imported (which Diana, in turn, christened Jack and Jill). But once the theme was established and executed, Dennis quickly lost interest. It ticked over but, like Diana, he grew bored without constant stimulation.

Diana returned to the world in style that autumn, when the British film industry decamped to Venice for the annual film festival. The Rank entourage arrived by plane on 3 September, but Diana had set out before them in her powder-blue Cadillac. The foreign media were curious to see the 'English Marilyn Monroe' and stars like Jack Hawkins, Donald Sinden, John Gregson and James Robertson were largely ignored at the press conference, where journalists and photographers flocked around Diana and starlet Eunice Gayson.

It was not a vintage festival. The year's big news centred largely on films being taken out of the competition – the Czech film *Jan Hus*, the Spanish film *Cato Del Gallo* – and the biggest American film, MGM's controversial juvenile delinquent drama, *The Blackboard Jungle,* was withdrawn after threats by Clare Booth Luce, America's Italian envoy, to cause 'the biggest scandal ever' if it wasn't. The film was replaced by *Interrupted Melody*, a movie biography of polio-afflicted opera singer Marjorie Lawrence.

It was into this highly charged political arena that Rank unveiled its magnum opus – *Doctor at Sea*. Critics took it with good humour, while acknowledging that the film was not 'a festival film', and enjoyed John Davis's hospitality at a midnight reception immediately after. They also enjoyed the sight of Diana being punted down the Grand Canal a few days later, wearing a bikini made entirely of mink. The paparazzi went wild and the image went straight back to Fleet Street.

When she returned to England, Diana inadvertently saw to it that Kim Waterfield also made the news before the month was out. Diana and Dennis were at the Embassy Club in Old Bond Street, watching Jack Jackson's *Gala Night* show being televised by the commercial channel – then restricted to the London area. Kim bumped into Dennis downstairs and there was an argument. 'Watch it, Waterfield,' sneered Dennis and suddenly Kim flew at him. People rushed to pull them apart, but they kept breaking free and throwing punches as they were escorted up the stairs. Kim was taken outside by the doorman but when Dennis appeared at the entrance Kim went for him. At that moment a policeman walked past and Kim was arrested on a charge of insulting behaviour. The papers were full of the mystery and the *Daily Mirror* led its report with the somewhat bald headline: 'Diana Dors says: "I cannot think what the fight was about."' The truth was rather less exciting. As Dennis was making his bullish threats, a fleck of spittle had flown out of his mouth and hit Kim square in the face. Kim was outraged, thinking Dennis had spat at him, but when he calmed down, when he really thought about it, he realized it was just part of Dennis's bluster, an accidental tic.

When the case went to court the following week, Kim was found guilty and fined twenty shillings, but magistrate K.J.P. Barraclough was fascinated by the accused.

'What are you?' he asked.

'I'm of independent means,' said Kim.

'Don't you do anything?' he persisted.

'I steeplechase as an amateur,' came the reply.

Diana played down the connection with Kim and denied any knowledge of a reported 'engagement'. She was more concerned with her latest film role, the one she'd discussed with J. Lee-Thompson on the set of *The Weak and the Wicked*. Like the previous film it was a prison drama scripted by Joan Henry, but this one had a more specific agenda. Henry had written it as a novel two years before but it clearly chimed with a story that had recently made the news, when nightclub hostess Ruth Ellis was charged with, and subsequently hung for, the murder of her lover, David Blakely, outside a north London pub. Called *Yield to the Night*, the script concerned a young blonde shopgirl, Mary Hilton (Diana), who becomes involved in a jealous love triangle with a nightclub pianist and his callous, wealthy girlfriend. When her lover commits suicide, Mary cold-bloodedly shoots her rival to avenge his death.

The press wondered why Diana, and not one of a more established and serious clique of actresses – like Margaret Leighton, Vivien Leigh or Ingrid Bergman – was chosen for the role. She was characteristically level-headed in her reasoning. 'Perhaps it's just that they've got so much more than I have,' she replied. 'They're all wonderful dramatic and emotional actresses. But maybe people think of me as an ordinary girl, and when this terrible thing happens to an ordinary girl, it's more . . . well, poignant. But you should ask the director, J. Lee-Thompson. When he offered me the part I didn't say, "Why me?" – I just said, "Yes, please!" At last I've got the chance to play a real human being and not just a cardboard character with curves.'

Diana had discovered she was pregnant before the film went into production and, though she wanted a family, the role was too good to pass up. The decision to have the pregnancy terminated was heavily influenced by Dennis's reluctance to start a family, but Diana was thinking about herself, too. There was a time limit on her looks, and if she took six months off, who knew who might take her place? And even if no one had, what effect would it have had on her figure? The decision, this time, was as much hers as Dennis's, and that hurt. Previously, she'd had mitigating circumstances to justify the decision and Diana had persuaded herself it was in the child's best interests — she had been unmarried, she had been broke. This time, she had a stable home life and an enviable lifestyle. She was simply thinking about herself.

Yield to the Night had originally been pitched to Rank, but the company had been wary of its controversial theme and so it was backed by an independent company, Associated British. Because she'd signed a non-exclusive contract, Rank was powerless to stop one of its most famous contract players taking the role, and the board grimaced when the first publicity stills were circulated, showing Diana without make-up and with her hair clipped. It seemed a far cry from the Diana who was telling the press of her plans to build a double-D swimming pool, the steps forming a large vertical D, the pool itself forming the other. 'What else are you going to buy?' she was asked. 'What else is there?' she retorted. 'Tell me and I'll get it!'

Filming began at Elstree Studios in October but the shoot almost had to be cancelled when Diana was involved in a car crash on 17 October. Dennis wasn't around, so Diana went to work in a hired car rather than the Rolls, which she wasn't at all happy about. As she climbed in she wondered whether to sit behind the driver or in the passenger seat; in the end she did neither, just curled up in the middle of the back seat and went to sleep. She woke with a start when the car slammed into the back of a lorry – a split second later, her head slammed into the back of the front seat and she was showered with glass from the splintered windscreen. She staggered from the car in a state of shock. When an ambulance arrived she was taken to nearby Hillingdon Hospital, where she was treated for cuts on her head, hands and leg. Doctors wanted to put three stitches in the wound in her head, but Diana refused – it meant shaving part of her hair. After a lot of pleading, they used plastic skin on the wound instead.

The accident kept Diana off the set for a week. Before she returned, she turned twenty-four and Dennis thirty-one, and they celebrated a day early on Saturday 22 October with a party that started at 8 p.m. on Saturday night and went straight on through till 5 a.m. on Sunday morning. Nervous insurers were worried that they might have to pay out £5,000 in lieu of lost earnings, but Diana reported for work, as scheduled, on Monday.

Journalists who visited the set found Diana in high spirits. Leslie Frewin, head of publicity at Elstree, even led a troop of writers onto the set to see one of the film's climactic scenes being filmed, in which Diana took her last agonizing steps from the condemned cell. The first rehearsal was rough but the second was better and the actual take went fine. Writer Derek Walker asked Lee-Thompson if it was really fair to expect Diana to do this in front of an audience – any audience, let alone an audience of critics – but he simply shrugged. 'A lot of stars wouldn't do it,' he said, 'but with Dors it's different. I think she is, if anything, different with an audience. She likes to have a reaction to her performance.'

Typically, Diana was worried that people might confuse her first major foray into drama with Marilyn Monroe's very public wish to be taken seriously as an actress, which she viewed with a certain amount of scorn. 'On the face of it, it sounds ludicrous to me. I might just as well say I want to play Lady Macbeth. Still, if Monroe thinks she can do it, good luck to her.'

Dennis wasn't around for most of the shoot, claiming to be looking after his property developments by dropping in on the El Toucan – or, more specifically, the waitresses he'd hired to work there. The coffee bar was bringing in £100 a week, which wasn't to be sniffed at, said Dennis, when times were bad. And in the film business, they often were bad. When reporter Robert Robinson asked Diana if she'd ever like to retire and go into business herself, Diana's reply was frank and to the point. 'Business, no. Retire, yes. When I've made enough money, I will.' What would she do, he asked? 'Stay home and knit. I already paint and embroider. But the public always thinks of me in nightclubs with buckets of champagne and somebody else's husband.'

When filming wrapped, Diana made a highly public attempt on 15 December to pass her driving test in Slough, Buckinghamshire. She took the test in the driving school's nondescript black Austin, wearing slacks, a windcheater jacket and scarf over her head. Dennis had bought her a steel-grey Mark 7 Jaguar, with red upholstery, as a present for passing and he paced nervously up and down while waiting to hear. She returned home, elated, with her newly qualified driving documents in hand. 'It was an uneventful drive,' examiner Thomas Winter told the press. 'Now I can go shopping by myself,' said Diana.

In the meantime, Diana had begun to think about writing. She told reporter Eileen Winncroft how she sat in the boathouse, mulling over ideas, but one of her favourites was considered too gloomy. A key character died – perhaps it was the one she wanted to play – and producers didn't want death in their movies.

'You'll have to be directed by a foreign film unit, then,' said Winncroft.

'Perhaps,' said Diana.

'Suppose,' suggested Winncroft, 'you wrote a script of your own in which a woman had a baby while she tried to work . . .'

Diana thought about it. 'That's a brilliant idea for continental audiences, who'll take realism and pregnancy and unglamorous faces,' she said. 'But not English audiences. They must have glamour, however false. But I shall go on writing. I've always wanted to. Actually, I don't read much. I stopped reading when the fairy stories gave out and all I had left were the schoolgirl magazines. I like a twist put on life. I like life dished up bigger and better and bolder and more exciting than lots of people seem to think it is.'

It was around this time that she finally found a story to match her title, *Mink and Millions*. In fact, it was a story she'd had all along but had been too shy to reveal – about a girl from the provinces who came to London in search of stardom. Producer Kenneth Harper said he was interested, and Diana promised to send him the story. Although the film was never made, the deal concluded Diana's most successful year to date which her mother had not lived to enjoy. But how would she follow it? *Yield to the Night* had been a gift of a role – would there come a role as good, as challenging, as rewarding? And if she was now, after Vivien Leigh, the second highest paid actress in Britain, would she ever take the number one spot?

The stakes had risen so high in 1955 she didn't know what to think. The press assumed she might consider giving up the pin-up work, but the answer was an emphatic no. 'I'll go on doing pin-ups 'till I'm too old to be any good at it,' she told *Picture Post*. 'All this putting of glamour and serious acting into separate compartments makes me sick. Just because a person is glamorous doesn't mean they can't feel real emotions. And I'll tell you another thing. I'm always getting the backwash of everything Marilyn Monroe does. Every time she stands up and says she wants to do The Brothers Whatsit by Dostoyouknow, everybody's on the phone asking if I'm giving up the glamour roles for the serious stuff. Why can't I do both?'

She apologized for cutting the interview short, explaining that a reporter from the *Daily Telegraph* was on her way. 'Fancy that!' Diana exclaimed. 'I didn't know they did things like me!'

The new year brought yet another change of address. Dennis was bored with Bray and in his thirst for investment had been to see another Thameside property in Maidenhead, Berkshire. Once owned, as Dennis claimed, by a multi-millionaire called Ernest Dunkles, Woodhurst was a huge, sprawling mansion, with over twenty rooms that he hoped to turn into flats. The centrepiece was a Roman-style swimming pool with white marble columns. 'It cost £26,500 in 1916,' Dennis boasted, 'it's bigger than most public baths, and the boiler alone' – which pumped in gallons of blue water – 'cost £5,000.' Diana wasn't impressed with Wood-hurst, but the more she thought about it, the more she was persuaded. Finally, they decided that since the swimming pool was already enclosed, they might as well build a penthouse on top of it. Dennis threw himself into the task. Three months later, the property would be theirs and ready for them to move into. Then he could start renovating the other flats – 'Dors them up', as he put it.

Curiously, although 1955 had been a watershed year, 1956 started very slowly. When Rank unveiled its £3 million, twenty-picture slate at the Dorchester Hotel in February, Diana was conspicuously absent. In fact, she had been offered a role, in John Paddy Carstairs' *The Big Money* – a comedy about a family of crooks whose black sheep is a bumbling, incompetent oaf – but the role was, inevitably, a small dumb-blonde part, the type she'd done five years ago. Diana felt insulted. After all, she thought, everyone agreed she'd come a long way since then. 'If that's the best you can offer me,' she told them, 'I'm rather surprised.' Belinda Lee took the part instead.

In any case, Diana wasn't the only one being left out – Kay Kendall and Jean Carson were in the same position – and she wasn't really too bothered. If Rank couldn't find any good scripts, that was their problem. She was still getting paid, wasn't she? And anyway, plenty of other things were beginning to happen for her outside Britain. For a start, she had an appearance on Bob Hope's television show, an international revue filmed in London and Paris, which aired in New York on 7 February, with the prospect of a Hollywood movie with Hope sometime in the summer. With another film offer from Italy, Diana's prospects were looking good all round the globe, and it seemed an amusing coincidence when news reports revealed that the Foreign Office was using her pin-up shots in the British government-sponsored *Al Alaam* magazine, as thinly veiled propaganda to promote the British way of life in the Middle East.

Despite the apparent lull in Diana's career, everything seemed to be happening around her, and on 13 March she was announced Showbusiness Personality of The Year at a charity luncheon hosted by the Variety Club of Great Britain. Diana was thrilled, though she gritted her teeth at some of toastmaster Tommy Trinder's lascivious double entendres about her 'outstanding' contributions.

A few nights later, the Hamiltons held a dinner party at Bray, and when Dennis read some of the news reports of the occasion he was enraged to see himself described, in the discreetly bitchy parlance of the time, as Diana's 'suede-shod Svengali'. It preyed on his mind all night, and as he grew more and more drunk his anger became more and more apparent. Diana went to bed early but was awoken around midnight by the sound of Dennis's drunken roar. 'Dors!' he yelled. 'Get down here!'

She pulled on a robe and walked to the top of the stairs. 'What the hell's going on?' she demanded.

'The press are here,' shouted Dennis.

Two journalists stood in the doorway, ostensibly wanting an interview but most likely in search of late-night hospitality.

'At this hour? Don't be ridiculous.'

She turned to walk away but Dennis charged up the stairs and grabbed her arms.

'You'll do as I bloody well say,' he yelled and wheeled her round. Diana lost her footing and tumbled to the bottom of the stairs, the robe flying open. She was naked underneath. 'There. Now fucking interview her,' snarled Dennis, storming back into the dining room.

A few of the guests still remained after the party. One closed the door and advised the pressmen to leave, another carried Diana upstairs to bed, where she lay dazed and shaking. She could still hear Dennis rambling drunkenly downstairs and realized she had to get out. She dressed hurriedly in sweater and slacks and grabbed her car keys, hoping to get away before he noticed.

Diana spent the night with some friends who lived nearby but returned the next morning to a scene of near-total pathos. Dennis was in tears, some of the guests were in tears, even the housekeeper was in tears. In a show of inspired, maudlin theatricality, he even begged her to think of the animals – a boxer dog, a poodle, two Siamese cats, a cockatoo and, of course Tweety-Pie the budgerigar. They both knew it was a cheap shot, but it worked. Diana's heart sank. Dennis was a difficult man to live with but he would be even harder to leave.

The spring of 1956 brought a lot of excitement when it was announced that *Yield to the Night* had been chosen, by default, to be the only British title to compete in that year's Cannes film festival. Rank had withdrawn its own offering, *A Town Like Alice*, based on Nevil Shute's novel and starring Virginia McKenna and Peter Finch. The film centred on a group of women and children POWs who were forced to march through Malaya by their Japanese captors. In case anyone thought it too subtle, the film's American distributor retitled the film *The Rape of Malaya*, but neither version was screened in Cannes since Rank was afraid of offending potential Japanese investors. This precipitated a bizarre spate of withdrawals and counter-withdrawals that culminated in the festival's German and Finnish delegates leaving before the festival was even halfway over.

This news was almost eclipsed, however, when it was revealed that Diana had agreed to sit for sixty-five-year-old artist Stanley Spencer after a chance introduction at a dinner party in Cookham. 'What I'd like from Mr Spencer is just a nice portrait,' Diana told the press, perhaps unaware that, since his creative prime in the twenties, and inspired by his experiences in the First World War, Spencer had begun to produce rather more provocative canvasses. Spencer considered himself a highly religious painter but his faith translated into disturbing images of sexual desire – some of which, he was warned, could conceivably be prosecuted as obscene if they were exhibited. Many regarded him as a spent talent and were disgusted by his new direction. 'I do not like these bloated, sausage-fingered puppets holding a mass meeting amid tombstones,' ran one memorable critique.

But Diana was not daunted. 'Why, I love all his pictures. But my picture will be a portrait, of course. No tombs, or anything like that.'

Cannes, however, was everything Diana was expecting, and she was mobbed as she walked down the Croizette on her first day there. Starlet Simone Silva had raised the publicity stakes two years before, when she whipped off her bikini top and clutched her breasts for a revealing shot with Robert Mitchum. Silva had wanted to be famous for years; she claimed to have been born in Cairo in 1928 to a French father and Italian-Greek mother, and that her original name was Simone De Bouillard. Whatever the truth, she was a secretary working in London when she met her husband, the wealthy textile merchant James Silver, and she customized his name several times – first to Da Silva, then Silvera – before arriving at the screen name she wanted. At the age of twenty-three, she was already frustrated. 'Sometimes I sob for weeks, I am so desolate,' she told *Daily Mirror* show business reporter Donald Zec. 'I would give anything to prove that I could be a star. The fact that I am still in London trying for parts, instead of taking my usual three months' holiday in the sun, shows how sincere I am.'

Silva's appetite for stardom had been whetted in 1950 when American director Walter Wanger spotted her at Cannes, where she was holidaying with her husband, and offered her a screen test. As Silva's luck would have it, Wanger was about to be bankrupted by the Bank of America over debts raised making *Joan of Arc* in 1948 which starred Ingrid Bergman. His Hollywood stock plummeted even lower in 1952, when he was imprisoned for shooting his wife's agent in the groin in a fit of jealousy. Silva became so desperate to be noticed that she appeared at every opening night in London's theatre district, wearing décolleté dresses that were really just the same basic design, with six different tops. 'If it's a bustline they want, I've got it,' she said. 'One inch more than Jane Russell. My neckline takes the plunge in the daytime as well as at night. I've been to twenty-two theatrical first nights – always with a daring neckline – and always I've had my picture in the paper the next day.'

By 1954, when an affair with Bonar Colleano ended her marriage in the divorce court, Silva thought time was running out: 'People criticize Marilyn Monroe for posing in the nude, but I say good luck to her. It's got her where she wanted to be. I only wish I'd thought of it first, and I'd have done it, too.' Her opportunity came at that year's Cannes, when her 'top' – two chiffon scarves attached to a grass mini-skirt and fastened behind her neck – came off, and Silva posed for a full thirty minutes, cupping her 38-inch breasts with her hands. In the scramble to get pictures, one photographer broke a leg, another broke an arm and three damaged their cameras when they tripped in the surf.

Silva immediately received an offer of work from a Hollywood producer, but when she arrived he reneged on the deal. The next year was a very public humiliation that started with a lambasting from evangelist Billy Graham. 'It was the worst type of exploitation of sex,' he declared. 'The lowest kind of publicity stunt. There is no doubt that this sort of thing contributes to immorality. I think any decent person would agree with me.' After dodging the American immigration board for nearly twelve months with a succession of appeals and applications for residency – paid for by cabaret routines in low-rent nightclubs – Silva finally returned to Britain with nothing. The only thing she got from her Hollywood deal was a pair of shoes, worth £4, and an eating disorder.

By 1956, Simone Silva's lessons had been learned by every starlet in the industry, and Diana took careful note of these 'moral' boundaries. By playing hard to get, she – or rather Dennis – found that she could tease the paparazzi into a photographic frenzy when she finally agreed to pose triumphantly on the beach at Cannes.

Two days before *Yield to the Night* received its world premiere, however, she discovered she was expected to pay half her expenses, which of course included Dennis's, too. She was furious and made her dissatisfaction public. 'I have never been so insulted and humiliated in my life,' she fumed. 'To think that I should have to indulge in this petty squabbling with Associated British over a sum like £100 or so.' Rank hadn't short changed her for last year's Venice trip, she pointed out, and she hadn't even been promoting a film. Her presence at Cannes was front-page material, the kind money couldn't buy, yet she was expected to subsidize the trip. 'Dennis and I feel like people who have been invited to a party and given a bill for the drinks,' sniffed Diana, perhaps forgetting that three years earlier, in Blackpool, that had been Dennis's precise definition of an hilarious practical joke.

The sum, it transpired, was closer to £40, but Associated British explained that the arrangement was necessitated by the Bank of England's Exchange Control regulations, and pointed out that her room and board were paid for by the Festival. Nevertheless, they agreed to pay the money and Diana, rather taken aback, decided to give the money to charity – in this case, the film's producer, Kenneth Harper, who had to pay his own bills. She then tried to top the gesture with an Evita-esque plan to throw £40 of her own money from her hotel balcony, but if she ever went ahead with it, photographers were mysteriously absent from the event.

Instead, she attended a supper dance thrown by Rank to showcase nine of its stars – Diana was one, the others included Belinda Lee, Muriel Pavlow, Susan Beaumont, Peter Finch, Donald Sinden and Tony Wright. Rank supported Diana's presence at the festival in theory, but did not appreciate the irony of the situation: it was effectively subsidizing one of its main rivals, Associated British. *Yield to the Night* premiered later that night, 4 May, and John Davis was there to witness its enthusiastic reception. When the film ended, Diana received a standing ovation, though it was as much for her outfit as her performance. It was a strapless turquoise chiffon gown with silver embroidery, pearl sequins, white fox trimmings dyed turquoise around the bottom, and a turquoise fox stole. She had been keeping it a secret until the premiere; the unkind, fashion-conscious French press suggested that she should have kept it a secret forever. *Daily Mail* columnist Majdalany perhaps hit upon Diana's 'look' when he wrote: 'This highly personal approach to clothes is not a question of good taste or bad, it is beyond the realm of taste altogether.'

It was a mixed festival. Hitchcock's self-remade *The Man Who Knew Too Much* and Nunnally Johnson's *The Man in the Grey Flannel Suit* headed a strong delegation from the American studios, but the Golden Palm and Special Jury Prize went, surprisingly, to two documentaries – Jacques Cousteau's *The Silent World* and Henri-Georges Clouzot's *The Picasso Mystery* respectively. Diana didn't win the Best Actress award, but many were surprised that she was even in the running – especially the Americans, who sneeringly nicknamed her Marilyn Bovril – alongside more established and obvious festival talent such as Susan Hayward, who won the award for *I'll Cry Tomorrow* (MGM's biopic of thirties starlet Lilian Roth), and Ulla Jacobsson, star of Ingmar Bergman's *Smiles of a Summer Night*. John Davis would doubtless have been more pleased with this state of events had the film not been such downbeat, obvious X-certificate material and, as he left the screening, Diana was convinced that he blanked her – a suspicion which was not dispelled when she found that there wasn't a seat for her on the Rank table at the dinner afterwards. She returned home the following day and, perhaps resentful of the Dors publicity, at least one newspaper reported that she was ignored at the airport in favour of Danny Kaye, who was flying in from Belgrade to promote a film he'd made for the United Nations.

At home, *Yield to the Night* was equally well received, and Diana had some of the best reviews of her career from the more strait-laced press. *Sight and Sound* commented that, 'the most important thing about *Yield* is not so much its quality as a film as the exceptional nature of its attempt. Here is a British picture which is daring enough to take as its theme the last few days in the life of a murderess condemned to be hanged, and brave enough to suggest that the whole business is not one that reflects the utmost credit on society.' Although it bemoaned the film's reliance on clichés and stock characterization, Diana was praised, albeit faintly, for her 'honest, suffering performance'. Despite all these good notices, her usual audience stayed away and when the film opened in London's West End on 10 September, it ran for just two weeks.

By this time, the Bob Hope movie had fallen through. He had wanted her for *Beau James*, a biopic based on the life of Jimmy Walker, Mayor of New York in the twenties, but to get the role as Walker's girlfriend she would have had to dye her hair black. 'Imagine me with black hair!' she wailed. 'My hair is part of my trademark. It has taken years to build up my personality and it would be silly to kill it now.' The role eventually went to Vera Miles. But this was a Paramount production and certainly a bigger deal than simply saying no to an independent producer like Robert Lippert or even Rank. Diana was relieved when another American studio approached her that month with a plan it hoped would kill two birds with the same stone.

RKO had a comedian on its hands, George Gobel, who was breaking through on American television, and they figured that signing Diana to play the lead would bring the right amount of publicity on both sides of the Atlantic – Gobel would break Diana in the States, Diana would break Gobel in Britain. Diana didn't play her customary hard-to-get routine, and the deal was announced in New York on 25 May. Gobel, for his part, had never met Diana in person or even seen her acting in a film. He was, however, shown a few stills from *A Kid for Two Farthings*, and his verdict came straight out of a Minsky's burlesque: 'They don't hardly make 'em like that any more!'

The deal swelled Diana's head a little, and when the BBC invited her to make a studio appearance on the film magazine programme *Picture Parade* – she assumed for its usual fee of five guineas – she refused. The commercial channel, she claimed, had already offered her 125 guineas for what amounted to a four-minute appearance. The BBC replied that no money had been discussed, which only exacerbated the situation. 'It looks as though they expected me to appear for gratis,' she seethed, 'which is even worse!' When the show was finally broadcast, presenter Peter Haigh was seen chatting with American millionaire and film producer Cornelius Whitney. As the interview concluded, he remarked, 'Believe me, it's nice to have somebody on *Picture Parade* who isn't short of a bob or two in these hard times.'

Diana was too preoccupied with her Hollywood adventure to really care. Ironically, it coincided with the arrival of the other movie blonde, Marilyn Monroe, who was flying to England to make a film version of the stage play *The Sleeping Prince* – later retitled *The Prince and the Showgirl* – with Sir Laurence Olivier. Although she was five years older than Diana, Monroe's story presented many parallels. Like Diana, Monroe was discovered by a Forces photographer, and her pin-up shots had brought her to the attention of a Hollywood studio. Also like Diana, she went under contract, to 20th Century Fox, in 1946. She was a bottle blonde, too, attended a studio 'charm school' and changed her name. The important difference, which Diana often took great pains to point out, was that Monroe didn't actually make her first movie until 1948's forgettable *Scudda-Hoo! Scudda-Hey!* – a year after Diana's speaking role in *The Shop at Sly Corner* – and even then she was cut almost entirely from the finished film. Monroe's career didn't really start until 1950, with the release of *The Asphalt Jungle*, and she certainly didn't take top billing until the release, in January 1953, of the noir-tinged thriller *Niagara*. As far as Diana was concerned, Monroe was a latecomer – yet she was always being compared to someone older and, in her body of work, far less prolific. She didn't yet know it, but she would never escape Monroe's shadow. Diana was always 'Britain's answer' to Marilyn Monroe, even though she had studied acting before her big break and despite her well-publicized early start in movies. If there was any justice, she thought, and if Britain had any kind of a film industry, Marilyn Monroe would be America's answer to Diana Dors.

Marilyn was due to arrive on 14 July, just two days before Diana started work on her Hollywood debut, so her agent suggested a house-swap while she was away. It was an interesting idea, but a location runner who came down to look at the house told her it was perhaps too public – because of river traffic – for the press-shy American star's needs. In actual fact, he had already decided it was 'much too small' for Monroe's purposes and, perhaps more importantly, had 'no class at all'. Diana didn't really care; she had the most crucial break of her career to think about.

She told reporters she'd be back when the film was finished, which would be about ten weeks. It seemed a little too convenient for some, and a letter to the *Daily Express* the following day articulated many people's suspicions: 'What a strange coincidence that DD should be leaving this country as MM is about to arrive. Afraid of the competition?'

Although she could be very touchy about sharing the limelight, Diana could hardly have planned the Hollywood trip; but even so, the timing was fortuitous for her. Only Rank photographer Cornell Lucas truly regretted the circumstances – he'd had plans for a shot that would have earned its place in history: Monroe in the foreground, facing the camera; Diana in the background, walking away, but looking back at the other blonde, turning her head in a double-take. It would have told, to some extent, the story of the British film industry in a single image.

Chapter Six

GO HOME, DIANA

RKO, OR RADIO-KEITH-ORPHEUM, was in the last stretch of an already chequered history when it signed a contract with Diana Dors. The company was formed during the talkies boom of 1928, when the Radio Corporation of America merged with the Keith-Albee-Orpheum exhibition chain to capitalize on its patented Photophone sound system and, together with MGM, Paramount, Warner and 20th Century Fox, RKO soon became one of the 'Big Five' studios that dominated the box office. It was a very distinct fifth, however. Since its inception, RKO had a highly quixotic production policy that, for some reason, made it unable to capitalize on the flood of talent that passed through its doors. Although producer David O. Selznick once headed the studio, and such classics as *King Kong*, *Top Hat* and Orson Welles' *Citizen Kane* were made on its premises, RKO was best known for its failures, in particular a much publicized bankruptcy in 1933.

In 1948, much to the shareholders' bewilderment, reclusive millionaire Howard Hughes bought a controlling interest in the company. Since inheriting the family tool company at the age of eighteen, Hughes' interest in the film industry had been well known – he had invested in his first film production in 1926, aged twenty – but his moods were capricious, and after a brief spate of unremarkable films that, among other things, brought Jean Harlow to the public eye, he began dabbling in aviation. His return to movies, nearly ten years later, was heralded by *The Outlaw* (1943), a daring launchpad for chiropodist's assistant Jane Russell's 38-inch chest measurement, although his star's cleavage so unnerved the censor that the film was shelved for a further three years. But when he bought into RKO, no one quite knew what was on Hughes' agenda – in fact, his efforts there now seem almost exclusively dictated by his anti-communist paranoia, so much so that he actually shut down production in April 1952 to weed out employees with overtly left-wing sympathies. Around 100 employees were sacked and, in at least one case, a writer's name was struck from the credits of a film he'd actually written. The Screen Writers Guild, which arbitrated the credit in the first place, sued Hughes and, such was the political climate, lost.

The remaining shareholders complained about Hughes' management style, which seemed to have no bearing on studio output and certainly had no effect on the company's failing fortunes, but they were finally silenced when he bought them out in March 1954, paying more than the going share price. Then, inexplicably, he sold the company in July of the following year to General Teleradio – a subsidiary of the General Tyre and Rubber Company – and although the new buyer mostly wanted to asset-strip the company's back catalogue, RKO was not a healthy purchase. Having divested itself of its profitable exhibition chain in the early fifties, after threatened legal action by the government on charges of monopoly and restraint of trade, RKO's domestic film revenues had dropped by over 50 per cent between 1945 and 1954. 20th Century Fox, on the other hand, was showing a small increase on its 1945 figures. Then again, 20th Century Fox had Marilyn Monroe. RKO needed strong returns if it were to survive the decade.

★

Diana boarded the Queen Elizabeth on 20 June 1956, and invited the press to witness her historic leave-taking. Her father came to wave them off. Also present was her dog, Crackers, who was brought on with a temporary boarding pass under the name of Mr Smith. She knew her brief emigration would be interpreted as a betrayal – even as an act of cowardice, with Monroe due any moment – but the line she gave reporters left them in no doubt of her position. 'I would like to retire in five years on a six- or seven-figure sum,' she announced. 'But I'd like a seven-figure sum because we're young and have expensive tastes.' Someone wondered if she was at all worried about piling on the calories in the land of plenty. 'No,' she replied, with telling lack of foresight. 'I never bother to diet – I'm lucky.'

A few hours before the ship docked in New York the following week, Diana got up early to see dawn break over the Manhattan skyline. By 6.30 a.m., reporters had arrived in a coastguard boat and were already gathering in the ship's lounge. She emerged in a knee-length white dress that emphasized her breasts with a single neck strap that crossed itself over her collarbone. 'I couldn't wear jeans for my entrance into New York,' she explained when she finally addressed a medium-sized delegation from the city press. As the impromptu press conference drew to an end, Diana looked around. Quite a crowd had gathered. 'Isn't this wonderful?' she laughed. 'We all speak the same language!' 'Lady,' quipped a passing porter, 'you don't need no language.'

Diana and Dennis left immediately for the Sherry Netherland Hotel on Fifth Avenue. New York was stifling, and RKO laid on an air-conditioned Cadillac for the journey. Diana was amazed by the city. Its busy grid system, rife with tail-finned traffic and yellow taxi cabs, made the sombre streets of London look very parochial indeed. Broadway, a snaking run of billboards and theatres, movie marquees and storefronts, flashed by with reassuring candour, and Diana began to identify with the city's energy and ambition. At the hotel she caught up with American television. The first show she saw was sponsored by a soap powder, but where Britain's commercial channel fumbled along with starchy, patronizing advertising breaks, its transatlantic cousin pulled out all the stops. There were boxes and boxes of the stuff all over the place – it was almost pouring out of the screen – and when she mentioned it to an acquaintance later, her interest was rewarded the following morning with a parcel of the powder, plus toothpaste, soap and after-shave, from the manufacturer. That, she thought, was New York.

After just an hour to change and rest, Diana was taken to the exclusive 21 Club for a cocktail reception and lunch. 'I want something completely American,' she announced, and although this was not graciously received in the kitchen, a hamburger and a mint julep duly appeared. After lunching, she hopped from table to table, taking any question that came. There were camera crews, journalists, columnists, photographers, and as two TV technicians bustled in front of Diana, laying cables and placing equipment, Dennis chastized them with mock outrage. 'Careful, boys,' he boomed. 'You're covering up what we're here to sell.'

For her part, Diana played the room well:

Q: Isn't that a rather revealing dress?

A: Yes. I don't know how much more revealing you can get!

Q: Is that a three-tier diamond bracelet?

A: Yes. And my husband was in tears when he bought it!

Q: Is he an actor?

A: No. He says he likes to eat regularly.

Q: Is he your first husband?

A: Yes – and my last.

Q: What did he think of those famous 3-D pictures?

120

A: Think of them? He thought of them! It's all part of our five-year plan to clean up and retire.

Q: And what do you think, Mr Hamilton?

A: I look on her pin-ups with detached amusement and personal pride. Dors has nothing to hide but a lot to show.

Q: Diana, what exactly do you mean by a 'five-year plan'?

A: There is a definite time schedule. I have five years in which to make a lot of money, and that's what I'm doing. The plan is to make enough money while I am young and to enjoy it while I'm still young. Five years, then a family and real living.

Q: Will you be looking for more roles in Hollywood?

A: Why not? I am completely independent. I can do anything I want. Isn't it wonderful? Particularly when I can make all this money. After all, five years is the run of a star, and some of the greats go on forever. But I never hope to be in their league.

Q: It's ironic that you should arrive in America just as Marilyn Monroe is heading for London . . .

A: Yes. It's lend-lease.

Q: Have you met Marilyn?

A: No, but I'd certainly like to.

Q: What do you think of the comparisons that are being made?

A: I don't mind. I'm 36.5–24–35. I don't know how that compares with Marilyn, but if you men don't know, does it matter? If I must be compared with someone, it's not bad company.

Q: As you know, Marilyn will soon be marrying playwright Arthur Miller. Would you like to be there? As a bridesmaid, perhaps?

A: I don't think I'd like to be a bridesmaid at anyone's wedding.

Q: Any chance of you and Marilyn working together?

A: No.

Q: Will you be staying in Hollywood permanently?

A: No. England is where my home is, and that's where my friends and my pets are.

Q: What do you think of American men?

A: You fellows seem awfully nice.

That night, an RKO executive invited the couple to dinner at his penthouse apartment. As their host barbecued steaks on the terrace overlooking Manhattan, Diana watched, tired but fascinated, while night fell on the city, stars reflecting in the East River on the one side, the Empire State Building standing brazenly tall on the other. New York was not afraid of the grand gesture, but its upfront commercialism – or vulgarity, as they called it in Britain – was softened by an almost religious faith in democracy. Eisenhower was running a populist Republican campaign from the White House, after crushing his Democrat opponent in 1952, and was set for a second term in November. The mood of the country was acquisitive and optimistic, which struck more than one chord in the Hamilton household. Diana liked America, and after reading headlines like the *New York Post*'s ('Britain's Dynamite Explodes On The City') and the *New York Mirror*'s ('A Fascinating Fabrication of Femininity') she truly thought the feeling would be mutual. As usual, things did not go quite according to plan.

The Hamiltons flew on to Hollywood a few days later. They'd sailed to New York because of Dennis's fear of flying, but this time there was no getting round it. Reporters were waiting at the airstrip and they whistled appreciatively as Diana stepped down onto the tarmac in tight pink trousers and powder-blue sweater ('It matches my Cadillac at home,' she explained helpfully). Squinting in the bright Hollywood sunlight, she lowered her sunglasses to look at them. 'I thought I'd slink in unseen!' she exclaimed, somewhat disingenuously, and the assembled press laughed. An inevitable soft mauling followed and Diana said what they wanted. Yes, it was wonderful to be in America. New York was the finest city she'd ever seen. Cadillacs were even better than

Rolls Royces ... At this rate, America was going to be a walkover.

From the airport, Diana and Dennis were driven to the lavish Beverly Hills Hotel. They both hated hotels but survived there with good grace for three days until an apartment could be found. Dennis admired the place, with its beautiful grounds and waving palm trees, but thought RKO had skimped on their admittedly overpriced suite – $55 a day for a small sitting room and bedroom – and hated dipping into his pocket to tip some hotel flunkey, on the hour, every hour. They ought to spell it 'Ho££ywood', he thought. Still, where there was money there was likely to be even more money – this wasn't grey old impecunious Britain, this was a grasping, entrepreneurial culture where his business contacts had an equal fondness for nice, round numbers. 'Only a failure could dislike Hollywood,' he informed the *Daily Mail*.

During the second night at the hotel, RKO arranged a second cocktail party, at which Diana debuted in front of her movie-town peers as well as the press. Hollywood's most infamous gossip columnists, Hedda Hopper and Louella Parsons, were present and Diana was terrified. At sixty-six, Hopper was arguably the most deadly of the two, having crucified Charlie Chaplin in 1943 over a controversial paternity suit brought by the actor's young mistress. Her conservatism bordered on the fanatical – Hopper's support of the 1947 communist 'witch hunts' culminated in her spending the summer vacation on a lecture tour of America's women's groups exhorting them to boycott Communist-tainted movies. Hopper wielded her power with an unhappy relish, spitefully referring to her expensive Hollywood home as 'the house that fear built'. Her rival, Parsons, then sixty-two, had an enviable platform in media magnate William Randolph Hearst's highly traditional newspapers, and her

123

power had already been exercised in the case of Simone Silva. While Silva was desperately trying to sort out her visa problems, Parsons noted solemnly in a Los Angeles newspaper that LA's head of immigration had received many letters from actors, producers and religious leaders criticizing Silva, adding that she had received many herself. When Silva's request was declined, Parsons gloated, 'I personally feel this is a good moral lesson for future cases. The day has passed when a notorious incident is enough for any man or woman to seek a place in an industry which is composed of many hard-working players who did not get to the top by the methods Miss Silva used to get here.'

Diana knew all about Hedda and Louella and was suitably awed, but Dennis flew straight into action. He took Hopper's hand and greeted her warmly, bubbling over with compliments and flattery, expressing surprise that such a 'wonderful lady' should have such a daunting reputation. Hopper cut him short just as soon as he'd started. 'All right, Hamilton,' she drawled. 'Don't overdo it.'

Diana, on the other hand, was doing very well, wearing a strapless outfit that caused plenty of consternation. After the royal treatment they'd received, Diana was even wavering in her determination to return to England. 'I have no studio obligations back home, and if I like the pictures and the roles here I may stay on,' she announced. 'I made it to Hollywood on my own terms. I was planning to come here eventually. I am on time.' RKO's head of production, William Dozier confirmed reports that Diana had driven a hard bargain and that his original attempts to sign her to a seven-year contract had gradually been whittled down first to three years, then two films and finally just one. Even so, he said, he had two more projects for Diana to look at, and if she was interested, they were hers. The following day, the Hamiltons moved into a Spanish-style villa, just off Sunset Boulevard. Previous tenant: Marlene Dietrich.

Diana and Dennis were well aware of Dozier's frustrations. Shortly after filming started on *I Married a Woman*, satisfied that they were making the right choice, Diana and Dennis began talks that they thought would cement her Hollywood career. First Dozier offered a three-year contract for one picture a year, but the Hamiltons held out for five. He was on the verge of relenting when Diana raised the question of options; instead, a three-year no-option compromise was reached, which Diana duly signed. She told the press it was worth £50,000 per picture, over twice her value at Rank, and made it clear that, in terms of moving, her hand was being forced. 'It's only in America I can get more money, better parts and a world-wide build up,' she explained.

The contract brought with it something of a crisis. Inclusive of any TV and radio work it would bring, the deal could feasibly be worth anything up to one million dollars over the next five years. In her existing tax situation, Diana stood to lose a substantial amount, although applying for resident alien status in the States would have reduced that considerably. Unsurprisingly, Dennis was all in favour of that particular solution, but Diana was undecided. The money was not the principle; she'd already alienated some of her British fans by taking the Hollywood dollar, but aside from that, she simply wasn't sure. Staying out there would change the game entirely. In Hollywood, Diana was another starlet, and making films was the equivalent of a nine-to-five. From what she'd seen, it was a very serious business, too – a stone-faced enterprise far removed from the irreverent, anarchic scene back home. In Hollywood, Diana was afraid she wouldn't be special – and she certainly had a fear of being ordinary.

The argument over relocation was the first and perhaps most dangerous crack in an already volatile marriage. Until this point, Diana had genuinely believed in her retirement plan – and perhaps even Dennis did, too – but the contract changed everything irrevocably. Dennis was getting very used to the high life, and the rewards seemed exponential. Why retire? Why waste money on a family? Why not push for every last cent? He was also beginning to over-estimate his role in Diana's career, and her opinions were brushed aside – sometimes in public, to her embarrassment.

When journalists called, they found the Hamiltons curiously split over the issue. Reporter Don Iddon pursued the story for the *Daily Mail* and received two very different variations on the story. Diana, for her part, was quite emphatic on the matter. 'I've no intention of staying in America indefinitely or becoming an American citizen,' she said. 'And that is that. I am trying to work a deal whereby I can divide my life and career between England and the United States. We can't possibly live here permanently. We have blocks of flats in London and Dennis has his property business in London. I suppose we could sell the property, but we have never thought of doing so. I am not giving up England or being English.'

Dennis, on the other hand, was giving a different brief altogether: 'If we sign this contract – and it's practically certain – it goes without saying that we'll become American. Everything in life depends on money – that's my philosophy and Diana's, too. Of course, it'll take a bit of wangling and it's necessary for us to go back to Britain and fix things up, but there's absolutely no question about what we'll do. What would you do, chum? Oscars are all right but they don't pay the rent.'

Dennis couldn't resist the final word. 'What I am saying is what Diana will do,' he said high-handedly. 'When you quote me, you're quoting Diana. And never mind what she says.'

The contract was eventually signed, and preparations began for Diana's next film – *The Lady and the Prowler*, provisionally set to co-star Ernest Borgnine – which would start shooting in September, just as soon as *I Married a Woman* wrapped. The news was not well received in Britain, and Diana received letters, cables and even a phone call from fans begging her not to leave the country. More serious was the press reaction, as it finally seemed that the dailies were beginning to tire of the Hamiltons' antics, and in an article on 20 July titled 'Close that Dors!' *Daily Sketch* columnist Candidus roasted Diana for her behaviour. 'If you are still feeling hot under the collar about the Docker expense account,' he wrote, 'I think you should forget about them for a while. Switch your indignation elsewhere and have a good, hard look at Miss Diana Dors. Whatever else you may think the Dockers may have done, at any rate they stay here and pay their taxes – and, believe me, the taxes are staggering. But what about Miss Dors?'

The column ended with a vitriolic snub: 'Perhaps Miss Dors will be at Cannes again next year, but this time sacrificing herself for the American film industry. No doubt she will have a London premiere for her first American picture. Well, I am just as tired of Hollywood tax dodgers nowadays as I was of Hollywood bomb-dodgers in 1939, and when that premiere comes along I hope not to be there. I also hope nobody else will be there . . .'

Ironically, the House of Lords was already of that view, but for somewhat different reasons. A bill to repeal capital punishment was due to start in the House, so, to aid the abolitionist case, writer Arthur Koestler and Gerald Gardiner QC had arranged a screening of *Yield to the Night* at the National Film Theatre. Only six peers arrived and, predictably, the bill was defeated, with 238 votes against. The act repealing the death penalty was not passed until 9 November 1965.

But Diana still had plenty of admirers, and *Sketch* writer Ker Robertson leapt to her defence the following day in a piece over-punningly titled 'I open the Dors!' 'Remember, nobody gave Diana Dors anything,' he remonstrated. 'She worked her own way for it. "Diana wouldn't cross the road without getting paid for it," Dennis Hamilton said a week ago. Would any entertainer? Would any bank manager, bricklayer, truck driver or typist?'

Diana, in the meantime, was relieved to see the relocation question temporarily sidelined when Dennis formed yet another company, Treasure Productions, to handle her American affairs. Back in Britain, however, Diana's friend and society hairdresser Raymond 'Teasy-Weasy' Bessone, was becoming highly interested in the sums of money that seemed to be causing her so much trouble. Raymond, the self-styled 'Toscanini of hairdressing', was born in Soho in 1911 to French and Italian parents. He trained in his father's barber's shop but branched out on his own as a young man when he bribed the printers of *Hairdresser's Journal* with a packet of Woodbines to let him procure an early copy of the magazine and get a steal on all the other stylists looking for work. Building up from his first job in a Deptford salon, Raymond dropped his surname and opened his first West End salon in Grafton Street in 1936. 'The majority of women in those days,' he said later, 'seemed to think that unless you were French and queer you couldn't be a good hairdresser. Well, to please the customers I styled myself 'Raymond' and adopted a heavy French accent, and to help the other part of the illusion I permed my hair and painted my fingers and toenails. The whole nonsense went down very well. It seemed to give women a certain confidence they wouldn't get from a heterosexual.'

Raymond was certainly mad about sex – orgies, anything – but he was profoundly heterosexual. He loved fame and if fame brought mistresses, that was an added bonus. He first rose to fame, in fact, quite by accident. In 1954, Frederick Mullally was then running a PR operation in Hay Hill, just round the corner from Grafton Street. He'd just lost a heavy libel action and didn't have the money to pay the damages, so he called on Raymond, for whom he'd already run a couple of campaigns, to see if there was anything he wanted. 'The only thing I want,' said Raymond, 'is to be on television.' At that time, there was only one channel – the BBC – and its policy was to be scrupulously fair in its coverage of every profession, so Mullally had his work cut out. He knew the producer of a BBC show and asked him what he wanted most. The producer replied, 'A decent review in the press. My ratings could do with a boost.' As it happened, a major tabloid TV critic was dating Mullally's secretary at the time, so Mullally paid him a visit. 'What would it take for you to give a good review to next week's show – really boost it?' asked Mullally. 'Obviously, we can't give you cash – that would be terrible – but supposing Raymond bought a valuable antique for your wife's next birthday?'

The deal was set. The antique was bought, the review was written, the ratings were boosted and Raymond was booked for the show. During rehearsals, Raymond ran around frantically, picking at the models' hair: 'A leetle teasy-weasy here . . . A leetle teasy-weasy there . . .' Mullally jumped on it straight away. 'Keep that going,' he advised, 'teasy-weasy, teasy-weasy . . .' The next day, 'Mr Teasy-Weasy' was a household name, and he held onto his fame with a Barnum-esque approach to business that always kept his name in the papers. Raymond was fastidious about his appearance, always wearing a fresh blue carnation in his buttonhole, because 'everybody' wore red. 'I do not like to look like other men,' he said. 'If I looked ordinary I'd *be* ordinary. Even when I was a little boy my mother dressed me in velvet and lace and my father curled my hair with an iron. I am trying to take male fashion out of mourning.' Raymond was always looking for ways to publicize his salon, even down to creating his own brand of red filter-tipped cigarettes to avoid un–ladylike lipstick smudges ('They're terribly pretty,' he enthused). And when Diana made her transatlantic trip, Raymond immediately cashed in on their friendship by announcing to the press that Diana had invited him over to Hollywood to bestow on her the most expensive hairdo of his career. Like Dennis, Raymond was careless with figures and dropped hints that he would be there for three weeks and that every day he was away from Britain would cost his business £100. A figure of £2,500, inclusive of flights, was arrived at, and Raymond did not dispute it. Wasn't that a bit expensive, he was asked? 'Not when you remember what a new hairstyle does for a woman's morale,' he countered. And he certainly had big plans. Raymond wasn't *entirely* sure yet but he knew it would be 'a hairstyle which may sweep the world like so many others I've launched – the Petal Cut, the Poodle Cut, the Teasy-Weasy, the Alice Bands . . .' This was, unfortunately, before Raymond introduced his masterpiece – the crash-helmet wig.

Without her knowledge, Diana's American publicists issued a flat denial of the story. 'I'll not pay him a penny,' she was reported as saying, although in actual fact she was amused by the affair. Diana's usual hairdresser was Leon of Shaftesbury Avenue, but Raymond offered to foot the bill for a lavish Hollywood party if she played along, so she conveniently forgot her loyalties. The publicists – a novelty for Diana, as most of her publicity was self-generated – were immediately sacked and a clarifying statement was issued. 'Raymond will be coming as a guest,' she explained. 'But I expect he will find it pretty difficult keeping his hands off my hair.'

To coincide with Raymond's visit, Diana had called their housekeeper, Frances Sholl, and asked if she would join them in the States. 'Sholly', as she was known, was not impressed with the stories she'd read in the press that the Hamiltons were paying their cook £20 a week, enough for her to be able to run her own Cadillac. The fifty-year-old Sholly, by contrast, was taking home just £3 10s. 'And for that,' she fumed, ' I do all the cooking, clean the shoes, wash Dennis's shirts – two a day – and I haven't a washing machine. And there's no other staff. I'm cook, housekeeper, everything. We had a daily once. But she gave one look at this place and took fright.' Diana wanted Sholly, and her twelve-year-old daughter Monica, to fly out on 10 August, but the short notice just incensed her further. 'How the devil can I get off on the 10th?' she fumed. 'Why, I haven't even got my passport pictures yet. There's Monica's, too. But the Dors . . . I started my education anew when I joined them. Everything is done at the last moment.'

As Diana's income skyrocketed, astute reporter John Lee turned his attention to Bert Fluck, still living in the family home in Marlborough Road. It was just a short piece, but the intention was clear – Bert was sat in his own armchair, cigarette in hand, posing wearily for the camera. Before settling down for the interview, the piece bluntly described Bert's evening routine, leaving work at 5.30 p.m. and paying his usual bus fare of 3½d. 'I like to go my own tin-pot way,' said Bert. The purpose of the article was to fathom his reaction to his daughter's apparent wealth, but Bert fielded questions with good humour and dignity. 'I am not affluent by any means, but I get by all right.' He shrugged. 'I live a quiet and simple life. I haven't got a car and I don't want one.' With retirement looming, it was suggested that he might like to cash in on Diana's affairs, but Bert ruled the matter out of hand. 'Not me. I think it's a great mistake to interfere like that. Parents should keep in the background – watchful, but in the background. And anyway, I know that if I ever need help in any way, my daughter will help me.'

Bert's retirement, meanwhile, was not uppermost in Diana's mind. Filming had started on the Gobel picture and she was amazed by the size of her dressing room, which made the facilities at Bray and Pinewood look amateur indeed. It was almost an en suite apartment, decorated in soft green and lime, with a dressing room, make-up room, kitchen, bathroom with tub and shower, and bedroom with TV, radiogram and hair dryer. She was even given a mink coat as a present, which Dennis hated because he thought fur made her 'look like a whore'.

This was the life, she thought. Finally, it all seemed worthwhile, but it was publicity that had put her there, not her work. After all, she'd made nearly thirty pictures in her time, but the only one worth a light, she reckoned, was the Carol Reed film. None of the others helped her more than a sick headache. Of course, she and Dennis could always go and live in luxury in the south of France every summer – but then she'd have to act in rep till she dropped, or spend her old age getting up at 5 a.m. to potter down to some third-rate film studio. No, thank you!

But if she was going to stay she'd need a base, and their ambitions were getting ahead of them. They liked the house they were renting but, socially, it left a lot to be desired. 'Nice, but too much glare,' as Dennis described it. 'No trees – and no tennis court.' Lana Turner's house was on the market, but they were only prepared to offer £53,000 and Lana's people were holding out for £67,000. 'I'd love to have that house,' said Diana. 'One only lives once – and I want to live big. I can afford that house and I want it.' In truth, of course, she couldn't. Even with his half-hearted property business in England, Dennis was sinking them deeper into debt. Finally, with money borrowed from the studio and offset against future earnings, the Hamiltons settled on a two-storey, white-walled mansion in the fashionable Coldwater Canyon area of Beverly Hills. The property had no particular star pedigree but its previous owner seemed to have been an eccentric oil millionaire who sold it to Dennis with more than the usual fixtures and fittings. Dennis boasted that the shrubbery alone cost £28,500, furniture £55,000 and swimming pool £7,000 – which, if true, made the final sale price of £62,500 seem ludicrously cheap. 'The only things the former owners were allowed to remove were the paintings,' said Dennis. 'I'm going out tomorrow to buy new ones.'

The house stood on three and a half acres of ground, complete with a rose and orchid garden, and orange trees that were planted in little redwood boxes, which could be wheeled around as the sun changed its position. This time, there was indeed a tennis court which could be floodlit at night, and the underlit, hundred-foot pool came with five changing rooms, each complete with shower. The house itself was equipped with four bedrooms, five bathrooms (including a sunken Roman bath adjoining the master bedroom), lounge, dining room and servants' quarters. The kitchen was a state-of-the-art spectacle, with dishwasher, infra-red grills, push-button oven and deep-freeze, while the five-car garage boasted its own petrol pump and an electronic eye that automatically opened the door when Dennis's specially adapted car approached. In Diana's absence her ghost-written columns tantalized British readers with stories of a lavish, fully automated way of life. After the wilderness of the war years and the post-war run for employment, America's labour-saving devices seemed to come from another, futuristic planet. Diana's reports of 'a portable electric broiler which wheels up to the dining table, if you want it there', or an electric shoe-cleaner and polisher, tapped into the nation's growing dissatisfaction with its lot.

A house-warming party was irresistible, and with Raymond willing to foot the bill, a date was set for 19 August. Telegrams went out just a few days in advance of the party to some of the film capital's biggest names – including Lana Turner, Liberace, Greer Garson, Doris Day, Eddie Fisher, Debbie Reynolds, George Sanders, the ubiquitous Zsa Zsa

Gabor and Diana's *I Married a Woman* co-stars Adolphe Menjou and George Gobel – saying, 'We would be delighted if you could come to a ding-dong in honour of the arrival in Hollywood of our good friend Raymond.' Someone asked Dennis what a 'ding-dong' was. 'A cocktail party that could develop,' he said, and he was right.

It was important for Diana to make a good impression, since her only recent film of any note, *Yield to the Night*, had been held up on its American release. Its US distributors had exploitatively retitled the film *Blonde Sinner* and slashed twenty minutes from its one hundred-minute running time, so Diana refused to promote it. A lot was riding, then, on a comparatively innocuous party.

Although by 1956, the studios were already losing some of their powers to television, they were still clinging to the old ways and were still in thrall to the likes of Hedda Hopper and Louella Parsons. Visibility was at a premium, and fashionable reclusivity and non-conformism, as perfected by Marlon Brando, still lay very much round the corner – even Marilyn Monroe was only proving difficult because her entropic personality proved beyond the bounds of studio policing. Though Diana didn't quite know it yet, these were testing times. Ever since 1953, studios had tried a variety of gimmicks, from 3D to Cinemascope and Vistavision, to keep audiences away from their TV sets, and Hollywood was trying hard to find a way to recapture the pulling power of its heyday back in the thirties and forties.

Diana's party certainly harked back to more opulent times. The price was pegged in the region of £1,000, and for that the Hamiltons' purple jacaranda trees were hung with Japanese lanterns, while strolling players performed for the guests. A huge barbecue grilled steaks and chickens for the catering staff to take round, while, in the house, the gramophone played music non-stop for anything up to twenty-eight and a half hours. Diana was dressed to kill, wearing a tight-fitting peacock-blue, diaphanous silk blouse and matching matador trousers.

Since it was an outdoor party guests gravitated to the pool and at 8.30 p.m., Diana and Dennis stood with Hollywood agent Louis Shurr, whom Bob Hope had introduced to them, and dress designer Howard Shoup for a photo. Suddenly, there was a commotion and all four fell backwards into the shallow end. Diana was completely doused, emerging with her newly styled blonde hair pushed back into a flat and unflattering slick, while the sixty-five-year-old Shurr, who could not swim, flailed bewildered in his ruined suit. Dennis was enraged and climbed out of the pool, screaming, 'Who did it? Who did it? I'll give $5,000 to anybody who tells me!' He picked on thirty-two-year-old United Press photographer Stewart Sawyer and knocked him to the ground, kicking him and screaming abuse. A few people tried to pull him away, but Dennis was too far gone. 'Any man,' he yelled, 'who comes to *my* house, eats *my* food, drinks *my* liquor then throws me in *my own fucking pool* deserves *everything he gets.*' In her anger, Diana forgot herself, too, and added a few choice words of her own, though Sawyer's later claim that she, too, had kicked him 'in the head' seems rather unlikely given that she was wearing now-sodden diamanté-studded sandals.

The guests were shocked to see Sawyer carried away, bloodied and unconscious, and though some stayed, the party was unequivocally over. The next day, doctors revealed the extent of the damage – Diana had suffered bruises and abrasions on her arms and a possible sprained back, while Dennis, predictably, found his knuckles grazed and swollen. Sawyer had easily come off worse, with cuts and bruises on his face, head and ribs and a suspected broken nose. Sawyer posed with his injuries, denying any collusion in the incident and claiming not to remember anything until he woke up in someone else's car. At first he flatly denied Dennis's accusations, but his story gradually changed, since he subsequently told Lionel Crane, 'I didn't do it deliberately. I may have bumped against them. All I remember is lying on the ground and someone hitting me. Then I passed out. Sure, I had a couple of drinks, like everyone else . . .' Sawyer's wife was furious. 'Just wait till I get my hands on that Diana Dors,' she seethed. 'I'll kick *her* where it hurts most.'

Despite all the evidence to the contrary – the clearest pictures came from the other side of the pool – journalists thought this to be another publicity stunt from the press-hungry Hamiltons. They seemed quite happy to believe that an image-conscious film star would willingly ruin an outfit, a diamond-chain wristwatch and a hairstyle for a photo opportunity that would show her at her worst. 'If that was a stunt,' said Diana, 'it looks as though it were laid on by the photographers. It's strange that they were all ready when we were pushed.'

After so many years using the PR machine to their own ends, the Hamiltons were learning the hard way that, in America at least, publicity was a two-way street. Dennis found himself grudgingly admiring the principle if not the deed itself. 'It's a good gimmick,' he conceded, 'but it happened to the wrong person.' This curious statement dovetails suspiciously well with Dennis's initial defence for the Sawyer incident, in particular his claim that the photographer had come to him with the idea that a picture of Zsa Zsa Gabor going into the pool would make a good, newsworthy photograph. 'I told him no,' said Dennis in a rare fit of piety. 'She was dressed up and it wouldn't have been a good idea.' Quite how this squared with Dennis the prankster – the man who once boasted that he'd sent a young Joan Collins to her local cinema for a fictitious premiere after tipping off the manager that a madwoman was on her way down – is unclear. What does seem likely is that someone was meant to cause a splash and that the whole sorry enterprise backfired.

The American press was appalled by Dennis's conduct, and the *National Enquirer* devoted its front page to the affair. Under the headline 'Go home, Diana – and take Mr Dors with you!', the *Enquirer* ran a 3,000-word diatribe by Lewis Onslow that railed against Diana and belittled her husband by repeatedly referring to his dropping of the name 'Gittins' as a vulgar, transparent attempt at DIY gentrification. 'America has two imports she can do without,' he wrote. 'They are a bizarre, boisterous couple who have thrived on publicity – good and bad – and whose zany, riotous exploits have reverberated on both sides of the Atlantic . . . Miss Dors is Britain's busty answer to Marilyn Monroe. Dennis Hamilton is her lusty husband – and nobody's answer to anything.'

Of the swimming pool incident, Onslow wrote, 'Some people may have found it amusing. We do not agree. The exhibition was sheer bad manners. Inexcusable bad manners – even if the whole thing was a publicity stunt . . . We have enough bizarre characters in this country without importing others who have no regard for the common standard of decent behaviour.'

Diana was once asked whether she thought her impact would be temporary. 'All impacts are temporary,' she replied. 'They're bound to be. It's like buying a new dress – soon, the effect wears off.' But even by her own cautious standards, it was getting clearer by the day that America's honeymoon with Diana Dors was over before it had even started.

Chapter Seven

TWO TINSELLY BORES

THE WEEKS FOLLOWING the party were not good. Raymond and his wife Jennifer hurried back to London, and Diana was quite conspicuously spotted being helped into a Beverly Hills medical centre – wearing heels, a white sundress and, so it was claimed, a mink stole. But United Press stood by Sawyer's account, boycotting the Hamiltons and even taking the unusual step of syndicating the story to non-subscribers. Lawyers at RKO, meanwhile, were looking hard at Diana's contract to see if they had reasonable grounds to fire her.

'Morals clauses' had been part of performers' contracts since 1922, when Will H. Hay, former Postmaster General in Warren Harding's Republican administration, was drafted in to head up the Motion Pictures and Distributors Association of America. Hays' job was to clean up Hollywood's image in the wake of such scandals as silent star Fatty Arbuckle's notorious rape trial, and the murder of film director William Desmond Taylor, which revealed the dead man's string of affairs with well-known Hollywood actresses and also brought the decadent underworld of drugs – marijuana, opium and morphine – to the public's attention.

In Diana's case, however, it was clear that nothing could be done, for the moment at least. The poolside fracas was not a clear-cut issue – Diana protested her innocence, and despite his vehemence, Sawyer never pressed charges. Besides, RKO knew that sacking an actress for her husband's bad behaviour would be difficult to uphold in a court of law. Instead, RKO pressed on with Diana's next film, as planned, although its co-star had changed. Borgnine was unavailable, and *The Lady and the Prowler*, a lurid drama about a woman whose attempt to murder her husband backfires horribly, was now to feature Rod Steiger, a formidable stage actor who made his name with a flurry of intense screen roles in the early fifties. Steiger was very much Diana's kind of man. Born in New York in April 1925, he had dropped out of high school and signed up with the navy at the age of sixteen, serving in the Pacific during the Second World War. In peacetime, Steiger used a scholarship from the government's GI Bill programme to study acting, which finally took him to the Actors' Studio, a workshop founded in New York in 1947 by, among others, film director Elia Kazan. Two years later, stage director and former actor Lee Strasberg became its 'artistic director' and pioneered a groundbreaking approach, known simply as the 'method', that would change acting style, if not the movies themselves, irrevocably. Strasberg's teachings derived from Stanislavsky and went beyond simple strategies of identification and empathy to go much deeper into character. Although a headache to studios and directors, method acting was popular with East Coast actors and, as well as Steiger, the Studio worked with the likes of Marlon Brando, James Dean, Lee Remick and Shelley Winters. Indeed, when Brando won an Oscar for his performance in Kazan's 1954 film *On the Waterfront*, Steiger's supporting role did not go unnoticed by the critics.

In Diana's eyes, Rod Steiger was something new. He was part of a generation that was taking Hollywood away from its roots, away from studio dictatorships and away from the established star system. Even Monroe was flirting with the method, and while filming *The Sleeping Prince* (aka *The Prince and the Showgirl*) in England she had taken Strasberg's wife, Paula, along for advice and support. Paula's tuition was certainly unique, and many people on the set thought her a charlatan — especially when Monroe needed help to cry on cue. 'Think of Frank Sinatra,' urged Paula. 'Think of Coca-Cola.' It wasn't Diana's style at all. She enjoyed acting but she could never take it as seriously as *that*.

While in Marilyn it seemed affected and silly, in Steiger it was altogether different. When filming started in September, the attraction was mutual, even though both were technically out of bounds (Steiger had been estranged for some three years from his wife, Sally Gracie). Diana was awed by Steiger's talent and said, many years later, she thought he was the best actor she had ever worked with. Although his usual roles were often heavy and intimidating, Steiger could be both funny and sensitive offscreen, clowning around or quoting lines of poetry. His commitment made her excited about acting again, and most importantly he didn't seem to need anything from her, either — not like Dennis, who had long given up making any kind of independent career for himself. 'Rod made me feel like a woman, not a child,' she wrote in *Dors by Diana*, 'and in him I imagined I saw a real man!'

RKO was more concerned with building Diana's profile back up again and hadn't really noticed what was happening. Diana was shooting at the studio all day, sitting for wardrobe and giving interviews when she wasn't needed. She arrived home at seven in the evening, too tired to go out. 'I hate this fast-paced life here,' she complained. 'There's no fun.' Dennis had been neglecting her for some time, and his behaviour in America made her feel cheap; she'd become a piece of meat, a body for hire, and his management style seemed more like pimping. The longer Diana stayed in America, the less she enjoyed it — the weather made things bearable, but with the exception of the ex-pat scene, the social life was careerist and vapid, and the work . . . well, it was work. She ran up huge phone bills, talking to her friends back in England, calling Sholly and asking to speak to the animals. Dennis's views on the matter were quite clear, however – this was where the money was, and this was where they must stay. If she did all the films that were being offered, she would be there for the next fifteen years, working solidly. Diana wasn't quite so pragmatic. She wanted success, but not at any cost. She began to realize that she wasn't as ambitious as she used to think.

The rumours first surfaced when suggestive pictures of Diana and Steiger on the set of *The Lady and the Prowler* began to circulate, without RKO's permission. Dennis knew something was going on, although he suspected one of the minor players, and when Diana told him she was in love with Steiger, all hell broke loose. Dennis drove down to the studio the next day, looking for him – Diana later dramatized the situation by adding a shotgun – but the actor wasn't around. After a turbulent week, Dennis suddenly announced that he was flying home to London, in the hope that Diana would realize how lost she would be in his absence. Instead, she drove him to the airport.

Dennis's arrival in London on 27 September, certainly surprised the press, but the Hamiltons were ready with their cover story. 'He had to leave in a real hurry,' Diana told the *Mail*. 'The whole situation over there blew up so quickly he couldn't handle it by phone any more. You see, we've been having lots of trouble with blocks of flats that we've been letting.' And remembering Dennis's advice, she added, 'There are hundreds and thousands of pounds involved . . .'

Dennis kept up the pretence, adding that he was also trying to negotiate two more films on Diana's behalf – one being *The Long Haul*, to star Robert Mitchum, the other *Pot Luck with Pomeroy*, to be directed by Robert Aldrich. 'It's a lousy title,' said Dennis, 'which we will change.' Either way, it was never made.

Curiously, neither denied that there had been an argument over whether to stay in Hollywood, and both agreed on the outcome. 'Diana has made a tremendous impact on Hollywood, but she has never been truly happy there,' said Dennis. 'This means leaving our wonderful home – and it means she will earn about £20,000 for her next picture, instead of £75,000. I am the commercially minded type and I tried to dissuade her. She won.'

Diana's account tallied. 'When we first came out here, we didn't know the score,' she told the *Daily Express*. 'I just didn't know where I was, and my husband Dennis and I thought of settling down for a while and making a home in Hollywood. Now I know where I stand. I know all about it. And I am coming back to London early in November. Maybe it will be better this way – to deal with things in Hollywood at a distance. Maybe it's not too good to be thought of as a fixture. Right at the beginning, there were offers, offers all the time, from producers. But I'm homesick and I want to come home. We had a row. I won.'

Dennis's stay in England was short, and he flew back just a few days later. On his arrival at LA airport, playing the dutiful husband, he immediately sent a bouquet of red roses to the RKO lot. In the meantime, whispers about Diana and Steiger had reached a crescendo, and both were busy defending their corners. Diana dismissed the talk as 'the worst possible balderdash', and Steiger added that it was 'utterly absurd'. Later, he told *Picturegoer*, 'Miss Dors was scared about those rumours. Where that sort of thing is concerned RKO is a very strict studio. Those rumours were not true. I almost wish now that they had been . . . just to spite the people that started them.'

In the middle of all this came Dennis, telling a journalist, as he prepared to fly back, 'Of course she likes Rod. She thinks he's wonderful – and so do I.' At this point, of course, Dennis was thinking of his investment. 'Morals clauses' did not necessarily include violent behaviour on behalf of the contract player's spouse, but they certainly included adultery, and any infidelity on Diana's part would not only sink her marriage, it would also sink her career.

Louella Parsons was on the warpath, and under the guidance of *The Lady and the Prowler* director John Farrow, a friend of Louella's, the Hamiltons tried to make amends. Farrow had worked in Hollywood for twenty years, and though only in his early fifties he was already in the last years of his professional life. He was also a Catholic, which endeared him to Louella, and had written several published works, including a biography of Thomas More and a history of the papacy. That he was a confirmed flirt had perhaps not reached Louella's ears, but the two got on well together, so Farrow arranged for Diana and Dennis to visit the columnist at home, in a bid to contain the damage.

If Louella saw through the charade she gave no sign, proferring instead her own grotesque benediction when Diana confessed all. They'd been having problems, said Diana, like all married couples. Steiger was a ghastly mistake, a distraction, and they'd only kept it from Louella because they wanted time to work things out. Now they were back together, she added, they were going to work at their marriage. Dennis nodded earnestly.

After what seemed like hours, they were free to go. Diana was mortified, and Dennis clearly did not enjoy this added humiliation. The atmosphere at home was dreadful and three difficult weeks passed slowly by. With the threat of cancellation hanging over Diana's contract, money was definitely an issue and Dennis was bemused to see the house at Bray attract minor attention on the market, finally going for little or no profit. Then, late in October, the Hamiltons came to the attention of the Los Angeles Department of Inland

Revenue, who reported allegations that they were attempting to evade Federal taxes by manipulating company books. Tax inspectors visited the Hamiltons' accountant without warning, although nothing at that stage was found to be amiss.

Diana claimed to know who the Department's source was, saying cryptically, 'We believe she is the wife of someone who became insulting to us and whom we were compelled to ask to stay out of our home' – perhaps a coded and ill-founded reference to photographer Sawyer's wife, who had already made her feelings about Diana abundantly clear. 'That woman,' added Dennis, 'can talk herself to a standstill as far as Diana and I are concerned.'

But Dennis was back in England within a matter of days, having flown back to London on 23 October, where he was met with a barrage of questions about his marriage, his wife and her co-star. This time the cover story was 'legal business', which he failed to clarify, but his good grace lapsed under questioning. Steiger's name was mentioned. 'Utter nonsense, all these stories,' snapped Dennis, stamping his foot petulantly. The press knew they'd hit a nerve, and the fact that Dennis was no longer prepared to play his usual games (there was no more of that 'She thinks he's wonderful – and so do I' rubbish) told them this marriage was about to implode. Dennis knew the story could no longer be contained by subterfuge and lies. It was only a matter of time.

In the States, Diana had been on the receiving end of some unsavoury investigative journalism herself, when reporters broke into her Hollywood home, looking for incriminating evidence. The reverential fan press of previous decades no longer existed, and the trail-blazing scandal magazine *Confidential* was at its peak, having notched up sales of four million a month the previous year. *Confidential* had been a major thorn in Hollywood's side since its launch in 1952, and frequently ran scurrilous, intrusive stories that made wild claims, some of them true, about the stars' seedy private lives. It was launched with self-righteous spleen. 'Here you will read about the famous who are infamous,' the editor promised in its first issue, 'about the glamorous who are deglamorized; about the mugs and the mobs; about high society and low society. Yes, you may be shocked, but at least you'll get the truth without any trimmings . . . You'll get what you've always wanted to hear – the real stories behind the headlines – uncensored and off the record.'

Following enquiries into its dubious methods and the truthfulness of its claims, *Confidential* hit trouble the following autumn, when one of its victims sued for libel and a grand jury indicted the magazine on a number of bizarre counts. Most damning was the charge of conspiracy to commit criminal libel and publish obscene and indecent material; more puzzling were the charges which involved disseminating information about abortions and 'male rejuvenation'. Publisher Robert Harrison attacked the charges in a blistering two-page editorial. 'Hollywood is in the business of lying,' he wrote. 'Falsehood is a stock in trade. They use vast press-agent organizations and advertising expenditures to "build up" their "stars". They "glamorize" and distribute detailed – and often deliberately false – information about private lives. Because of advertising money, in these "build-ups" they have the co-operation of practically every medium except *Confidential* . . . They can't influence us. So they want to "get" us.' Harrison ended on a defiant note. 'We doubt,' he said, 'that the time has arrived when Americans can be gotten for the crime of telling the truth.' Such fighting talk was swiftly forgotten; the magazine pleaded guilty to a token charge and settled out of court.

Confidential continued in a toothless tame new version and its publishers eventually sold it in 1958. But in 1956, *Confidential* pulled few punches and it set the trend for blue-collar publishing. Diana was used to the genteel, old boys' network that was Fleet Street, but even that was soon to change.

In a bid to avoid prying journalists and gossip columnists' stringers, Diana arranged to meet Steiger at his Malibu beach house, where they could be alone. It required a lot of subterfuge to dodge reporters and other scandal-sheet tipsters, but Diana thought it was worth it. The affair had only been going on for a few months when Steiger broke it off by phone, having left for New York, where his estranged wife Gracie was appearing on Broadway. Diana was heartbroken. She thought him callous, but in retrospect he was being more realistic than she was. There was clearly no future in the affair – Diana was just a distraction for him, while she was clearly rebelling against her husband and her unhappiness in Hollywood. '*Après moi, le deluge,*' he told her. Three years later, in 1959, he married British actress Claire Bloom; the relationship lasted ten years.

Diana didn't even consider the possibility that Dennis might begin an affair of his own, which he did almost as soon as he landed in England. It was to be the first of many – he was planning a counter-rebellion of his own. Some time before, Dennis and Raymond had sealed a gentleman's agreement with a handshake, swearing that neither would make a move on the other man's wife. The agreement was unilaterally broken when Dennis began making early morning appointments with Jennifer while Raymond was out. Raymond thought it strange when she drove him to the station wearing a nightie and dressing gown and full makeup, but he accepted her reasoning when she told him, sweetly, 'It's not worth dressing just for this trip.' He found out later that Jennifer was going straight back home to meet Dennis.

Diana broke the news of the split herself on 2 November,

when she issued a statement to the press. Without going into details, she explained simply that, 'Dennis and I are separating,' and that he would continue to be her business manager. Diana immediately went to ground, staying with her actress friend Irene James and leaving another friend, Peter Reynolds, to look after the house. The added complications involved in separating from one's manager were not lost on the press, and its reporting on Diana's financial affairs was suitably bleak – it was claimed that Dennis was withholding money and that Diana had sold her Lincoln Continental to raise cash. She hit back instantly, denying the car story and claiming she had £14,000 to live on and that she would get £80,000 on completing *The Lady and the Prowler*.

Dennis responded with his own statement, rashly calculated to have the most immediate and damning impact. 'Diana has ended it all,' he told Donald Zec. He was asked why. 'It is a matter which concerns only Diana, Mr Rod Steiger and myself. I have no intention of going any further than that.'

Dennis played the wounded party, talking up phone bills of over £1,000 in which he claimed to have tried in vain to beg Diana to reconsider. 'All our dreams are smashed to smithereens,' he wailed. 'When I think of all that we achieved in just five years . . . She always wanted a house with a swimming pool – I built it for her. She wanted a Cadillac – we got that, too. She wanted a cream telephone – I gave it to her. I just can't understand her.'

Considering that Diana had paid for all these luxuries herself, with the profits from her own hard graft, Dennis had quite a nerve. He even went so far as to call a press conference in a Leicester Square bar, where he was accompanied by Shirley Ann Field, a twenty-year-old actress he claimed to be managing. It was his turn to shine, his turn to field the questions:

Q: Are you still in love with Diana?

A: **No comment.**

Q: Is there any chance of a reconciliation?

A: **None whatsoever.**

Q: Do *you* want a reconciliation?

A: **None whatsoever.**

Q: What part did Diana Dors play in the break-up of your marriage?

A: **I don't wish to say anything about that. All the steps have been taken by Diana.**

Q: What about the property you share with Diana?

A: **Oh, I don't think we'll start throwing bricks about.**

Q: Isn't it possible that somebody in America will be able to look after her affairs as you did?

A: **Of course it is. So far as I'm concerned, I'm going to take 20 paces backwards, put my hands over my ears and wait for the splash.**

Q: Do you think this would have happened if you hadn't gone to America?

A: **Well . . . I don't. As a matter of fact . . . No, I don't think it would. You have to remember that, over there, there are two columnists for every star, always prying for information and writing it up – women with hats that need a gardener – creating a cancer in the press.**

Q: Have you anything to say about Rod Steiger?

A: **No comment.**

Q: Have you ever thought about going into films yourself?

A: **I was once an actor, a very hungry actor, a long time ago. You might think I was a very bad actor . . . and you'd be right.**

But, as always, Dennis was proving to be rather a good actor, and his remarks about the suitability of an American agent were strategically timed. In the last week of October, Diana had sacked Louis Shurr, without explanation, and the agent was not pleased. Neither was Bob Hope, who had introduced them, and Hedda Hopper wrote a scathing editorial. 'But for Hope and Shurr,' fumed the woman with the hat that needed gardening, 'she'd be unknown here. Her popularity seems to be slipping even before her first film is shown.' Dennis went overboard in his bid to position himself as the only person who could possibly manage Diana's affairs successfully, claiming he hadn't even decided yet whether he wanted the burden. 'Diana is committing professional suicide,' he said dramatically. 'Whatever happens, she must not get into the hands of cheapjack Americans who can do her career *immeasurable* harm.'

The rebounding claims and counterclaims were considered surprisingly newsworthy given that the winter of 1956 was hardly lacking in international news. There were reports of rioting in Kowloon, an anti-Soviet uprising in Budapest and, most seriously of all, there was the escalating Suez Crisis, with the prime minister, Sir Anthony Eden, building up to war in the Middle East. In protest at lack of western funding for the Aswan Dam, Egyptian president Abdel Nasser had nationalized the Suez Canal, effectively a lifeline for the west as a conduit for the export of oil. Eden launched a military response without consulting his American allies, expecting their approval. When the US condemned the action, Eden's humiliating climbdown resulted in the withdrawal of a British presence from the country. The Empire had been dying slowly for quite some time, but now the coffin was finally being measured and the full, depressing impact was beginning to hit home. The Hamiltons were, at least, a cheerfully British distraction.

The split was played as a soap opera, and even Mrs Sholl had a walk-on, coached admirably by Dennis. 'This whole wretched business is *her* fault,' she insisted. 'I can't stand by and see Dennis take the blame.' Dennis, for his part, played the cuckold to perfection, mooning about 'the Diana I used to know' and hinting at the Steiger affair with an artfully wounded dignity. 'Maybe the truth about our troubles will come out some day,' he mused. 'That is up to Diana. I have tried to make her understand how much her personal life can affect her career.'

If his own future was really so secure, if he really didn't need the bother of managing his wife's career, Dennis certainly seemed to be protesting too much. Diana, on the other hand, didn't exactly help herself. 'I'm no business-woman,' she said blithely. 'I don't think I'm in a financial mess, but I won't know until I talk with my business manager and lawyer. I know nothing at all about figures . . .' a quick flash of the old Dors, ' . . . except, of course, my own.'

The saga escalated with the news that Diana was to return briefly to England on 12 November. Stopping off in New York, she held an impromptu press conference in the VIP lounge at the airport, where she caused a stir by checking in enough excess baggage for six more passengers. To please an RKO photographer, she posed with the enormous pile of suitcases, waving a phoney farewell to the USA.

Wearing a sober, black two-piece suit with matching high heels, rhinestone-studded shades and a mink stole, Diana valiantly tried to scotch the Steiger rumours and dealt tactfully with her crumbling marriage. 'What a mixed-up mess it all is,' she sighed. 'The public may think I'm just a blonde sexpot making bundles of dollars, but I'm human and vulnerable.' Someone asked what the future held, but she didn't know. 'Well, at least I've got my work,' she replied, 'but a woman wants more than work.' She talked so much, she made her flight with only six minutes to spare.

The Diana Dors that arrived at London Airport was much more guarded, and photographers were confused. Good-old-Di, do-anything-Di, refused their requests for cheese-cake poses and only fleetingly removed her dark glasses. 'I'd rather not answer questions about my marital affairs at the moment,' she snapped. 'I want to be left alone to try to work things out for myself – if I can.' Someone observed, pointedly, that Dennis wasn't there. 'I wasn't expecting him,' she retorted. And with that, she was gone – heading straight for the Dorchester Hotel in Park Lane, one of London's finest. But Diana wasn't retreating from the limelight. After checking into her suite, she held a series of press conferences that only served to encourage cynical rumours that the Hamiltons were separating for tax purposes. 'Mr and Mrs Perpetual Promotion' they were called.

The image she presented that day was a considered attempt to put an end to the old Diana Dors – the publicity stunts, the practical jokes, the mink bikinis. She'd even lost fourteen pounds, she said, taking a fraction from her fashionable curves but nothing, she insisted, from her bust. In Diana's eyes, the separation was a chance to start again. 'Diana without Dennis is going to be a different girl,' she promised. To prove she was serious, she explained that she was even willing to let Dennis have the pool. 'I can manage to live without a swimming pool,' she said stoically. She said she'd grown up, that her outlook had broadened, that she knew people were sick of her protected tenancy in the headlines: 'People must be as fed up with reading about the exploits of Diana Dors as I am. My whole outlook has changed. I've had a very hectic and exciting five years with Dennis, and I've made a lot of money. But the money hasn't given me any happiness, and I don't want to work and live just for money.'

Diana talked frankly about her marriage and spelt out the reasons for its collapse. 'Our life was like a balance sheet,' she said. 'Perhaps the reason Dennis and I split up is because he was inclined to treat me more as a business than as a wife.' In summing up, Diana meted out a suitably catty riposte to the 'Mr Rod Steiger' reference that her husband had made to Donald Zec. 'Dennis is a wonderful business manager,' she enthused. 'Nobody can deny that. And he's going to go

151

on handling my career – unless he's too busy running Shirley Ann Field's career.' And after the first round of interviews, Diana took her leave. First, she said, she was going to go out and buy a Cadillac. Then she was going to have lunch.

Diana had booked a suite for the night, but it was never occupied. Instead, she climbed into a waiting Rolls Royce and drove down to meet Dennis at the Penthouse in Maidenhead. The meeting was tense, but Diana stayed the night and slept alone in the spare room while reporters kept a vigil outside. She and Dennis drove back to London the next day, taking lunch at the Dorchester and hiring a suite, but at around 7 p.m. the booking was cancelled and the Hamiltons drove back to Maidenhead. Rumours of a reconciliation were further fuelled a few days later when camera crews received a tip-off that Diana was holding a press conference at Leon's salon in Shaftesbury Avenue. Dennis looked surprised, not to mention embarrassed, when he brought his wife for her hair appointment, and he quickly disappeared. Diana hadn't known about it either, and she wasn't happy, but she dealt politely with the first few questions. As Leon's stylist teased her hair into a style based, optimistically, on a character in Tolstoy's *War and Peace*, someone asked whether they would be getting back together. 'I would like it,' she replied tersely. 'I imagine Dennis would, too.' When Diana's red-faced publicity consultant cleared the room, it was obvious that, contrary to his misguided opinion, the Hamiltons' marriage really *was* on the rocks and not about to be saved by a photo opportunity.

Diana was putting a brave face on it, but the strain began to show. She cancelled an appearance on the BBC's *In Town Tonight* show, alongside Norman Wisdom, and for a few days the Hamilton phone line was unobtainable – 'Temporarily out of order at the subscriber's request.' Diana was jet-lagged and emotional, but there were rumours in the media of a nervous breakdown. Perhaps this was wishful thinking on their part.

Although Diana still had her supporters, many members of the press were starting to tire of the whole circus. When she did finally appear on *In Town Tonight*, a *News of the World* columnist yawned the following day that, 'we had the privilege of hearing about that Hollywood swimming pool incident. Why, I can't imagine – we've heard it all before'. Journalists were beginning to feel jaded and used; where Diana used to oblige them with a quote and a photo, they now felt she was trying to turn things round and take more than she was giving. For a start, her outlook on life now seemed almost indistinguishable from Lady Docker's. It was one thing to be a provincial glamour girl, in awe of bright lights and big pay cheques, but Diana was now twenty-five and her once-quaint naivety was crystallizing into greed. The *Daily Mirror* ran a long and incredibly personal article on 1 October, headlined, 'A Word . . . In Your Pretty Ear', about the Hamiltons' attitude to money. It savaged Dennis, saying that he spoke about his wife 'in a way a gold prospector might talk about a gold mine in them thar hills', and described Diana as 'still playing the same gold-plated record about the Dors dough.' It ended with a backhanded compliment: 'We all know you're a nice kid at heart. We believe that in your own way you're also quite an actress. Maybe this harping on cash-cash-cash is just another act. Maybe it isn't. But here's some advice – FREE OF CHARGE. When you shake the dust of Hollywood off your feet, rub the gold dust out of your eyes as well and leave this money-grabbing talk behind. It isn't cute. It isn't clever. It doesn't win friends or influence people. Why not give it a permanent rest?'

A rival paper ran a similar diatribe unsubtly headlined,

'Dear Diana and Dennis – YOU MAKE ME SICK!' which described them as 'two tinselly bores' whose only talent was 'an ability to wash their dirty linen in public better than a laundry with glass walls.' Not only did the article cast aspersions on the authenticity of the separation, it also boldly called the rumoured Steiger affair 'fake'. But she only had herself to blame for the position she was in. Only a few years before, any publicity was good publicity. Now, any publicity was simply publicity, and it was starting to devalue her life, to the extent that no one knew what was fact and what was fiction. Everything she said or did was open to interpretation, and when she took part in the BBC's *A–Z of Showbusiness* in November, her brief appearance brought one of the most damning reviews of her career. In the programme, she was asked, 'Don't you want to be anything more? A serious actress?' She replied, 'The answer to that was supplied in my last dramatic picture, *Yield to the Night*. But the fans who saw the picture said, "We want our Dors to be just the way she is."'

Dennis had always called her 'Dors', but the way he said it always sounded more like a trademark, and she was beginning to realize what he was getting at. But what was actually a forthright and realistic way of dealing with the film's lack of success was seized upon by TV critic Herbert Kretzmer, who fumed, 'She actually said it – "Our Dors". How dare this blonde headline-hunter set herself up as the mouthpiece of the British cinema-going public of Great Britain and refer to herself as "Our Dors"?'

Dennis immediately saw that some damage limitation was necessary and proposed a vague truce. The couple were reunited at their Maidenhead home, but it was a reconciliation of convenience that only satisfied the press and the public. Dennis even went on record in the *Sunday Pictorial*, with a glib, ghost-written series that explained his wife's frustrations and her dream of starting a family – one of the articles was helpfully headlined 'Diana Wants A Baby'. 'I put her career, her success, before motherhood,' he gushed, in a somewhat unconvincingly over-penitent way.

Diana was not aware of any sudden transformation in her husband, especially at the end of the year, when his unreconstructed, freeloading friends descended on their Christmas party. There was also the small matter of assault a few days after, when Dennis was involved in a fight in Maidstone High Street with the driver of a car which refused to pull over and let his Cadillac overtake. Dennis stopped the motorist, a thirty-eight-year-old fruit and vegetable salesman, and punched him in the face. Charges were pressed, but before the case could go to court, a settlement was reached and they were swiftly dropped. This time, Dennis perhaps realized, they couldn't afford the publicity.

Chapter Eight

THE FORMER LADY HAMILTON

WHEN RKO BEGAN making plans for its 1957 production schedule, it seemed obvious that Diana Dors was not a priority item – in fact, release dates for her two completed films had not yet been set. Ironically, *Yield to the Night* made its American debut in January to perfectly respectable reviews. 'The extremely trim Miss Dors, in case anybody wonders or cares, *can* act,' remarked the *New York Times* dryly. 'Her restrained, haggard transition from listless empathy to numb terror is a pip in a shattering, haunting and generally sterling little picture.'

Diana was due to start work on *The Long Haul*, which began shooting in February, so she and Dennis took a two-week break in Malaga with Sandra Dorne, a friend from the Rank days, and her husband, Patrick Holt. When she returned, Robert Mitchum had dropped out of the film, and Dennis was very wary of his replacement, Victor Mature, a middle-aged actor whose rugged good looks and self-deprecating humour had made him Hollywood's king of beefcake. It also made him a hard man to marry, as a string of ex-wives may have testified, and his reputation set alarm bells ringing in Dennis's head. But Diana was making a concerted effort to revamp her image, and she was growing tired of the increasingly personal 'scandal' stories she was reading in the press. 'I don't give a damn if they're true,' she insisted, 'but it doesn't exactly please me if they're not.' She even went so far as to endorse a pamphlet issued by a society called British

Temperance Youth, warning against the dangers of drink. 'Famous film star Diana Dors hates champagne,' it claimed, 'and stays away from all cocktail parties.'

But despite her intentions, Diana did begin a relationship on the set, right under Dennis's nose. Tommy Yeardye was a stunt man and bit-part actor who was playing Mature's body double in some of the action scenes. Yeardye was muscular and good-looking, much like Mature himself, and had in the past doubled for Rock Hudson. Diana took a shine to him, but she hadn't expected things to go much further than an on-set flirtation.

It was Dennis's voyeuristic tendencies that finally brought the affair into the open. They were entertaining some guests for the weekend, their old friend Jon Pertwee and an actress friend. Pertwee had a theatrical commitment to honour and, while he drove down to Croydon, Dennis went out for a drink with friends. Before he left, Dennis tripped a switch that started a hidden tape recorder and when he returned that night he listened to a fragment of the women's conversation. It wasn't what he had been expecting to hear; in fact, Dennis was the first to be humiliated. Diana had been telling her friend about Yeardye. There wasn't much to tell, but Dennis knew, or could imagine, from the way Diana described him that this was not a platonic friendship. He was furious and embarked on a wrecking spree, smashing ornaments and glasses, and finally throwing the two women out of the house. Terrified, Diana and the other actress drove back to London. When Pertwee arrived back at the Hamilton's house, tired from the evening's performance, the scene that met him was extremely tense. Dennis sat slumped in a chair, babbling about his wife. When Pertwee tried to lighten the atmosphere, Dennis played him an extract from the tape which, Diana claimed later, featured the other woman talking candidly about a man she found attractive. Dennis knew very well that Pertwee's relationship with her was not

rock solid, and when the relationship foundered soon afterwards, some of their friends held Dennis personally
responsible.

After a couple of very awkward days, it became clear that
Diana could either suffer an awful atmosphere in someone
else's house or face one at home, so she returned to Dennis.
Again, his forgiveness was a compromise – *The Long Haul*
was still shooting, and Dennis knew that his 10 per cent cut
as manager depended on her completing the film to the
producers' satisfaction. He also knew, unbeknownst to
Diana, that the BBC were planning to feature her in *This Is
Your Life*, a flattering show in which unwitting celebrities,
sometimes has-beens, were surprised with friends, relatives
and fellow celebrities often in dire need of exposure. It was
primarily a show for stars in the twilight of their career and,
at the age of twenty-five, Diana was an unusually young
choice.

When 1 April came around, *The Long Haul* was still
shooting a lot of night scenes, so Dennis suggested a trip to
the theatre to break up the monotony of waiting. He told
her they were going to see Sophie Tucker, an ageing
Russian-American vaudeville singer, but when they arrived
at the King's Theatre in Hammersmith, Diana was surprised
to find *This Is Your Life* host Eamonn Andrews waiting for
her and she was taken up onstage. He brought out her father,
who played a nostalgic piece on the piano, Aunt Kit, and
some uncles she hadn't seen in a long while but it was the
show business guests who made it a memorable night. In
fact, it was praised for its directness, especially for the way in
which Andrews broke with tradition, opening with a barrage
of tongue-in-cheek criticism from *Mirror* writer Donald Zec.
'Let's face it, Diana,' Zec told her, 'you represent the most
calculated, hardboiled, exploitation of sex I've ever seen in

British pictures. Do you want me to go on?' 'Not really,' she replied. But, of course, there was a sweetener. 'Although I think at times you are brash – perhaps at times very outrageous – I would also like to say that I think you are unique,' he concluded. 'No one can ignore Diana Dors. You have that rare quality which I admire and I write about all the time . . . You are a star.'

But this was still quite a combative show, and Diana was amused when Wolf Mankowitz, the journalist turned screen-writer whom Diana had known since his work on *A Kid for Two Farthings*, rather nicely described her as: 'The bleached blonde the whole world knows is bleached.' She had to compose herself when Andrews introduced another special guest – Stewart Sawyer, flown in from Hollywood at an estimated cost of £361 13s. 'I've come 6,000 miles to shake your hand,' said Sawyer. 'If I'd known you were coming,' Diana replied, 'I'd have worn my swimsuit.'

The Hamiltons' marriage was now a complete sham as far as Diana was concerned; it was a part she was playing for the film industry as well as the public. She was dissatisfied and bored but, in some ways, Dennis was right – she would have been lost without him to handle those dull financial invest-ments and tax returns – and with her silly affairs and flirtations she was just testing her limits, like a petulant child. But Diana wasn't stupid. She also knew that Dennis would be lost, or more specifically broke, without her, and this was perhaps her way of hurting him back. In the light of all that friction, it seems astonishing that Diana went along with the whole *This Is Your Life* charade, but the Hamiltons were able to bury the hatchet for business reasons: Dennis was simply protecting his investment, while Diana still had one eye on the clock and she knew she needed to keep her profile high. Besides, divorce was still frowned upon in Britain and had yet to become a show business prerequisite, as it was in Hollywood.

In the weeks after the show it was warfare as usual, but Diana was still surprised when Dennis suddenly announced that he was leaving her. While the whole Yeardye affair was brewing, Dennis had been making plans to open a drinking club in Windsor. Provisionally called The Swinging Door, it was, like El Toucan, exotic in its decor, with bamboo panelling and fishing nets. The prospective manageress – a photogenic twenty-year-old Anglo-Indian model – hammered the point home by posing in a midriff-revealing Indian costume ('It will be *some* club,' members were promised). Dennis told Diana he'd met someone else, and that they were moving into a room above the club, which he'd now retitled El Dors.

Diana took this as a sign that the marriage was now finally, officially over, but when she took advantage of her freedom on the last Saturday in April by holding a late-night party at the Penthouse, the news travelled quickly back to Dennis. Some of the guests stayed over, but the following day a wealthy businessman named John Hoey drove down at around noon in his green Cadillac. He suggested a ride in the countryside, and Diana, Yeardye and starlet Shani Wallis happily accepted his offer. When they returned that evening at about 6 p.m., Dennis was waiting for her. Sholly met Diana in the driveway to tell her the news. 'It's all right,' she said, 'he just wants you to sign some papers.'

The way Diana told the story, it was rather more serious than that. Leaving Yeardye, Hoey and Wallis outside, she later claimed that she went upstairs to find Dennis brandishing two sheets of paper. One was a list of alleged 'infidelities', including the names of some men Diana barely knew, and the other was a contract listing most of their joint properties – the Penthouse, Woodhurst, the coffee bar and the club. Dennis wanted her to sign both – the property list would give him ownership, while the other list would be his insurance, a ham-fisted attempt at blackmail to deter her from trying to renege on the deal.

Diana claimed that she signed them under duress, but this version of events perhaps suited Diana in later life, when the tax man needed mollifying yet again, and her claims in both *Swinging Dors* and *Dors by Diana* seem a little far-fetched. In the first account, Dennis punched her then broke a window with the barrel of his shotgun and aimed it at her three friends outside. In the second, he was aiming specifically at Yeardye. In both, the actor came charging through the front door, up the stairs and sent Dennis crashing to the floor with one blow. Presumably, Diana's proud, violent husband completely forgot that he was holding a shotgun, and meekly allowed Yeardye to escort his wife from the house, taking her to stay with his parents in Mill Hill.

There was no mention of this in Tommy Yeardye's account. In his version, Dennis asked to speak to Diana alone, and it was only when he tried the front door and found it locked that Yeardye realized something was wrong. He broke a pane of glass with his fist and ran upstairs to find Diana in tears. Dennis lunged at him. 'He had rather a surprise when he found that, when it came to a fight with me, he had met his match,' he said. There were rumours that Dennis had pushed Yeardye through a window, probably circulated by his friends, but Yeardye took great delight in quashing them. 'It is not true,' he said simply. 'Although he *tried*.'

In fact, it's unlikely there was ever a gun involved, or perhaps even any documents – this was simply a matter of Dennis's burning jealousy. Dennis really thought she'd be nothing without him, all those jibes about not being able to find the garden gate by herself must have suddenly rung pretty hollow. If Dennis really was a deranged gun-toting gangster, would Diana have been quite happy to leave Sholly in the house and ring up an hour later to ask if she could stop by and pick up some clothes? When they got there Dennis had dumped a pile of clothes and jewellery in the middle of the driveway. Diana loaded them into the boot of the car and drove off. 'That is the last I have seen of her – or want to,' he said later.

Dennis had quite a field day with the press that day, and many papers obliged him by running the news that El Dors was due to open on 11 May. In case they might have overlooked it, he made dual-purpose statements to the press at Yeardye's expense. 'Is it too late to change the name of the club?' he asked. 'I want it changed from "El Dors" to "The Film Extra".' He made a lot of Yeardye's status, putting him down at every opportunity. 'Diana has thrown away everything,' he said, disdainfully. 'She is a very silly girl. A very silly girl indeed.'

Uncannily, to mark the end of filming on *The Long Haul*, Diana appeared at the Savoy on 2 May to 'christen' a lorry used in the production. Wearing a green dress described by one eye-witness as having 'not so much a plunging neckline as a rising waistline', she poured champagne on the vehicle, which bore the name 'Diana' on its grille. 'Please,' she said, 'I don't want to talk about my private life. Please don't ask.' But someone did. And she talked about it for an hour and a quarter. 'Why do your marital troubles always coincide with the end of one of your films?' she was asked. 'Maybe because of the tension I work under,' she replied. 'Maybe just coincidence . . .'

Dennis moved out, but he didn't go very far. While Diana kept the Penthouse, he settled into another flat at Wood-hurst, just twenty yards away and separated only by a tall fence. Sholly went with him and so did the animals, including Joe the cockatoo and Crackers the boxer. Diana stopped wearing her wedding ring. To get away from it all for a couple of weeks she and Tommy booked a flight to Majorca. 'I don't care if I never come back,' she said, and a bored section of the public hoped she would seriously consider the option.

When she returned in the first week of June, she decided to go ahead with the divorce and filed a petition a few weeks later, on grounds of adultery and cruelty. Not to be outdone, Dennis claimed he'd prepared a petition a few weeks earlier and that Diana had persuaded him to hold back. He announced his intention to issue a cross-petition, on the same grounds.

Diana, meanwhile, was packing for Rome. Many British actors were being courted by continental film producers, and some of Diana's peers – specifically Belinda Lee – were soon to establish whole new careers in Europe. Director Vittorio Gassman wanted Diana for a film called *The Girl Who Rode in the Palio*, about a girl who wins a trip to Siena in a competition and falls in love with an Italian prince. Diana graciously insisted that a role be found for Yeardye, who was fast becoming something of a celebrity in the fallout from her marriage. His role was never quite clarified – sometimes he was just a friend, at other times her 'business manager' – but he played the game and knew the value of good publicity. 'I'm not one of those physical fitness maniacs, like Joe Robinson and Micky Hargitay,' he modestly told reporters. 'I just like to keep in shape.' Just in case anyone missed this, Yeardye made sure a few barbells were to hand, and if they weren't, he went to fetch them ('Shall I get the weights, Diana?'). Her more sophisticated friends were not impressed.

The Gassman film was hard work, but she enjoyed herself. There was a nagging doubt about Tommy, however, that even the warm Latin nights and romantic open-air settings could not erase. Yeardye was a good man, strong and reliable, but she felt he was too keen to stay in her shadow. Since moving into the Penthouse with her (which he strongly denied in the press), he hadn't worked much, and Diana wanted a man with plans and schemes and a glint in his eye, a man who'd try anything, just for the hell of it. A man like Dennis.

When they returned from Rome, the Penthouse seemed very empty. She missed Dennis and the pets, even Sholly, although she drew the line at feeling too sorry for herself. She'd made a lot of money and had a lot of good things from life. 'Let's not fool ourselves,' she once said. 'I'd rather be unhappy in luxury than unhappy in poverty.'

She was feeling especially down when Dennis phoned. He'd been working on Woodhurst – 'Dors-ing it up' – and he wondered if she'd like to come round and see the results. She accepted his invitation and was duly impressed by his rather haphazard arrangement of ornaments and antiques – including a library of leather-bound books (for show, not reading), and a piano, an instrument he had never learned to play. This was the Dennis Hamilton others saw – the uncultured showman who liked to throw his money around but didn't seem to care where it went, the vulgar playboy who bought the look of a rich man's lifestyle in the belief that that was much the same as really living it. That night, however, Dennis romanced her with wine and poetry, and Diana remembered the charming devil who courted her and whisked her into marriage. He asked if they could try again, and Diana said she would seriously consider the matter but she needed time to think. Deep down, though, she knew it was out of the question.

The news stories did not please Rank and, although Diana was still under contract, no projects had been mentioned for nearly two years. She didn't know what to think when she was invited to Pinewood Studio on 30 September to celebrate the film company's twenty-first anniversary. She was relieved they hadn't snubbed her, but the thought of mixing with the same people who had treated her so shabbily at Cannes the year before filled her with horror.

She'd heard the company weren't happy with her demeanour, and the whole publicity problem was getting out of hand. Did those people think the Diana Dors who made the headlines was really her, not just a character she played for the public? She just did what was expected of her – a saucy remark, a provocative smile, a teasing pose – though she found it, ultimately, rather tiring, and she'd thought Rank had understood that. She was depressed to realize that, like the rest of the country, her paymasters couldn't see past the image. But in their defence, that was what they'd paid for, and Diana was perhaps naive to expect more from a company that consistently put entertainment before art.

Nevertheless, she expected better from them. 'The Americans and the Italians can't understand it,' she said. 'They think it's crazy. I haven't been told officially why I don't make pictures for Rank but I gather they don't approve of me. What am I supposed to do? It's the publicity that's put me where I am, not the parts I've had. People expect me to be what I am – that's my value at the box office. Why should I change?'

But there was more to it than that. Divorce offended J. Arthur Rank's own religious principles to start with, but the very public way in which Diana and Dennis were bickering in the daily press, plus the none too subtle allusions to what was really an extra-marital affair with Yeardye, made the break-up much worse for her career. It didn't help that Dennis was so often in the news, especially when the El Dors club was raided one weekend and fifteen customers questioned over an after-hours drinking session. But perhaps the final straw for Rank came when Dennis announced that he was suing *Confidential* magazine over an article headlined

'What Diana Dors Never Knew About Her Ever-Lovin' Hubby' which was plastered over two pages of its September issue. The article made it plain that he was chasing other women: 'There were naughty doings behind the doors of the Dors household. Dennis figures that faint heart ne'er won fair floosie ... so while Diana snoozed upstairs, he cuddled downstairs.' In actual fact, it was quite a mild exposé, which 'revealed' how Dennis had made several crude passes at a friend's girlfriend behind his back, first while Diana was at the studio and again when Diana was upstairs in bed and the boyfriend was out buying liquor.

Dennis's bravado in announcing a lawsuit was no doubt encouraged by the news that Irish-born Hollywood star Maureen O'Hara was suing the same magazine for libel over claims that she was spotted being over-intimate with a lover at Grauman's Chinese Theatre. When O'Hara was able to prove that she wasn't even in the country at the time, *Confidential*'s defence collapsed and the Los Angeles County grand jury was left to decide its fate. It was going to be easy for Dennis to align himself with the outraged parties and close ranks on a clearly doomed magazine, but the story left a sleazy residue on both his and his wife's career.

Dennis's womanizing continued at Woodhurst, and Diana soon tired of the sight of his starlet harem as they paraded into his flat, which she could see quite clearly from her sitting-room window. Aside from the emotional complications of living next door to her estranged husband there were also pragmatic problems: Diana had the lawn mower; the boiler and pump for the swimming pool were both on Dennis's side of the fence. It was an intolerable situation and in September Diana decided to put the Penthouse on the market. Her plans for a new place – 'I'd love to buy a farm' – were greeted with scepticism in the press. 'Everyone roars with laughter when I mention it,' she said, 'but both my mother's and my father's people were farmers, so I suppose I just want to get back to it . . . I'd like to find something that's working for me. With this place,' she said, referring to the Penthouse, 'I'm working for *it*.'

Diana was still unsure about Yeardye, much less sure about Dennis, and made plans to spend a few days in October in New York while she made an appearance on Perry Como's TV show. What began as a three-day visit turned into ten days; extra TV appearances were pencilled in and Diana made an impromptu showing at a luncheon being held for the Queen by the city's mayor. 'I'll wear something discreet,' she promised. 'After all, I'm English first and sexy second.'

Diana even met up with Rod Steiger who, she claimed, asked her to marry him and backed up the offer with a bunch of red roses. But her passion had cooled. She had been shocked to meet a recent girlfriend of Steiger's who quoted the same lines of poetry he had once quoted to her. Where she once found him caring and tender she now thought him calculating and presumptuous, expecting to pick up exactly where they'd left off. Now, even she could see they had no future together.

Dennis was also keeping a New York florist busy, sending love notes with each delivery. When Yeardye flew out to join her for a week, her lovelife could not have been more cluttered. Thinking it over, she decided she was happiest, for the moment at least, with Yeardye. He offered support and stability, and that was what she needed most at that point. Dennis had been fun but he objectified and patronized her, blithely telling her not to worry and bringing home stuffed toys as presents. She used to think they were sweet, but as they piled up in the bedroom she came to detest them. 'I'm not a child any longer,' she protested to columnist Godfrey Winn. 'I've been in show business for ten years. It makes you tough whether you want to be tough or not. It's a jungle, I guess – but not that kind of jungle,' she added, gesturing to a pile of teddy bears and other cuddly animals.

When they returned, it was announced that Diana's contract with Rank had finally been cancelled 'by mutual consent.' 'They have no plans for me,' said Diana. 'So we decided to call it a day. I'm not weeping about it.' She was more interested in the farm she was planning to buy, a fifteenth-century farmhouse near Horsham, Sussex, with fifty acres of land and livestock including a herd of dairy cows, pigs and a chicken run. 'I can't bear being alone, ever,' she reasoned, 'so if the worst came to the worst, there would always be the animals.'

Her career was about to take a brand new turn when it was announced that she would appear on ITV's flagship entertainment show, *Sunday Night at the London Palladium*. Many people saw it as part of the show's desperate battle to stay on top of the ratings by using names rather than talent. Because no one really knew what Diana Dors could actually do, the show's producer, Brian Tesler, was asked what kind of act she would be putting on. Would she sing? Dance? Appear in a sketch? 'All of these,' said Tesler, adding a tell-tale 'We hope . . .'

The show was to be hosted by her old friend Bob Monkhouse and in rehearsals the day before transmission, Diana attended a press conference wearing a figure-hugging pink dress and a silver mink stole. The question was repeated: what would she – or what could she – do? 'I shall probably fool about with Bob a bit,' she shrugged, 'but you've got to do something else. It's always such an anti-climax when a film star walks onto the stage and has nothing to do or say except talk about their latest film.' She was going to sing, she said, and even though she'd never had any lessons she thought she had enough to work with. 'I don't intend to stand in front of the microphone and husk my way through a number,' she said. 'But I feel so nervous about it that all you'll probably hear is a squeak of fright.'

Diana made her entrance with a troupe of male dancers,

wearing a dress that revealed as much cleavage and leg as was legally possible. The show's special guest star was Walter Chiari, an Italian comedian billed as his country's answer to Danny Kaye, which was quite an accolade. Monkhouse introduced her to Chiari as 'The former Lady Hamilton', and when they embraced in an innuendo-heavy extended clinch, he circled the couple, yelling, 'Are you in there, Diana?' She finished her twelve-minute appearance on the show with a ballad, 'I'll Take Romance'. When someone played it back to her after the show, she cringed. Perhaps she did need singing lessons after all.

Although her appearance, not to mention the show itself, was not considered a success by the critics, who roundly panned it, she was generously received by the audience. The subsequent publicity eventually led to an upsurge in bookings as a cabaret artiste, which basically entailed making her old variety act a bit more upmarket. The first offer was an eight-week season in Las Vegas in the New Year, for an estimated £3,500 per week. 'I've already been to scout the territory,' she said. 'I shall sell myself on glamour, with the slinkiest gown money can buy.' It was a reference to Marlene Dietrich, who at that time was bowing out of movie work and starting a new career as a singer, giving stately renderings of classic songs with a never less than stunning wardrobe. Dietrich was not an accomplished singer but her personality gave her voice a gravitas that few could rival. Diana wasn't in that league, and her singing style owed an awful lot to Doris Day in pitch and delivery, but she liked the idea of an artist being more important than the content of their performance. She signed up with a singing tutor in Hampstead, Georges Canelli, who was duly tracked down by a reporter. 'She's gifted. Very gifted,' said Canelli. 'But it's too soon to say much yet. She's only had two lessons.'

★

With Dennis out of the picture, Rank off her back and a singing career opening up in front of her, Diana was feeling very good about herself indeed. RKO had effectively annulled her contract, and she felt she was at last free of the hoopla and shameless hustling that surrounded her early years as a star and could at last try to shape the future. Time was running out, and, being a blonde, she firmly believed her chances of survival were shorter – brunettes lasted much longer, she thought. Which was why the farm was so important to her, it was somewhere she could go, something she would still have, if it all fell through: 'It's when you're living in a bedsitter in Bayswater that you miss your career and the bright lights.' The split with Dennis had brought a new Diana into the world, a woman who shied away from stunts like mink bikinis and poolside parties.

It was obviously the old Diana, then, who made an unexpected appearance at Hammersmith police station on 29 November, in connection with the assault and obstruction of a policeman. Driving into London, Yeardye had been driving Diana's blue Cadillac when he made a right turn from Hammersmith Bridge Road into Queen Caroline Street. According to the statement he later made, he was about to pull out when PC Roy Anderson stopped the car and banged on the window. 'The door was wrenched open,' he said, 'and PC Anderson said, "Where do you think you're going?" I replied, "I had indicated I was going right . . ." The officer said, "You are bloody well *not*."'

Diana was carrying the latest addition to her menagerie – a poodle puppy called Amanda Jane and a Siamese cat called Juliette – so she reached across and grabbed at the doorhandle, afraid they might jump out. Diana claimed the PC grabbed her hand, pulled it off the handle and shouted, 'Just because you're a bloody film star you needn't think you can bloody well do what you like!' Yeardye made as if to drive off and the policeman stood in front of the car, at which point Yeardye got out and pushed him away. Climbing back into the driver's seat, Yeardye defiantly started the engine. 'I ran in front with my hand raised and told him to stop,' Anderson told the court. 'He revved the engine and accelerated at me. I was forced to leap onto the bonnet to save myself being run over. I was carried along on the bonnet for ten or fifteen yards.' By this time, quite a crowd had gathered – after all, they were outside a post office, just down from the Hammersmith Odeon and a busy café. Diana sank into her seat while housewives parked their shopping bags and stood to watch, some of them waving.

Yeardye was arrested, and when he appeared before the magistrates the next morning, Diana went with him. She was wearing a sombre black dress, silver mink stole and a fetching sling made from pink silk as she applied for a summons of her own, alleging assault and abusive behaviour on behalf of the PC. Mysteriously, the sling was gone when she made an appearance at the Wood Green Empire that night, in a variety show called *Saturday Spectacular*. 'I left it in my dressing room,' she explained. 'There was no question of my not appearing in the show. For ten minutes I had a very hectic time in sketches and a song and dance act. Most of the time my arms were moving about a lot, I was grinning and bearing it.' But there didn't seem to be any bruises, either. 'No,' she said, 'there are no visible ones. They must be inward bruises.'

A few days later, one of the pretenders to Diana's throne, Simone Silva, failed to appear at La Ronde, the Piccadilly restaurant where she was booked to perform a nightly cabaret routine. Her film career was over but, after appearing on a TV talent show as a singer, she was hoping to reinvent herself. It was never anything more than a hope; on the night of 31 November she was found dead in her bed at her flat in Brook Street, Mayfair, clutching a teddy bear. The cause of death was a stroke, attributed to a heart complaint brought on by kidney disease. Silva had not been well for a long time – she had collapsed three years earlier after losing seventeen pounds in just eight days, and in the last week of her life her stage costume had to be taken in three separate times. Little was known at that time about anorexia nervosa, but Silva's manic desire to be loved, to be wanted, perhaps predisposed her sad, destructive relationship with her own body.

The newspapers were not kind; headlines claimed that she tried to buy success and described her as 'Miss Make-Believe', 'The Star Who Never Was', 'The Beautiful Girl Who Lived A Lie'. She was twenty-nine.

Chapter Nine

DEATH OF A SALESMAN

DIANA'S PINK SILK sling and wounded pride didn't amount to much when Yeardye's case finally came to court on 20 December. He was found guilty and fined £30 plus 30 guineas costs, plus 40 shillings for obstruction, with no separate penalty for the assault charge. Diana's own counter-accusations were respectfully heard – 'I felt extremely humiliated,' she claimed, 'with a policeman across the bonnet of my car' – but magistrate E.R. Guest tactfully mediated between both claims. 'I think it was done as tempers had risen,' he decided. 'The policeman was pretentious and perhaps not tactful. I think it was done with the object not of hurting him but of frightening him out of the way.' Perhaps unsurprisingly, Diana's accusations were never answered in court.

In just six months, despite what she clearly thought were her best efforts, the Hammersmith affair had brought Diana's name back into the headlines, and it was there at the year's end, when her Boxing night party took a dramatic turn. With Dennis out of the way, some of her old friends had come back into her life, including Kim Waterfield who, in his absence, had been sentenced to four years imprisonment by a French court for his part in the Jack Warner robbery. The party was beginning to wane and many stalwarts were leaving, when a sudden noise and a flash of light at 2 a.m. caught some of the guests' attention. Dennis's riverboat – a sixty-foot barge called *De Bries*, which was moored on a nearby towpath – blazed merrily in the darkness, causing an estimated £6,000 worth of damage. Many guests were unaware of what was happening and, in fact, the first Diana heard of it was the commotion when the fire engines came.

She later said she suspected one of Dennis's tenants, a stuntman who was less than happy with his landlord's cavalier attitude to rent increases, but the boat-burning incident followed uncomfortably close to a phone call made by Dennis to the police at 8 p.m. on Boxing Day evening. Dennis claimed he had 'a hunch' that something would happen that night and asked the police to keep an eye on his boat. He later coloured his stories with claims that he had been pestered for the previous fortnight by an anonymous caller who threatened to smash up his home. More bizarrely, Dennis also alleged that his mystery assailant said he would 'slice me up and throw me over a weir.' Perhaps the relevant authorities were not paying close enough attention when Dennis told one newspaper that 'the insurance expired at midnight, but I understand investigations show the fire broke out earlier in the evening.'

On a superficial level, Dennis blamed Diana, and cold-war relations between the two hit permafreeze. The situation wasn't helped when, two days later, a bottle sailed through the Penthouse's dining-room window. Diana called the police, who duly arrived and took away fragments of glass, for whatever purpose, but nothing was established. Dennis, in the next flat along, performed indignantly for the media, claiming that he, too, had taken delivery of a bottle through an unopened window but he 'hadn't bothered' to report it. 'I know who set fire to my boat,' he fumed. 'I am convinced there will be an arrest soon!'

But there was no arrest. In fact, there was, broadly speaking, no crime. Diana had served a restraining order on Dennis to prevent him disposing of joint property and since the boat was all he really had, it seems likely that he had paid someone to set fire to it in order to claim on the insurance policy. The situation with his estranged wife only made things more amenable, and he milked it for all it was worth. 'Life is getting very difficult,' he insisted. 'I'm taking precautions to safeguard my property. There'll be a hot reception for anyone who comes looking for trouble.'

Strangely, Diana didn't mention the disgruntled tenant for many years, and when she did, she was uncharacteristically shy, describing him simply as 'a stuntman'. Given Britain's libel laws, this was perhaps to be expected, but until the publication of *Dors by Diana* in 1981, she denied any knowledge of the mystery arsonist's identity. This perhaps suggests that, far from being the international impresario he liked to portray, Dennis was reduced to burning his own belongings (or rather his wife's, since the boat was a joint purchase) in order to make ends meet. Like the 'shotgun' incident, the boat-burning was simply a detail in the history of the Hamiltons' troubled finances, and any suggestion otherwise would have seriously undermined Diana's subsequent claims that Dennis took everything and had profited from her assets.

At the time, Diana still felt some kind of loyalty to Dennis and protected him even when people expected her to sanction his public execution. She actually received a letter in January 1958 from a man, who signed himself 'Max', offering to murder Dennis for £2,000 – all she had to do was take out a small ad in the London *Evening Standard*, using a certain phrase as a coded signal. Diana declined the would-be hitman's offer, just as she refused to rise to the bait when reporters tried to aggravate the war between them. 'I'm not bitter,' she said. 'I won't run Hamilton down – he's an extraordinary man. Maybe he really does believe he made me what I am today.'

She was even thinking of settling down. 'I should make a New Year's resolution,' she decided. 'To shut up. Or marry some nice character and raise a family.' Yeardye was the obvious candidate, and she described him as 'a wonderful friend', but when asked about her other friends she snapped, 'Friends? There are people who come and eat my food and drink my drink. They aren't friends.'

It was a difficult time. Workwise, there was clearly little happening for Diana in Britain, and *The Lady and the Prowler* – now retitled *The Unholy Wife* – had yet to be released in America. There was no decisive course of action to be taken, but Diana knew that if she did make the move back to Hollywood, it wouldn't be permanent. 'I won't stay,' she said. 'I'm a nervous person deep down. Sometimes I get such a sick pain inside I can't move. Places like Hollywood aren't good for the nerves. It's too easy to end up slashing your wrists in the bathroom or drinking yourself to sleep.'

By the beginning of January 1958, Diana had started work on a British thriller that was being produced by George Minter, a wealthy, dapper man who always wore a carnation in his buttonhole. He promised it would be 'the most dramatic role Diana has had since *Yield to the Night*.' Minter made his money by distributing movies through his company, Renown, and he occasionally financed them, but he wasn't a man of great artistic talent, to put it kindly. The film was called *Tread Softly Stranger* and her co-star was George Baker, a young actor with Rank Charm School good looks – although he was actually under contract to Rank's rival, Associated British, who didn't pay quite as well, but treated their actors with the same condescension.

Seemingly against the odds, *Tread Softly Stranger* was an interesting movie, filmed at Walton studio and on location in Halifax, with superb cinematography by Douglas Slocombe. It was about two brothers in love with the same girl (Diana), but Baker's character had a moral complexity that was quite unusual for its time. In essence, he was a conman, but Baker thought you couldn't be a conman without charm, and if you didn't have charm you were simply a robber. Diana's vamp, too, seemed strangely out of place in the cotton mills and industrial landscape of the north.

Baker was impressed by Diana's professionalism, and he knew – as, indeed, almost everyone knew – she was having a bad time. Early in production, producer Denis O'Dell was heard complaining that whole days were being wasted due to 'illness', and he nearly hit the roof when Diana took a whole week's leave of absence. Legal wrangles with Dennis were becoming more and more convoluted when the courts granted him an injunction to stop her disposing of alleged 'joint' properties, the unpleasantness seemed never-ending.

But many on the set thought she kept her private life out of it. She didn't sulk, cry or throw tantrums, she never missed a cue or a line. She even spoke to the press during filming, which was more than Monroe had managed, although the interviews she gave were preoccupied by the amount of negative publicity she was getting. 'These days,' she sighed, 'I have only to poke my nose outside the door and everyone thinks it's a publicity stunt.' Diana laid the blame squarely at Dennis's door. 'Oh yes,' she said, somewhat testily, 'Dennis is a hustler all right. A real Mike Todd.'

Well, no, thought Baker when he heard about the piece in *Picturegoer*. Mike Todd had talent – a former Broadway producer, he'd pioneered widescreen cinema techniques and had had major hits with *Oklahoma!* and *Around the World in 80 Days*. But Dennis Hamilton? They hadn't met very often, or talked much, but Baker knew all he needed to know about 'Mr Dors'. He wasn't a pleasant man, to say the least. In fact, he sometimes wondered where you actually *found* a man like that.

Diana was always able to laugh. The production was actually in a bit of trouble with its backers and some of them insisted on sitting in on a few scenes. Among those they saw was a scene that required Baker to burn a sum of money in the sink. He set fire to it while there in the background stood four grey-looking men. 'Ah well,' said Baker, 'here goes the end money.' Diana looked round. Not a smile. Not a crack. That absolutely finished her, and they both rolled about. The more they laughed, the more serious the men in suits looked. Diana still enjoyed a laugh at someone else's expense, especially if they were asking for it.

Tread Softly Stranger was a curiosity and rather better than the flat reviews it received. But Diana's public was undecided about her more adult work, and after the commercial failure of *Yield to the Night*, she began to get the uncomfortable feeling that the silly, fluffy comedies she despised were actually what the fans wanted. In fact, *Picturegoer* magazine – which, despite its populist slant, was a more intuitive and perceptive publication than many of its successors – actually said as much while the Minter film was shooting. 'Comparatively speaking,' ran the editorial, 'Dors has never been as popular on British screens as she was in the little comedies she made long before producers got the idea she was a big dramatic actress.'

When she finally saw *The Unholy Wife*, Diana began to think they had a point – it was edited so badly, she couldn't believe it was the same film. When it previewed to American critics a few weeks later, it was almost unanimously panned ('An unholy mess!' exclaimed one, and probably many more, of the film's unflattering reviews). If Diana's time in Hollywood was a very black joke, *The Unholy Wife* was surely the punchline.

Her whole future was suddenly looking very shaky. *The Long Haul* had not been warmly received and producers were staying clear. In fact, the next offer after *Tread Softly Stranger* was a melodrama about prostitution called *Passport to Shame*, which brought in less than half her usual rate. She'd always been mindful of her own career arc, but at twenty-six, it suddenly seemed to be dipping at an alarmingly sharp rate. The serious roles were losing fans, the stunts had worn out her welcome in the media and both Rank and RKO had made their excuses and left. But, surprisingly, the first people to bear the brunt of her frustrations were not producers, or directors, or agents, or even journalists. Instead, she spoke out harshly against some of the people who thought they were closest to her, and the rift it caused was not quickly repaired, if it ever really was repaired.

Swindon Scooter Club had asked Diana to become their vice president, and she'd refused. But she didn't just refuse. Remembering the business with the hockey club, and acknowledging that the Scooter Club people were 'probably very nice', she told the *Sunday Express* that her home town could 'go and jump in its railway yard.' 'I've *had* Swindon,' she said curtly. 'What has Swindon ever done for me? Most towns are proud of local people who achieve success, but in Swindon I only get criticized.' It was a hasty, hurtful speech, made not by a movie star but by the little girl who once so felt imprisoned there, and it was addressed as much to Ruth and Daisy Cockey at Bath Road school as to the hockey club or anyone else, for that matter. Bert Fluck maintained a discreet, fatherly silence, but Diana's comments caused a lot of bad feeling in the city, and the weekly paper carried a number of letters about the affair.

Ironically, Diana had inherited a lot from Swindon but she had yet to realize that the values she sometimes thought of as silly and provincial were actually more valuable than those held by the witheringly cosmopolitan Hollywood set. In fact, they could even save her life.

The Penthouse was finally put on the market for something in the region of £14,000, considerably less than the original asking price of £20,000. The buyer was a wealthy business-man involved in the nebulous trade of 'war-surplus materials'. Dennis did not oppose the sale, in fact, when Diana's divorce petition went to court a few months later, she asked for the case to be dismissed. This may have had more to do with British libel laws than any sudden change of heart – Diana had rashly cited Shirley Ann Field in proceedings, whose solicitor aggressively denied the suggestion. Sensing a long, degrading expensive court case, which she could ill afford, Diana chose not to pursue the matter and withdrew the petition.

Together with Yeardye, Diana planned to move much further out, into what was known as 'the stockbroker belt' between Horsham and Guildford, to the south-west of London. The property she had her eye on was a much more stately affair than any of her previous homes, a fifteenth-century farmhouse known as 'Palmers', since the land it was built on was given as a present by Queen Elizabeth I to Sir Percival Palmer. It was a wide, two-storey cottage with oak beams and leaded windows, boasting six bedrooms, three bathrooms and fifty acres of land. There was no pool, as yet, but she was planning to add a tennis court and, she claimed, a landing strip. 'I'm having a private plane!' she said; it might have been Dennis talking. To keep up appearances, Diana also took her gay Irish butler, Patrick, a dandy of twenty-four, who'd recently started work at the Penthouse and referred to Diana primly, and unbelievably, as 'Her Ladyship'. 'I hate the country,' he said. 'But madam makes up for it. She is so wonderful. So fabulous. Looks exactly the same first thing as she does at a film premiere in the evening.'

Palmers was not cheap, possibly as much as £20,000, and Diana needed to earn quite a bit of money if she was to keep it. But the questions she'd caused to be raised in Parliament just a couple of years before were already coming back to haunt the business she was in. At first, Diana was amused by the aura of wealth film stars exuded, but the joke wore very thin when she realized the tax man was closing in on entertainers. The first to suffer was Bonar Colleano, whose taste for foreign holidays, tailored suits and sports cars made him the perfect target for the Inland Revenue and the press when he was landed with a bill for liabilities of almost £9,000. The *Star* went after him in a deeply sarcastic editorial:

> How much income tax do you owe?
> Oh, of course, you're a PAYEr. Week by week, month by month, your pay is trimmed. You're not allowed to owe any.
> How much does Mr Bonar Colleano owe? £8,067.
> Taken the wife to Trinidad? He did – for £700.
> How much pocket money do you allow yourself?
> His is £65 a month.
> How much housekeeping for the wife?
> He allows £130 a month.
> How's the wife's Jaguar?
> Going well?

While the investigation was under way, Colleano determinedly fought his corner, claiming his practice of signing property over to his wife, Susan Shaw, was a kind of informal 'insurance policy', just in case anything happened to him. As for the amount he was spending, he saw nothing untoward. 'Look,' he said, 'I just have to live it up. I'm not a man in the street – no one would want to see me if I were. I'm not a star but I'm established and I have to live expensively. Picturegoers, while maybe not understanding it, expect it. I can't ride on a bus or on the tube. It would be embarrassing.'

Colleano protested that absolutely everyone benefited from the image, from producers – who needed to be wined, dined and entertained (preferably on a yacht) – to the public, who clearly liked to see a young man at the peak of his physical presentability. 'Haircuts?' he continued. 'No three-bob trims for me. It costs thirty shillings a time because I must look right about the head. Then there are the suits and shirts and shoes – I have to dress impeccably at all times. All that costs money.'

The tax inspector never got his hands on Colleano's money, and neither did his wife. He'd spent it. Colleano died in a fatal car accident a few months later, in August 1958, aged thirty-four, driving back to his hotel from Liverpool's New Shakespeare Theatre, where he'd been appearing in a presentation of George Axelrod's play *Will Success Spoil Rock Hunter?* About a mile from the Mersey Tunnel, he ploughed through a corrugated iron fence and smashed into the two-foot levee behind it. His last film, ironically enough, was called *No Time to Die*.

Susan Shaw never recovered and, because she couldn't cope, handed the upbringing of their three-year-old son, Mark, to his grandmother, Rubye Colleano. The business rallied round for her, though, and a charity football match was held at Hayes Stadium in Middlesex – Film Stars XI versus Showbusiness XI – where Yeardye turned out along-side the likes of Stanley Baker, Alma Cogan and Alfie Bass. Shaw made a few films after her husband's death but she was totally out of commission by the end of the fifties. The former Rank starlet tried office jobs and bar work, to no avail, but by the tail-end of the sixties she had found a full-time occupation – drinking.

Tax was not too far from Diana's mind at this time, with Colleano's private life splashed all over the tabloids, so she was delighted when booking agent Joe Collins, father of starlets Joan and Jackie, called to ask if she would be interested in taking a revamped variety tour – *The Diana*

Dors Show – on the road. Variety, as she had discovered, was still an excellent source of money, or more specifically cash, which didn't all have to appear on the books.

It added up to eight weeks' work, on a percentage basis, taking in all the major towns in Britain. The twist, which was perhaps Collins' own inspiration, was that the venues should be movie houses, but the whole tour was swept along by the news that Diana had been booked for a cabaret season at the Desert Inn in Las Vegas the following October. She was positively bubbling over with plans for 'really super-super' gowns that would put Dietrich in the shade. 'I want them to be real eye-openers,' she said. Collins recommended Eric Darnell, an incredibly flamboyant designer who'd dressed Collins' daughter Joan several years earlier, before she left Britain to take up a Hollywood contract with 20th Century Fox in 1954.

While filming *Passport to Shame*, Diana began making the final plans for the tour, which would open in Coventry on 28 July and move through Birmingham, Bristol, Gloucester, Plymouth, Hull, Stockton and Dublin. Collins said he could take care of the acts, but he needed the name of a good comedian as an anchor for the show. Diana racked her brains but couldn't think, and it was Yeardye who suggested a young comedian they'd seen recently at the Stork Club in London. Richard Dawson was born Colin Emm, in Gosport, Hampshire, but his comic style was strictly transatlantic, a rapid-fire barrage of gags and impressions, mostly of Hollywood stars like James Cagney, Jerry Lewis and Robert Mitchum. He made little impression on Diana at first, but their relationship grew in rehearsal and especially on tour.

The opening night in Coventry, accompanied by singing combo Group One and pianist Albert Sadler, was Diana's first variety appearance in four years, but very little had changed. Topping the bill, she was onstage for a little over half an hour, opening with a song called 'I've Got the World

On A String' and running through a set that just about balanced comedy and cabaret. Dawson held the pace, mugging furiously as the show's demented MC, with corny jokes ('Who booked this audience?') and a steady patter that owed a lot to the wisecracking, much funnier Marx Brothers. Along with quips like, 'The train now approaching platforms 5, 6, 7 and 8 is coming in sideways', Dawson even had the audacity to use one of Groucho's classic routines, even then one of the oldest gags in show business. 'I didn't come here to be insulted,' said Diana, wide-eyed, on cue. 'Oh really?' came the reply. 'Where do you usually go?'

Diana's own contributions were, perhaps amazingly, even more creaky. The quick-fire Little Miss Muffet routine received yet another airing, and so did the poem about J. Arthur Rank with which she had amused everybody at Highbury Studio back in the Charm School days. She told little anecdotes about Hollywood – 'At Gary Cooper's birthday party, there were so many candles on the cake three people collapsed from the heat!' – and sang a song called 'Too Young', which she customized with tongue-in-cheek references to her own life ('While other girls filled their minds with letters/I filled mine with sweaters'). For the finale, she joined Dawson in a duet for a hokey rendition of Cole Porter's 'Let's Do It'.

It wasn't high culture, but that wasn't why people were there and Diana knew it. They were just curious. She obliged them with two costume changes, appearing first in a £400 strapless white cocktail gown hung with diamante teardrops which gathered at the feet in a huge feather-trimmed float, and then, for the encore, a tight, figure-hugging red dress, slashed right up to the thigh. It was a trial run for Vegas and a clear signal to the fans that, after a string of gloomy roles in gritty, heavily film noir influenced crime movies – *Yield to the Night*, *The Unholy Wife*, *Tread Softly Stranger*, *Passport to Shame* – she was ready to have a bit of

Above Diana faces journalists at a press conference staged to reunite her with her then-estranged husband Dennis after a hairdressing appointment at Leon's salon in Shaftesbury Avenue (15 November, 1956).
© HULTON-DEUTSCH COLLECTION/ CORBIS

Left Arriving at London airport with escort Tommy Yeardye. Both are flying out to Rome to start filming on Vittorio Gassman's *The Love Specialist* (2 June, 1957).
© HULTON-DEUTSCH COLLECTION/ CORBIS

Above Rock Hudson feigns interest in Diana during shooting in Rome (20 July, 1957).
© UPI/CORBIS

Left On set with Rod Steiger, filming *The Lady and The Prowler*, later retitled *The Unholy Wife* (1956).

Above right Diana feigns interest in Victor Mature at a press conference to launch *The Long Haul*, her first film after the abortive Hollywood trip (2 October, 1957).
© UPI/CORBIS

Right Attending a premiere at London's Empire Theatre with second husband Dickie Dawson (18 March, 1959).
© HULTON-DEUTSCH COLLECTION/ CORBIS

Above Well into her thirties, Diana takes her first unflattering role as a faded beauty in Michael Winner's *West Eleven* (1963). © UPI/CORBIS

Right Diana's cabaret act makes its successful debut at the famous Dunes hotel in Las Vegas (6 November, 1960). © UPI/CORBIS

A typical moment in British popular culture brings Diana together with entertainer Des O'Connor, comedian Charlie Drake and singer Jessie Matthews on long-running BBC TV series *Juke Box Jury* (mid 60s, date unknown). © PICTORIAL

Diana with third husband Alan Lake (late 60s, date unknown). © PICTORIAL

Left Orchard Manor, Diana's first permanent address, bought in 1967 after her divorce from her second husband Richard Dawson. She lived there until her death in 1984. © PICTORIAL

Opposite At home with her third son, Jason, Diana's only child by Alan Lake (early 70s, date unknown). © PICTORIAL

Below As a man-eating nympho who terrorizes a young man in Jerzy Skolimowski's *Deep End* (1970). © PICTORIAL

Centre On stage with her husband Alan Lake in Donald Howarth's *Three Months Gone* at London's Royal Court Theatre (26 January, 1970). Diana plays a sex-crazed

landlady, Lake one of her lodgers; six months later he was arrested on assault charges. © HULTON-DEUTSCH COLLECTION/CORBIS

Far right At Violet Kray's funeral, with Alan Lake (August 1982). © BRYN COLTON; ASSIGNMENTS PHOTOGRAPHERS/CORBIS

Diana shows off her vital statistics (36½–24–35)in a classic cheesecake shot from the mid 50s. © CORBIS-BETTMANN

fun. 'I think I've done enough of those downbeat parts,' she said.

While Diana was on tour, she began spending more and more time with Dawson. She found him funny, attentive and romantic, and finally had to confront Yeardye with the news that she'd fallen in love with someone else. He was philosophical – 'I have never fooled myself that I'm the only fellow in Diana's life,' he later said – and took it so well that Diana allowed him to stay at Palmers while the tour was completed. She was blind with love, and after the Pygmalion-esque relationship with Dennis, she was flattered to be on a more equal footing with a man who did not want to make or mould her. But some of Diana's friends doubted Dawson's motives and thought he was just using her as a stepping stone. Terry Gardener and his partner, who used to be great friends with Diana and Dennis, considered Dawson a man of little talent and very little charm. Not only that, he was extremely possessive and awfully jealous of her. Gardener didn't see much of Diana after Dawson appeared on the scene. But then other old friends thought they were perfectly well suited. In Lionel Jeffries' opinion Dawson's personality was absolutely right for her – patient, firm, guiding – after the tumultuous Hamilton years.

When the tour drew to an end, Diana called Yeardye and asked him to leave, so the house would be empty for her return. After a harsh exchange of words he agreed, but Diana knew she had handled the affair badly. Even so, she was more than a little surprised when she went to take some money out of her safety deposit box at Harrods, which doubled as a tax-free bank account. The box was £11,000 lighter, and since Yeardye – who really had been operating as her business manager in the previous months – also had a key, she jumped to a hasty conclusion.

Diana went straight to Chelsea police station, and when the story hit the media she added another £7,000, without really thinking of the consequences. When the tax implications sank in, the extra money was quickly forgotten. Tommy Yeardye flew in from France a few days later and denied any knowledge of the supposed 'theft'. 'The whole thing is a complete misunderstanding,' he said. 'There is no missing money. Not a single penny. It is merely that I have transferred money on her behalf to safeguard her interests. Every penny of it is here and will be given to her.' Yeardye pointed out that he had been left in charge of the farm for three weeks while Diana was on tour, and that much more lucrative possibilities had presented themselves in the meantime. Deep down, Diana knew Yeardye wasn't so stupid – but she also believed he was really so hurt. She thought the missing money was his attempt to pay her back for the affair with Dawson and, although she knew she'd asked for it, she'd had enough of men using her own money against her. She could be silly with her money, as old friends like Terry Gardener knew, and very silly with her men. She was a country girl at heart who thought that no man could do the dirty on a woman if he loved her, or even if he was attracted to her. In some ways, she was really very foolish.

Yeardye was 'sacked' from his post as business advisor, and Diana was reunited with her money at her solicitor's office in Holborn, London. Subtle as ever, Diana even held a press conference, wearing a pale gold cocktail dress, gold belt and heavy gold earrings. Dawson waited for her outside in the car – she was, after all, still a married woman – while Diana counted up piles of notes and, after an hour, called Chelsea police station to confirm that all her money was there, every bit of it. 'Counting that money took *such* a long time,' she said. 'But what a very nice pastime!' As for Yeardye, he went on to do very well for himself indeed. After a brief stint as proprietor of The Paint Box, a club in London's Holborn district where diners could sketch *deshabillé* models while they ate, he moved to the west coast of America as business manager with Vidal Sassoon's burgeoning empire.

Diana didn't really know what to do about Dawson. Her relationship with Dennis was so very tense that both parties had agreed in private not to discuss each other's business in the media. To complicate matters, the stand-off thawed slightly at the beginning of October, when Dennis was admitted to the London Clinic, ostensibly suffering from serious heart trouble. Diana was on tour again when she heard the news, playing to two houses a night at the Liverpool Empire, but when she called the hospital she was asked not to visit. So instead, she sent roses. As soon as the tour hit London she went to see him, and the sight of Dennis lying there in his pyjamas, frightened and vulnerable, affected her a great deal.

The tour continued its shaky run, stopping in the capital at Finsbury Park Empire on 7 October. Diana was distracted, and *The Times* was quietly scathing in a review, printed the following day, headlined 'Upholding Celebrity's Mask'. 'The fate of some performers is to be overtaken by their own celebrity,' it read, 'whatever talent they had is progressively masked and stifled by the habit of maintaining the personality the public expect to see. Miss Diana Dors, judging by her performance last night at the Finsbury Park Empire, seems to be halfway through the process; and it is this which makes her performance instructive and supplies its only appeal as entertainment.' But then, Diana didn't read reviews. 'I should worry,' she said. 'I'm getting £2,000 a week for it. Anyway, it's the audience that counts with me, not the critics.'

With the success of the tour and the extra dates, it seemed churlish to point out, although many did, that Diana was actually meant to be in Las Vegas by this time. Her answer was simply this: the variety tour had been so well received she had 'postponed' her visit there until the following year.

No one was unkind enough to suggest that Vegas might not take kindly to taking second place to a hick tour of Britain's variety theatres, and so the matter rested.

Instead, Diana accepted cabaret work in Johannesburg, apparently totally unaware of the volatile political situation that existed in South Africa. 'Coloured' and native African voters had been actively disenfranchised since 1951 and were required to carry identification at all times. This situation would culminate in a violent incident in the township of Sharpeville in March 1960, when a peaceful protest was broken up by government forces, killing 67 people and injuring a further 186. Over half were shot in the back.

Diana didn't particularly care about the political scenario, much like the rest of the world, and she accepted the £1,000 fee for a short season in Durban and Johannesburg. She remembered it as going 'well', but the South Africans saw it slightly differently. Treating her time off as holiday Diana, according to columnist Unity Hall, 'proved as popular as Lady Docker was in Monaco', a reference to Norah's behaviour the previous year when she and her husband arrived at the christening of Prince Rainier and Princess Grace's first child. The Dockers had, without informing their hosts, brought their own child, and when told he could not be accommodated at the reception, Bernard and Norah stormed off. That night, fortified by drink, Norah slandered the prince in public and tore up a miniature version of the principality's flag. The Dockers were subsequently banned from Monaco and therefore, by reciprocal treaty, the Cote D'Azur.

Diana wasn't actually banned from South Africa, but her behaviour was certainly misinterpreted at every turn. It was claimed that she had refused to stay at a hotel where fans had gathered, turned down radio interviews and that an attempt to welcome her with a gift of a souvenir Zulu spear and shield was met with the words, 'What do I do with it? Eat it?' Every invitation she turned down was considered to have been 'snubbed', and at the one official function she did attend – a special Sportsman of The Year dinner – her style of dress was frowned upon. 'I came to South Africa to relax and have a holiday paid for by cabaret engagements,' she said. 'I bargained for no other arrangements.' From any country in the western world, the press would have been poisonous. Coming from South Africa, it barely drew any attention.

Diana was back in England in time for Christmas, and treated herself to a brand new Cadillac (registration DD 200). But she was travelling again within a matter of weeks. She'd been booked onto American comedian Steve Allen's show, for a fee of £7,000, and a flight to New York was arranged for her and Dawson on 3 January 1959. Dawson was beside himself; he'd always wanted to work in America, which was, after all, where the bulk of his material came from.

But Diana still had Dennis to think about. He'd shown signs of improvement while she and Dawson were in South Africa, and had actually checked out of hospital for a few weeks. It didn't last, however, and he was soon back at the Clinic, looking just as grim. Diana called him before she flew to the States and he didn't sound good. She told him she'd see him when she got back, which would be about a month, but from the way he was talking, Diana got the impression Dennis thought he wouldn't live that long. How dramatic, she thought, when he was only thirty-four.

The Steve Allen Show went down well, and she was invited back for several more guest appearances, which, at £7,000 a throw, she wasn't inclined to turn down. In fact, it was through the show that she later bumped into one of Allen's other guests, a Jewish comedian called Lenny Bruce, whose 'shocking' nightclub act amused her greatly. Diana became very fond of him and they kept in touch over the next few years. She defended him loyally, even after his death from a heroin overdose in 1966, and once provided sleevenotes for an album of his routines.

At the end of January 1959, she and Dawson flew to Hollywood for a short holiday, and for a few days she ignored the calls that were coming through, making herself unavailable to the press and even her new agent. Finally, after calling Liberace's swish Palm Springs villa, film columnist Lionel Crane tracked Diana down on 31 January by placing a phone call to the Hollywood home of Roger Moore and his wife, Dorothy Squires. Diana tried to dodge it, but Squires said it sounded serious. Taking the call, Diana heard the news that no one had so far been able to get to her – Dennis was dead.

Diana was shocked, she hadn't thought he was really that ill, and she immediately made arrangements to fly back, a lengthy affair that involved a stopover in Denmark and took almost an entire day. She arrived back and faced the press in full force, wearing shades and a sombre black coat, but her comments only reflected the fullness of her confusion. Her tributes were hesitant and her criticisms strangely admiring. The good times still didn't outweigh the bad, but she couldn't find it in her heart to do the man down. They had been like lucky charms for each other, she thought, each helping the other forward. It worked both ways. She was grateful for the plans and schemes, the stunts that put her in the news and kept her there, but Dennis just didn't know how to move on – maybe because all he cared about was money, or maybe he really was just a one-trick showman. But could he really be explained away so easily?

Dennis had certainly been a complex character, and Diana discovered another level to him when she learned that he had converted to Catholicism just a few weeks before his death. Arranged by his parents, the funeral took place at 11 a.m. on 4 February 1959 at St James' Roman Catholic Church in Spanish Place, London W1, causing scenes of near-riot both inside and out. On the streets, curious bystanders flooded round the funeral cortège, almost blocking access to the church. Diana had to push through the crowds to get in, but the general level of decorum was about the same inside, with people racing to find seats and standing shoulder to shoulder in the aisles. As she knelt to pray, four photographers had to be ejected from the building, and when she followed the coffin outside, Diana was almost lost in the throng. It was a curious mix of people; there were old friends like Jon Pertwee, Sandra Dorne and Paul Carpenter, a few faces she knew – like Vera Day, a model once proclaimed 'Shape of the Year' by the *Daily Sketch*, whom the media had romantically linked with Dennis before his death – and hordes of unknown women whose motives for attending were really quite dubious. She was shocked to see them posing quite eagerly for the cameramen outside. 'It was,' noted a bystander, 'more like a society wedding than a funeral.'

Afterwards, Dennis's body was taken off to Westminster Cemetery in west London's Uxbridge Road, where he was to be buried. Diana did not attend, going home, instead, to Billingshurst. Even had she wanted to go, no one had actually told her where the cemetery was, they hadn't even made the slightest effort to get her there. As Dennis's body went into the ground, Diana's wreath was added to the many others: 'To my darling Dennis. With loving memories that words can never express. My love always, Diana.' Nearby lay a wreath from Raymond's wife. 'For Dennis, peace,' it said, and was signed simply 'Jennifer' – a very daring move considering she was embroiled in an ugly divorce battle that had only hit the courts the previous month.

Amid the claims and counter-claims, Jennifer alleged that Raymond had beaten her and that he was having an affair with actress Rosalie Ashley; Raymond denied the affair but admitted slapping his wife, claiming that her affair with

Dennis had driven him to it. He added that she argued violently, and often threw dinner plates and other 'household articles' at him. Mr Justice Karminski had the difficult task of settling the case and determining which of Raymond's two properties – the town house or the country house – should go to which party. 'I can't help feeling that these are excitable people and that sooner or later some dreadful scene will break out,' he sighed. Dennis was well out of it.

Dennis's death prevented a few unsavoury news items coming out that, had he lived, would undoubtedly have ruined him – and perhaps taken Diana, too. In the last years of his life, Dennis had found a new 'business' partner, a man whose needs and tastes almost perfectly matched his own. Together they had held parties, where the champagne flowed freely and the girls behaved accordingly, but his new friend was surprisingly anonymous. Although this man owned huge areas of property in west and possibly even central London, he had barely spoken to the press and only allowed himself to be photographed on extremely rare occasions. Few people knew of his existence and, when he died of a heart attack three years later, in November 1962, it was claimed that he had faked his own death. But in the aftermath of a major political scandal, this short, fat, balding man became much more of a media sensation than Dennis could possibly have imagined.

Chapter Ten

COME BY SUNDAY

PEREC RACHMAN ARRIVED in London in 1949 with little or no money in his pocket. Born in Warsaw in 1920 to a successful Jewish dentist, he had seen his entire family arrested and taken away when the Nazis invaded Poland at the onset of the Second World War. If he hadn't escaped in time, Rachman might have joined them – a brush with certain, cold-blooded death may go some way towards explaining the brutish, short-term management style he perfected over the next few years.

His first real job in London was working for a highly disreputable Soho letting agent in Old Compton Street, but as soon as Rachman found his feet he set up on his own, moving west to Paddington, then Notting Hill and Ladbroke Grove. As part of a drive to find workers in the fifties, London Transport had advertised in the British colonies, particularly targeting the West Indies. Many people responded, but when they arrived they found Britain to be an inhospitable, closed society, a situation 'Polish Peter' (as he came to be known) moved quickly to capitalize on by providing cheap accommodation. His modus operandi was very simple. He would buy a property, or a series of properties, and install a landlord. The landlord had to guarantee a certain sum of money per week – or even per day, if the rooms were used by prostitutes – and no questions would be asked. To meet Rachman's needs, the landlord would sublet and sublet until every room in the house was occupied, sometimes by entire families. Rachman thrived on chicanery, and his empire was designed to cause maximum confusion – landlords and rent collectors would regularly change addresses, and ownership of properties would change from name to name. Complaints from tenants were met with aggression and intimidation, but non-payment resulted almost certainly in violence.

Before 1960, when the Building Societies Act tightened control on lending and even closed down some of the companies Rachman had used for finance, mortgages were easy to obtain through crooked means – usually by paper collateral, which, in turn, bought more and more properties. After a point, it all seemed perfectly legitimate. Dennis Hamilton knew how to work that particular scam, and his friendship with Rachman worked both ways. Rachman could show him how to organize his own, largely fictitious, property trade, while in return Dennis could show Rachman how to organize his sex life. This they did from Woodhurst, where Rachman 'shopped' for models in the pages of high-class magazines, so that Dennis could contact the photographer and get their numbers.

Many starlets and models were fooled and used in this way, and a former henchman claimed Dennis even had a secret room at Woodhurst, which could be viewed through a two-way mirror. Voyeurism was perhaps the strongest link Dennis and Rachman had in common; Rachman was rather fussy about women, preferring to maintain a coterie of regular 'mistresses'. He shared Dennis's cruel streak, right down to taping his friends' conversations and inveigling them into sexual situations in the hidden room, where they would be watched. In fact, the two-way mirror idea impressed Rachman so much that he went on to have one installed in a property in Bryanston Mews West, central London, later the home of Stephen Ward.

When Dennis died, almost all his property vanished at the

same time. Diana believed Dennis had sold Woodhurst to Rachman, and quite probably the coffee bar and the club (which closed, suddenly and with no explanation, seven months later), too, but whether this was legally effected or not, she didn't think to check. At the time, Rachman was sheltered by a modicum of respectability, and even the Notting Hill race riots of 1958, one of the causes for which were poor housing conditions, had not broken his cover. It would not be until the summer of 1963, nearly a year after his death, that the slum-king of London was finally unmasked when Rachman's then girlfriend, Marilyn 'Mandy' Rice-Davies, emerged at the centre of a sex scandal involving the Secretary of State for War, John Profumo.

But Dennis had left Diana another bombshell, far more personal and far more devastating. The day after the funeral, Diana later claimed she was contacted by Jon Pertwee who asked to see her as a matter of some urgency. She drove over immediately, and he explained to her that a doctor friend of his had been working at the London Clinic, where he had been made privy to the true cause of Dennis's death. It wasn't a heart attack – he had been suffering from tertiary syphilis. This is a dramatic but highly curious story. Why would a team of professional doctors not inform a dead man's widow of the potentially fatal disease she might be carrying – or, more bizarrely, leave the task to a friend of a friend? More intriguingly, why was Dennis in the London Clinic in the first place? Just after his death, Diana told the *Express* that she couldn't remember him having a day's illness. 'He was so vital, so strong, till this happened,' she said, 'yet he was always afraid of death.' If he was 'seriously ill', as she later wrote, why was she so surprised when he died? In her memoirs, Diana makes no mention that she had contracted the disease – or Yeardye, or Dawson – or had taken any course of treatment, in those days a long, unpleasant process.

Since Diana was left nothing in Dennis's will, Pertwee's news gave her the grounds to contest it, since tertiary syphilis would undoubtedly have compromised his sanity. She chose not to, most likely because the resulting publicity could have killed her career, but there is also the slim but entirely plausible possibility that there was no syphilis, or if there was, it was more recently contracted.

In later life, Diana made something of a habit of rewriting history to suit the tax man, retroactively blaming the tertiary syphilis for Dennis's violent moods. The condition opened a two-way avenue. If Dennis really had been insane at the time of his death, it could prove he had managed her money unwisely – and, more importantly, there was at least the vague possibility of getting some of it back.

A couple of weeks after the funeral, Diana and Dawson flew back to the States for TV and club work, but it seemed as if the old Dors had died along with Dennis. The most striking press shot, which appeared in the *Daily Mirror*, showed her waiting in the departure lounge at London Airport. She was wearing light, tailored clothes – tight-fitting slacks, moccasins and a fitted, fur-collared jacket – and craning her neck as if something had suddenly caught her attention. Beside her sat a dour little old lady in a long black coat, wearing sensible shoes and carrying a handbag which looked more suitable for the transportation of surgical appliances. 'The camera that is always at the elbow of people whose names make news was primed,' ran the article. 'But the personality that has dominated a hundred, thousand exposures is for once briefly eclipsed. By an ordinary woman.'

It was a cruel blow, especially from the press, whom Diana preferred to think of as an ally. She doubtless sensed that her time was up in Britain, for the moment at least, and turned her attention abroad. American TV was bringing in work and Vegas was still a possibility. Hollywood, however, seemed to be a closed book; her relationship with RKO had degenerated so badly she finally served them a writ. Filed on behalf of Diana and Treasure Productions, it hinged on a contract signed on 29 August 1956, for three films to be produced by Treasure and distributed by the American company. RKO, claimed Diana, had cancelled the contract with a note saying she had become 'an object of disgrace, obloquy, ill-will and ridicule' and had acquired 'an international reputation for insobriety, unchastity, intemperance and exhibitionism.' In return, and fully mindful of the ailing company's financial situation, she accused RKO of 'false and sham accusations made in bad faith as part of a scheme to avoid its obligations', claiming damages of $1,275,000 (£455,000).

Returning to Britain at the end of February, Diana began to re-evaluate her life. With Dennis out of the way, she was now free to marry Dawson, which she did with undue haste. Diana wanted to wait and hold a big party at home, but twenty-eight-year-old Dawson had his heart set on a Stateside wedding, which was duly arranged. The service was to take place at 9.30 p.m., on 12 April 1959, at the New York apartment owned by Diana's American agent, Harry Steinman but, true to form, it was by no means low-key and private. Diana was appearing on the Steve Allen show that night, a nationwide broadcast, and spent most of the day in rehearsal, practising her song and dance routine with the four male dancers who would accompany her. At 7.30 p.m. sharp she was ready, standing on a raised pedestal and singing a song called simply 'Love', while pink smoke billowed round her heels. A few minutes later, she joined Allen for a sketch, then, just after 8 p.m., she jumped into a cab and headed for her rented apartment. After changing into her 'wedding dress' – a short, gold lamé sheath dress overlaid with white lace, plus matching gold shoes – she raced over to the apartment on Riverside Drive just half an hour before the seven-minute civil service, which was conducted by a New York state judge. Surprisingly, it made the papers.

Back in England, the newly weds settled into Palmers and, for the first time in her life Diana thought she might actually be in a position to start a family. She was no longer reliant on the movie industry, which made her image that little bit less important, and a small line in cosmetics she'd recently put her name to was actually doing quite well. 'I'm selling half a million shampoos a week now,' she claimed. 'It's bringing me more money than selling my dignity to be a film star ever did.' In fact, she even began thinking about retirement again. 'I have called a halt to making films,' she said, 'because I have enough self-respect not to want to be in any more stinkers.' Funnily enough, the one film she did make that year was something she'd worked on only a few weeks before, a cameo-packed novelty production called *Scent of Mystery*, filmed in a bizarre process its director called 'Smell-O-Vision' – which meant that carefully distilled odours were wafted into the auditorium – on the rare occasions it was ever shown.

The retirement rumours gathered strength, and they weren't exactly quashed by some of the things Diana was saying, or her boasts that she was giving up acting to become a businesswoman. 'I have been working for 13 years – since I was 14,' she said. 'I have worked hard and I would like to sit back and enjoy the fruits of that work. I am not stage-struck.'

She denied reports that she had only two more years in show business, but agreed that she was no longer the same woman: 'No one can go on being a bright puppet once their brain gets bigger. That's where Marilyn Monroe was smart. She made publicity by the blonde routine, then she made a new reputation by disappearing and becoming an actress. In a way, though it sounds conceited, I suppose I underestimate myself. I can survive as a person anyway, although I never saw it like that. Now I think the worst thing in the world to be would be an ageing glamour queen . . . with clips to hold my face up and false curls to cover the clips. I would rather become a fat, frowsy character actress when the time comes.'

Speculation about the reasons for this sudden change of heart became fact early in August when Diana announced that she was expecting a baby, due in February the following year. All work dates were cancelled, Diana put Palmers on the market, and the Dawsons quickly found themselves a new home. It was another sprawling estate, a five-bedroom, comparatively modern house, in Virginia Water, Surrey, which Diana christened Springwoods. The main sitting room was L-shaped, with turquoise walls, fitted carpet, velvet sofa, tiger-skin rug and a cocktail bar in the corner. The property, as yet, had no swimming pool, but the Dawsons were making plans for a glass-enclosed pool that would be attached to the house ('So we can step straight from the drawing room into the pool all year round.'). She set to work on the nursery, choosing lemon and white for the colour scheme, but refused to say whether she was hoping for a boy or a girl – they had names either way. If it was a boy, Mark Richard. A girl, Caroline Jane.

But Diana had not been entirely idle, as she claimed. Shortly before she became pregnant she had been approached by music publisher David Platz, who put Diana in a studio with bandleader and arranger, Wally Stott. When the album was finished, it would be put out to tender and the highest bidder would get the UK rights to its release. Pye eventually saw off the competition and released the album in February 1960 as *Swingin' Dors*, on tinted pink vinyl, in a lavish cover with a swinging-door gatefold front that opened outwards in two halves.

The arrangements were very strong and Diana's deceptively good voice carried the recordings beautifully, though she had a tendency to steer clear of standards (with the exception of 'Let There Be Love') and opt instead for songs with horribly twee lyrics and simple melodies that fitted comfortably within her range. But the album, to some extent, told the story of her life so far and as it would be lived in the future – songs about loving and losing were common enough, but Diana chose songs about breaking up ('Tired of Love'), making mistakes ('That's How It Is'), and taking dangerous lovers ('Rollercoaster Blues'). 'The Gentleman is a Dope' was seen by some as a tactless reference to the Yeardye affair, but most surprising was a song called 'April Heart', using strange meteorological metaphors to describe a volatile relationship ('Crash! The temperature drops and your eyes say stormy/Up the mercury pops and they're shining for me'). Diana clearly saw this as a song about Dennis, and its closing lines had a special resonance: 'But half a love's worth more than none/So I'll go on as I've begun/In again/Out again/Of your April heart.'

One other track in particular had an especially autobiographical slant. Called 'Come By Sunday', it described a woman whose working week was one long social whirl but who took stock of herself and dropped the façade, once every week:

I always make appointments, at least a week ahead
For six long days I go like mad, the seventh day I stay in bed.
The whole week through, I'm on the town,
But Sunday always gets me down
So come by Sunday, make it after three
Come by Sunday – spend some time
Come by Sunday and stay a while
Come by Sunday and spend some time with me . . .

Diana had hated Sundays ever since she was a child, and in repressed post-war Britain, it was still governed by trading laws and licensing restrictions. Officially, it was dead time and in some ways, Sunday represented the one part of her life that was missing, the hole she could never fill. In the excitable, devil-may-care Hamilton years, Sundays were usually occupied by the overspill from Saturday's all-nighter, but now she had her family to think of and Sunday would be a quiet, more private time. Within the next ten years or so, she would even turn to religion.

Wally Stott's conversion was even more dramatic. Several years after the album's release, he became Ms Angela Morley, a film composer of some repute. Even Diana couldn't top *that*.

Although the baby was due in February, Diana went ahead and accepted bookings for an American tour starting in March and lasting through to mid-April, playing the Flamingo Hotel in Vegas and the Chi-Chi club in Palm Springs. The press were already calling the baby 'The Cabaret Orphan'. No difficulties were taken into account, despite her mother's ordeal, and when she finally went into hospital, Diana spent nearly twenty-four hours in labour. Fortunately, there were no ill effects, and Mark Richard Dawson was born in the London Clinic at 9.55 p.m. on 4 February 1960, weighing a little under 7 lb. Dawson immediately called Bert to tell him the news. He was at home, watching television.

Diana's pregnancy was featured regularly in the press, and quite a few people were willing to see a change in her personality. Many were not, including sixty-seven-year-old Mary Stocks, a member of the BBC's General Advisory Council known for her plain speaking and bizarre grasp of reality after she 'revealed' that post-Suez petrol rationing did not apply to MPs and that they were happily helping themselves. During a live appearance on the BBC's *Any Questions?* show, the panel was asked, 'What advice would [you] give Miss Diana Dors on bringing up the son born to her yesterday?' Stocks replied, 'My advice is that she should get it adopted.' The rest of the panel disagreed, but Stocks stood by her remarks, adding later, 'The life of a child whose parents live in a blaze of publicity must be very undesirable. That sort of thing can do a child no good at all.'

Diana's 'homely' new image was not helped by the serialization of her memoirs, ghost-written with her co-operation, in the *News of the World*. She made a lot of money, somewhere in the region of £36,000, but hated the finished product and felt her life had been cheapened in the process. The series dwelt heavily on Dennis's two-way mirror and secret 'blue cinema', which Diana wrote about with wide-eyed, fake horror. When she finally wrote her own life story in 1981, with much less ghosting, these memories were pointedly underplayed. The public, however, was shocked and appalled – every week for three months – in exactly the way the *News of the World* had hoped. Even the Archbishop of Canterbury joined the fray, describing Diana as a 'wayward hussy', and the paper was subsequently rapped by the Press Council, who described the memoirs as containing 'grossly lewd and salacious' material and accused the *News of the World* of 'debasing the standards of British journalism.'

Thomas Wiseman, in the *Evening Standard*, noted correctly that the sensational bits were nearly all about Dennis Hamilton, who was in no position to complain. 'Indeed, I imagine he would have been flattered,' he added. 'He should be. Miss Dors has served him as a kind of boudoir Boswell. She has done him proud – in a ghastly sort of way.' Wiseman was also one of the few not to be fooled by her 'confessions'. 'Somehow,' he wrote, 'I can't quite believe in the Diana who, on discovering the purpose of the mirror in their

Chelsea flat, finds "a ripple of horror [starting] at the base of my spine and [filtering] slowly to my brain." Diana Dors doesn't take sex that seriously. Though she tends to use intimate endearments as small talk . . .' one of her favourite ice-breakers was 'How's your sex life?', '. . . though her language is pretty basic, Miss Dors' attitude to sex is that it's all a big joke. Her whole exaggerated personality is a parody of sex; the movement of her hips; the flicker of her eye-lashes; the inflammatory eyes – they all suggest the downright absurdity of sex.'

'What I really am, you know, is a sentimentalist,' said Diana. 'I'm very sentimental. I'm a show-off about sex because it's expected of me, and maybe there are other psychological reasons, too. And then, let's not kid ourselves, it pays.'

Unfortunately, few others saw the joke, and there were furious rows when her name was added to the bill at the Royal Variety Show on 16 May. Despite calls for her withdrawal by the Church of England newspaper, she attended but was not presented to the Queen.

Amidst all this unwanted attention, the appearance of a sinister ransom note seems all the more threatening:

> *Miss Dors, at 7 p.m. on Friday 29th of April place £2,500 in notes*
> *at the entrance of your right-hand drive. Inform nobody. Failure to*
> *obey these instructions will mean death to your husband and son.*
> *We can assure you it won't be pleasant. To save a lot of grief and*
> *suffering, understand you must comply with these simple instructions.*

Diana warned the police, who advised her to make the delivery using envelopes stuffed with old newspapers, and when the would-be blackmailer arrived he was immediately caught and arrested. The culprit was a sixteen-year-old Royal Naval Cadet, with no previous convictions and an above-average school record, who claimed he was paid one pound by a stranger to make the collection for him. He was tried as a juvenile at Chertsey Court, where he changed his story and pleaded guilty. Because of his age he narrowly escaped a custodial sentence, instead he incurred the maximum punishment – a fine of £10. His defence described the ransom note as 'a weird lapse' by a cadet of 'impeccable background and above average intelligence'. The boy said he wanted the money to buy a sports car.

After the Vegas booking, Diana took her first dramatic television role at the end of April. After apparently turning down Rediffusion's offer of the lead in Thomas Hardy's *Tess of the D'Urbervilles*, she appeared as a singer accused of murdering her lover in an *Armchair Theatre* presentation called 'The Innocent'. By amazing coincidence, the part required her to perform two songs, 'The Point of No Return' and 'Tired of Love', from the recently released *Swingin' Dors* album. The play was not well received, but Diana was open to other serious offers.

Television was taking over in a big way, and anyone with any degree of foresight could see it was going to be a nail in the coffin for the British film industry. While many actors tried to adapt, some, like Lionel Jeffries, weren't even prepared to try. He remembered cinema as a magical experience – the curtain which rose when the lights went down, and the single beam of light piercing the darkness – but that magic, as far as televison was concerned, had totally gone. You couldn't get lost in the story; your attention was always being distracted. There was nothing magical about your sitting room. In the early days Jeffries did a TV show with Peter Sellers, but they both decided never to do it again. Sellers may have done some talk shows, but television was a totally different form of entertainment from anything Jeffries was used to. He just couldn't adapt to it – there was something soulless about a camera that didn't even have a film in it. No, television was not his thing. Get rid of them all, he thought. Keep one and put it in the British Museum as an example.

But cinema was changing as well – especially British cinema, which was on the verge of a major shake-up. The seeds had been sown several years before, when writer and documentary filmmaker Lindsay Anderson formed the Free Cinema movement in 1956 with Karel Reisz and Tony Richardson. Free Cinema was an attempt to break away from middle-class melodrama and escapist fantasy and instead use film to explore more mundane realities. 'Implicit in our attitude,' the group announced, 'is a belief in freedom, in the importance of people and in the significance of the everyday.'

Reisz, in particular, had already gained critical plaudits with a documentary filmed in 1959, called *We are the Lambeth Boys*. When filming began on his adaptation of Alan Sillitoe's controversial play *Saturday Night, Sunday Morning*, the producers mailed a copy of the script to Diana. The money was lousy, the leading man was 'some unknown' called Albert Finney, and any curiosity she had was finally dispelled when she read that her character would be involved in an abortion scene. The part went instead to Rachel Roberts and, although Diana regretted missing out, she took it very well. For her part, Roberts went on to make quite a niche for herself in the kind of sexy older women roles Diana later seemed overqualified for. But her early success did not bring happiness; Roberts' death by overdose in 1980, at the age of fifty-three, was treated as suicide.

Diana's generation was facing another grave new threat. In the wake of Richard Burton's groundbreaking perform-ance in *Look Back in Anger*, the matinée-idol grooming of the Rank years began to look very out of place, and the likes of Richard Todd, Anthony Steel and George Baker found

205

actors like Oliver Reed, Richard Harris, Peter O'Toole and Albert Finney, the near overnight star of *Saturday Night, Sunday Morning*, taking their places. Some, like Dirk Bogarde, made the change with astonishing ease, but others were not so fortunate. 'We had to look to our laurels,' said Baker, 'and most of us faded.'

At the time, Diana was more concerned with the RKO case, which was finally withdrawn in July when she settled the claim for $200,000 (£71,400). It was a hollow victory, since not only did RKO not retract its comments, but the payments were to be split – half the money would be paid to Diana over two years, and the other half to Treasure Productions over five years. Since the company had been set up by Dennis, she had no reason to believe she'd ever see anything of it.

At that time, Diana was performing at the Dunes Hotel in Vegas, a handsomely paid but gruelling ten-day booking. She was used to doing two shows a day from variety, but Vegas expected three, one at 8 p.m., another at midnight and a third at 2 a.m. She did her usual set, incorporating songs like 'Ain't Necessarily So' and 'How Long Has This Been Going On', which, together with a few impressions – Eartha Kitt, Lena Horne, Mae West and Marlene Dietrich – brought the act up to just over half an hour. She went down well, and even before a flattering write-up appeared in show business trade magazine *Variety*, the hotel had extended her booking to 4 August.

Dawson enjoyed the high-rolling Vegas lifestyle and its electrifying mix of characters, but Diana was feeling overworked and began to miss her son terribly. Just a few months old, Mark was still at home in Surrey, so Dawson arranged for their nanny to bring the boy over. Diana was delighted. After just a year with Dawson, she was already becoming bored, the laughter had long since stopped and she found her lively, gag-a-minute husband turning into a moody, distant man who preferred his own hermetic company, sometimes even when guests called round. Dawson was unknown in the States and was still waiting for his big break, so Diana was doing the lion's share of the work and, wherever it came from, she could ill afford to turn it down.

Her stock was certainly rising and, almost immediately after the Dunes booking, Dawson took other cabaret offers on her behalf. He even managed to swing two weeks in September at the prestigious Ciro's club in Los Angeles. Competition was fierce: Count Basie was appearing over the road, and her first night there clashed with the first night of Hollywood's biggest ever ice show.

She was even approached by film director Ken Hughes with a view to filming her *News of the World* memoirs, which had just been published in paperback. Hughes, who had directed her in *The Long Haul*, had just had a success with *The Trials of Oscar Wilde*, starring Peter Finch, and was trying to get a biography of Oliver Cromwell onto the screen, although that project would take another ten years to complete. He saw Diana's story as 'the struggle of a girl to win the respect of the world', but he conceded that libel and censor problems were going to prove difficult. 'I expect we'll have to wade through fourteen councils and ten lawyers,' he sighed. Perhaps unsurprisingly, the film was never made.

In the meantime, Diana was making plans to move full-time to the States. Film work hadn't dried up entirely, but there would be no more lead roles; instead she took smaller parts in films like *On the Double*, with Danny Kaye, and *The Big Bankroll*. For the Kaye film, probably as a nod to the change in fashions, she had even allowed her hair to be cut fashionably short, for the first time in her career. She said she was still looking for good roles – 'But don't misunderstand me,' she added hastily, 'I've no illusions about doing Shakespeare. I shouldn't *dream* of inflicting myself on the public in that way.'

While Dawson sold the house in Surrey, Diana made plans to take up residence in a big house on Angelo Drive, Beverly Hills, which would cost something in the region of $175,000. But because they were still not naturalized American subjects, the Dawsons were forced to work on six-month visas, which necessitated trips outside the US, sometimes just over to the Mexican border, to renew them.

While doing TV work in Hollywood on a series called *The Racers* she met a young actor called John Ashley and began a torrid affair that flourished when Dawson flew back to Britain to see his accountant. When he returned, the child's nanny told him what had been happening behind his back, and there was a terrible scene. Ashley begged her to leave her husband, but Diana had little time to think – she was about to leave on a three-week tour of South America, taking in Caracas, Venezuela and Brasilia. She went alone, but the sight of Dawson with their little boy, waiting at the airport when she returned, softened her heart. Ashley withdrew from the running and Dawson promised to be more attentive.

When Diana finally returned to Britain, she was top of the bill on *Sunday Night at the London Palladium*. She had been out of the country for the best part of a year and she was greeted with suspicion, which confused her. 'Everybody keeps on about the "new" Diana Dors,' she said, 'but I don't know who she is, really. I'm not quite sure who the old one was, to tell you the truth. I'm exactly the same person I was when I went away, like I shall be for the rest of my life.'

Reviews for the show were mediocre, and Diana was surprised that many still hadn't forgiven her for selling her memoirs. After declaring that 'her life was an open newspaper', the *Evening Standard* felt the full force of Diana's spleen when it suggested to her that selling her confessions was somewhat 'cheap'. 'Listen,' she snapped back, 'for £36,000 I don't mind being cheap. It was my story that I was selling and I didn't involve anyone else who could be hurt by it.

'I suppose it's true that I've often done things for money,' she continued, 'but you mustn't forget that for a long time I didn't have any. There were times when I was very famous and had trunkfuls of cuttings about the fabulous Diana Dors and I literally didn't know where my next meal was coming from. In this business it's very easy to be famous and broke, and I'd perhaps have to make a joke about it and say I didn't know where my next Cadillac was coming from. But I have been very broke, and that's why I had this idea to amass money, to give myself some security.'

Diana spent a lot of that summer travelling backwards and forwards between Britain and America, usually to make cabaret appearances, and the frequent travelling became more arduous with the onset of autumn. Diana was pregnant again, and Dawson was delighted, but on one of her regular trips to London there was a dreadful incident that nearly lost her the child. To celebrate Guy Fawkes night, an agent by the name of John Kennedy held a bonfire party at his home in Wraysbury, Buckinghamshire. Kennedy had launched Tommy Steele's career, among others, and there were plenty of show business people present. For her part, Diana was especially pleased; she had just signed a contract with Soho club titan Paul Raymond to appear at his new restaurant, the Bal Tabarin, for £1,500 a week.

All this was soon forgotten, however, when someone threw a jumping jack into the house, thinking, for some strange reason, that everyone would be amused. Instead, an open box of fireworks caught light and the subsequent explosion set fire to the house. Along with actor Sid James and his wife, Diana backed into the kitchen and was forced to climb out of the window, cutting her leg in the process. Two people were trapped in the building and killed by smoke fumes, a third guest suffered a fatal heart attack. Not only was Diana lucky not to have lost the baby, she was lucky to be alive. Amid all the confusion, someone managed to find her mink coat, worth £2,000. It wasn't even singed.

The Bal Tabarin was Paul Raymond's big move upmarket, a restaurant with floor show in Mayfair's Hanover Square. Raymond was considered off colour by many in show business for his touring theatre shows, which had culminated in the opening of his self-titled Raymond's Revue Bar in London's Brewer Street in April 1958, where nude artistes like Melody Bubbles, Trixie Kent, Mika Mingo and Bonnie Bell, The Ding-Dong Girl, moved freely on the stage. The Revue Bar was a private members' club and therefore uninhibited by the kind of censorship that the Lord Chamberlain imposed on stage plays, which prevented any form of movement by nude 'artistes'. This had prevously resulted in an absurd situation at the Camberwell Palace in January 1956, when a performer called Peaches Page was sacked for moving during a nude tableau – because a mouse ran over her foot. Raymond had already got round that particular problem by putting his girls on a moving stage and rotating them.

Born Geoffrey Anthony Quinn in 1926 in Glossop, Derbyshire, Raymond began his career at sixteen, as an office boy in a cotton mill, making extra money as a dance-band drummer, then joining the RAF for two years' service. He came to London in 1950, where the money he saved from his bar job went towards making his break in the entertainment business. One of his first attempts supposedly included buying a mind-reading act from a duo called 'Mr And Miss Tree' for £25, another involved putting together a variety show in a local theatre in the Midlands area. It flopped horribly, and he repeated the experiment unsuccessfully in Lowestoft. In fact, it wasn't until the following year, when Raymond discovered the pulling power of naked performers, that his audiences began to increase, and in 1952 he hosted his first nude revue, called *We Strip Tonight*. 'Titles are an art,' he said. 'They can come in a flash.'

From there he went from strength to strength, staging bigger and bigger revues with vignettes like 'Paris After Dark' and 'Piccadilly Peepshow', promising special added extras like 'The Banned Reefer Dance' and 'The Eurasian Voodoo Dance' (helpfully subtitled 'A Raging Torrent of Emotion That Even Nature Cannot Control'). His posters regularly got him into trouble, with lurid captions that screamed, 'Look! The Dance of the Pound Notes! Dressed Only in Pound Notes . . . She Even Gives her Last Pound Away!'

Raymond's revues were by no means sleazy, and he toured some of the most reputable theatre chains in the country. His wife helped choose and dress the girls and the shows themselves were often comparatively lavish, including the popular and self-explanatory 'Nudes In The Lions' Cage'. 'It's a first-class act,' said Raymond. 'And, honestly, the lions *could* maul the girls. Costs me £18 a week in insurance.'

The opening of the Revue Bar in 1958 marked a new era in permissiveness, which made redundant the pout and tease of Diana's early career and was defiantly at odds with the Rank Organisation's contempt for adult entertainment. Raymond was both a businessman and a realist ('Look,' he said, 'there's no such thing these days as a family audience.'), and his ways and means were proving irresistible. Every man over the age of eighteen who bought a ticket to his 1956 revue, *French Postcards*, was given an 'art photograph', and several years later the Revue Bar broke new ground by hosting a striptease quiz show, where the audience was asked a series of questions. Each correct answer led to an item of clothing being removed.

Raymond's stunts became progressively stronger (for their time), including 'amateur nights', where excited provincial girls would strip indelicately, and 'historical episodes' that featured exotic slave girls and scenes of simulated whipping. This led to prosecution in April 1961, when he was tried at the London Sessions, along with the Revue Bar's manager, charged with running a disorderly house. Raymond denied the charge and claimed a well-heeled clientele that, he said, included many prominent peers, politicians and high-ranking members of the legal profession. Raymond's wife Jean backed this rebuttal, insisting their girls wore G-strings at all times, and his defence barrister, Edward Clark QC, spent an hour and a half trying to convince the jury. 'We have come a long way since the dance of the seven veils,' he assured them. 'We are, in fact, progressing, for better or for worse. You may think for better. We are more broad-minded . . .'

Nevertheless, Raymond was found guilty by an all-male jury – undoubtedly reflecting the 'sexual' nature of the crime – and fined £5,000. In a tellingly bombastic summation, Chairman Reginald Seaton told Raymond, 'Your establishment and others have been vying with each other to see what degree of disgustingness they can introduce to attract members from all classes who are only too ready, out of curiosity or lust, to see the filth.'

The Bal Tabarin, however, was intended to be a more respectable establishment with a strictly no-nudes floor show policy. As well as Diana, Raymond was in talks with such talent as Buddy Greco, Billy Daniels and Mel Torme, proving his commitment to the idea. Opening her five-week residency, Diana performed her customary half-hour, nine-song set at the club's gala opening night, introduced by her husband. She was wearing a low-cut black velvet dress, decorated with gold brocade and gathered at the waist with a diamante belt, which didn't really try to cover the early signs of pregnancy. 'What do you think?' she asked. 'It's one of Alma Cogan's tea cosies!'

Singer Cogan, who was sitting in the audience with Lionel Bart, laughed uproariously. She was seven months younger than Diana but almost as famous, having been a household name in Britain since her first recording, at the age of twenty, in 1952. They called her The Girl With The Laugh In Her Voice, but she was just as well known for her wardrobe, which comprised over fifty-seven gowns – indeed, a 1962 press release claimed that her expenditure on dresses alone would have bought her a Rolls Royce, a Bentley, two Ford Zephyrs, two Jaguars and three bubble cars. Cogan was liked and respected by stars of all generations, from band leader Ted Heath to Paul McCartney, and her parties – at her flat in Kensington High Street – were legendary. Sadly, she was in the last stretch of her life, and died as a result of untreatable stomach cancer after an eighteen-month illness on 26 October 1966.

For the duration of the booking at Raymond's club, Diana rented a West London mews house, which she shared with her husband, child and nanny. It was a comfortable time; her swinging days were over, and she was looking forward to the birth of her second child, who she wanted to be born in the United States. The *Daily Mirror* called Bert Fluck, to see if he would be going over for the occasion. 'No,' he said. 'Diana is always asking me, but I couldn't stand the trip at my age.' Diana and entourage left London Airport for Hollywood on 14 February 1962, and she made no bones about the finality of her departure. 'I certainly won't be back this year,' she said.

The Bal Tabarin did not last long in Diana's absence – the club closed suddenly and without any apparent warning at

4 a.m. on 8 April, when Raymond announced his intention to sell the property to a secret buyer. 'People have been saying that this was the sort of sophisticated, late-night restaurant the West End wanted,' he said resignedly. 'I'm afraid they were kidding themselves. The West End doesn't want it.'

Chapter Eleven

DISAPPOINTING THE
VULTURES

DIANA WAS STILL a star, or at least a media phenomenon, but somewhere, not far below the surface, there
was still a trace of little Diana Fluck, fussily mothering her
tiny neighbour as she wheeled her pram up and down
Marlborough Road. She didn't just want to be a mother, she
wanted the same special closeness she'd had with Mary.
Although she had been dead for several years Diana hadn't
stopped missing her and always thought they'd shared a
special bond which others would never understand – which
was certainly true. Mary's indulgence of her teenage
daughter now seems wholly inappropriate if not actually
irresponsible – watching her flaunt her underage sexuality
and letting her go off to London at a very young age. But
perhaps Mary understood that Diana was not satisfied with
childhood; indeed Diana never voiced any regrets about her
youth.

Diana loved her son, and clearly preferred the company of
men, but she would have very much liked a daughter – an
heiress, a confidante, a partner in crime – to experience
some of the same intimacy she'd shared with her own
mother. The name 'Caroline Jane' was again on stand-by,
but Diana was more thrilled than disappointed when she
gave birth to the healthy, 10 lb 2 oz Gary on 27 June 1962,
at the Cedars of Lebanon Hospital in Hollywood. His
godparents were Steve Allen, Liberace, Terry-Thomas and
her good friend Pamela Mason – then James Mason's wife

and a formidable, almost aristocratic figure in the ex-pat movie colony.

Diana was working again within a matter of months, and it was during a cabaret season in Vegas, on 4 August 1962, that she heard the news sweeping Hollywood: Marilyn Monroe was dead, killed by an apparently self-inflicted overdose of barbiturates. Diana was stunned. Monroe was a fragile, unstable talent – it was common knowledge – but no one thought her neurosis was so serious. There was something frightening, something awfully frail, about the death of a woman who had become a myth in her own lifetime, and Diana was forced to reappraise her own lack of success in Hollywood. Maybe it had been a blessing. She thought of her two children and how they balanced out her life, giving her something to live for now that her own career was in tailspin. 'Children wipe out any suicidal thoughts in your mind,' she said. 'If Marilyn Monroe had had children she never would have died.'

Monroe's death made her closest rivals seem almost ghoulish in their blondeness and had a profound effect on their careers – especially Jayne Mansfield, whose whole screen persona worked largely in counterpoint to Marilyn's. Mansfield was dismissed by many as a female female impersonator, and when her subject matter died, the joke suddenly seemed to be in very poor taste.

Diana, however, was out of that particular rat race and had embarked on another – touring her cabaret set round the clubs and hotels of North America just to keep the house on Angelo Drive. It was well paid but wearying. Now, whenever she faced Vegas she felt none of the old thrill. 'Funny,' she said, 'I used to imagine it must be so tough. In fact, it's just like playing Blackpool.' One night, to fill in some time while she changed for the next number, she showed a short, 8 mm film of Mark playing. After the first night, the manager made her take it out. It was killing the glamour, he said.

Diana flew back to Britain in January 1963, when she was due to start filming on Michael Winner's *West 11*, a dour, quasi-realist portrait of life in the bedsits and jazz clubs of London's W11 postal district. The part was that of a much older woman, trying to recapture her youth, and Diana was looking forward to the challenge. When the plane was diverted, however, she began to regret her enthusiasm; London Airport was in the grip of a terrible blizzard and the plane was forced to land in Manchester. A train was being laid on at midnight, but she could not wait, so a taxi delivered her to Stockport, where she caught an earlier one. Welcome home, she thought.

Diana wanted to stretch herself as an actress but was still undecided about the future. 'I don't like being a sex symbol,' she said. 'It's good for business, and when I stop attracting men I'll have to take a good look in the mirror – something must be slipping. But the reason I attract men en masse is because they see something they think easily attainable. They look me up and down, no limit to their imagination. As a person, I resent it. As Diana Dors, it's good business.'

She was still thinking of starting her own company, outside of show business, and claimed to have sunk £300,000 into a DIY beauty kit, to be called The Diana Dors Hairdryer and Manicure Set. It was an odd venture, which perhaps reflected her own insecurities about her fame and, more significantly, her looks. Despite her 'sexy' image, Diana wasn't extraordinarily pretty – and she knew it. The Diana Dors she presented was a package and she considered her hair and figure a vital part of her camouflage. 'The odd thing, really,' she said, 'is that over here it was the women who liked me.

All my letters used to come from women. My image was attainable, I suppose. Women working at a factory bench looked up at me on the screen and saw hope for themselves. I was within reach, unlike a lot of actresses. The odd thing, really, is that despite my looks, I'm not a sexy girl. Average, I suppose. Maybe not even that. I've never taken a poll, so I wouldn't know.'

When filming wrapped, Diana returned to Hollywood – and the cabaret work that was fast becoming her major source of income. Dawson's parents had come to stay, and showed no signs of leaving, but it was a help with the children whenever she went away, which was often. She was midway through a booking at New York's International club on 28 April when Dawson's agent called to tell her that Aunt Kit had sent a cable to Diana's home, which was proof in itself that something was very wrong. Diana steeled herself for the news, and it *was* bad – her father was dead. She called Swindon immediately and Kit answered. Between sobs, Kit explained that Bert had gone out, as usual, to the railwaymen's club the previous night, and that when she went to wake him in the morning she'd found him lying cold in his bed. At the age of sixty-nine, after forty years in the shadow of heart attack, Bert Fluck had died in his sleep.

The funeral was arranged for the following Friday, but Kit did not pressurize her niece into attending; instead, Diana chose to fulfil her contractual obligations in New York. It was a callous, pragmatic decision, which she later regretted but, to her mind, Bert Fluck's funeral was just a formality, not the terrible nightmarish experience her mother's had been. Her later remorse was ascribed to a sense of 'duty', which was a sad indication of the way their relationship had been strained. Even when he died, Diana could not bring herself to love her father.

★

The summer of 1963 was a political and cultural watershed for Britain. For several months there had been murmurings about impropriety in the highest level of government, culminating in the secretary of state for war, John Profumo, taking the unprecedented step of denying rumours of an affair with a 'model' to prime minister Harold Macmillan in the House of Commons. It was a rash move, and as more damning evidence mounted, Profumo resigned on 5 June.

Five days later, Stephen Ward was arrested at his home in Bryanston Mews, a property formerly owned by Perec Rachman, and charged with living off immoral earnings. Ward was not initially granted bail and he was held in custody for two weeks, when further charges were brought – including five more counts of living off immoral earnings, and the procurement of an illegal abortion. When the case came to court, the trial hinged on the testimony of Ward's two most recent protegées, Christine Keeler, the model in question, and Mandy Rice-Davies. The nation became obsessed with their stories. Keeler, twenty-one, was dark and mysterious, if only by her absence (she fled to Spain the moment the story broke), but eighteen-year-old Rice-Davies was sassy, confident and blonde, causing laughter in the courtroom with her remarks (told that Lord Astor denied that they had ever made love, she famously replied, 'Well, he would, wouldn't he?').

Born in Birmingham, Mandy Rice-Davies had, like Diana, fled a provincial lifestyle to find herself in London, first becoming a model at the Earl's Court Motor Show, then a dancer at Percival Murray's club, on the fringes of Soho, at the age of sixteen. Through Murray's club, she was inducted into a strange and sexually-charged high life that culminated in her briefly becoming Rachman's mistress before his death in November 1962, which in turn brought Mandy her own Jaguar and, as she put it herself, 'enough in jewellery and mink to keep me'. In many ways, she was Diana's linear successor, and when she described herself as 'the new Lady Hamilton', it was perhaps an unintentional double entendre.

As the story poured out, the jury heard stories of easy women, satyric men and bacchanalian sex parties, though it was, in fact, the libidinous set of the fifties who provided much of the intrigue. Indeed, the fateful meeting between Keeler and Profumo by the swimming pool at Cliveden had happened two years previously, and was not part of an ongoing affair. Diana's name was even mentioned indirectly, with regard to the two-way mirror at Rachman's place in Bryanston Mews, which was quite obviously due to Dennis's influence. But of course, the comparatively tame parties Dennis and Diana held in Chelsea bore little resemblance to some of the more bizarre revelations, like the whipping parties hosted by a woman known as Marie Ella, and rumours involving a very famous public figure and his strange masochistic tendencies – wearing nothing but a leather mask, he would serve the food at dinner parties where the guests were encouraged to abuse him.

Personally, Ward could handle the charges, but the effect on his livelihood was crippling. Not only that, but a fund-raising display of his sketches which had been filmed by the BBC, was dismissed with the most callous disdain. Released on supervised bail, Ward was in a coma when the jury's inevitable guilty verdict came in, having taken an overdose of Nembutal while staying at the home of a friend, Noel Howard Jones. He was taken to St Stephen's Hospital in Chelsea, where he died at 3.50 p.m. on 3 August. 'I'm sorry to disappoint the vultures,' he said in his suicide note.

Stephen Ward's suicide blew the lid on London's underground sex scene, and though the Profumo affair is often credited, at least by poet Philip Larkin, with kick-starting the sixties in Britain, it also revealed, finally, the previously hidden decadence that lay beneath the squeaky-clean veneer of the supposedly 'wholesome' fifties. In a letter to the *Sunday Telegraph*, dated 11 August 1963 and headlined 'Was Stephen Ward a scapegoat?', journalist Thomas Wiseman wrote an eloquent analysis. 'A terrible charade of punishment had to be enacted,' he wrote, 'to show the public that the wages of sin are not Jaguars and parties at swimming pools, and international celebrity, and fat fees from newspapers; somebody had to pay dearly – and be seen to pay dearly – for all this fun, or else the envy of the sexually-underprivileged masses would have vented itself on the Establishment.'

It would not take a great leap of the imagination to see how the Profumo scandal reflected the Establishment's dim view of the sexually over-privileged Diana Dors.

In the meantime, life with Dawson was becoming strained, and Diana was bored. She'd become involved with a New York playboy called Frankie, but his attentions were cloying and she hoped to stall him with the news that she had been booked for an upcoming tour of Australia. The prospect unnerved her – she'd be alone in a strange country. But, once there, she made friends soon enough and within days she was introduced to a singer named Darryl Stewart, who was appearing on the same bill. They began an affair and when Diana's tour was finished she was so smitten, she made immediate plans for Stewart to join her in America. Through Pamela Mason, Diana acquired the use of a flat just off Sunset Boulevard and she installed her lover there for the next few months.

Dawson learned about the affair via a letter from Stewart's wife, who included in her note the news that she was about to give birth to her husband's third child, and he hit the roof. Confronting Diana with the letter, he ordered her to leave the house and – or so she claimed – threatened to burn her possessions if she didn't get out within two hours. She went straight round to Pamela Mason's for advice, and stayed there for several days. Fast-acting and unsentimental, Mason made Diana an urgent appointment with her lawyer, Marvin Mitchelson. Mitchelson was a legal heavyweight and one of the finest divorce lawyers in the world. After bringing Pamela one of the most lavish settlements in movie history, legend had it that he went on to win the biggest payout in divorce history – somewhere in the region of $81 million – in the case of Sheika Dena Alfassi. The alimony payments crippled Mason financially, causing him to embark on an indiscriminate round of movies – good, bad and awful – to keep up payments.

Under Mitchelson's instructions, Diana withdrew all the money in their account – about $1,500 – and filed for divorce on 17 January 1964, accusing her husband of cruelty and alleging that, when not performing, she had been kept 'a virtual prisoner' in her own home. She used the suit to claim custody of the children and half their joint assets but made no request for alimony, and Dawson was ordered to file his answer by 30 January. 'If things go well,' said Mitchelson, 'she should get an interlocutory decree within two months.'

Bizarrely, Diana regretted the decision almost immediately and was thinking of withdrawing the divorce petition. 'I may have given a slightly exaggerated version to my attorney,' she said. Dawson was, she added, 'a very gentle type of man. Violence is not in his character. The complaint gives the impression that he may have beat me up. Well, that isn't so.' The letter from Stewart's wife had upset her, and she realized one of her own defences was no longer true – in the fall-out from Dennis's death, and in her bid to stress that she was very different from her public image, she liked to insist that 'in all my life, despite everything said, I've never hurt a living soul or broken up a home or stolen another woman's husband.' Well, in the last week or so, she'd just about done all three. She returned to Dawson reluctantly, but the affair with Stewart was taking her further than she was prepared to go, for the moment at least. On 1 February, the Los Angeles Superior Court removed the hearing from its calendar.

When she arrived in England on 8 March, the press made a great deal about the luxurious platinum mink coat she was wearing. It was 'just a present' she told them, not a reconciliation gift, as they hoped she might say. 'Husbands do this from time to time,' she said, somewhat disingenuously. She insisted that Dawson and she were very much together, which was very much not true.

Plenty had happened in her homeland the previous year, and she knew it. 'Say, what's been happening?' she asked. 'When I was here last summer the whole government seemed about to collapse!' Whether or not she knew Macmillan had resigned and that a general election was in the offing was, sadly, not for discussion. Even so, she was not oblivious to the changes in youth culture. In many ways, Diana served some of the functions of rock 'n' roll before it arrived, and it was inevitable that as pop, and later rock, music progressed, it would push away the repressive boundaries that had enhanced her image in the early fifties. She was never really happy in the role of pioneer, and though she was never afraid of sex, she'd always fancied a bit of company in the front line. The Beatles, with their unmasculine, collar-length hair and borderline-foppish stage suits, were clearly working in the same territory, and that impressed her; she grew to like long hair on a man. 'London has changed fantastically,' she told the *Express*. 'I don't just mean the buildings. People are so very much more on the ball, especially the youngsters – new waves of them, setting the pace.'

She was in England for a month, principally to film a Sunday night TV play for ABC Television, called *A Nice*

Little Business, which was ITV's bid to combat the recently launched BBC2. To make the trip worth her while, Diana also squeezed in a slot on ABC's *Big Night Out* variety show and a few weeks' cabaret in Selby and Manchester, plus a week at Newcastle-upon-Tyne's La Dolce Vita club, soon to become the unwitting backdrop to a brutal killing.

A local crook was found shot dead in his car, which was parked near the club, and the British–Italian Landa brothers – businessmen apparently involved in a lucrative fruit machine racket – were immediately suspected. One was arrested, the other fled, but many had the feeling that the murder was a set-up orchestrated by an enterprising London gang. It was symptomatic of the times that criminals were feeling the same buoyancy the consumer was to feel in the first three years of Harold Wilson's Labour government, best exemplified by the so-called 'legitimate' attempts by underworld gang lords, Ron and Reg Kray, to invest in South African property with their good friend and Tory peer, Lord Boothby. As gang boss Harry Flowers, played by Johnny Shannon, later said in Donald Cammell and Nicolas Roeg's 1968 film *Performance*, which dealt explicit with this theme, 'Business is business and progress is progress.'

The Krays were at that time enjoying the relaxation of Britain's gaming and licensing laws, setting up clubs in the West End of London which ushered in a boom time for the city's night life. Only the previous year, Diana had placed the opening bet at the Isle of Man's first ever legal casino. 'I'm in favour of people gambling,' said James Cain, Manx MP and chairman of the government's Gaming Board of Control. 'We have been impressed with [the management's] integrity and enthusiasm to do something different for the island. We have found that they are not the cigar-smoking, pistol-packing Americans everyone expected.' Britain was beginning to feel the same way. Too late to help Diana's movie career, her homeland was finally trying to do things the American way.

The trips back to LA were becoming a chore. She and her husband were drifting apart, and their house together was, in her mind, as soulless as the city. Dawson cluttered the place with gadgets and toys that Diana thought their two toddlers were far too young to appreciate. Visiting in January 1964, *Express* reporter [Sir] David English had encountered ' . . . a sprawling bungalow decorated in what I can only call penny arcade style. Bright yellow chairs fronted by glass and chromium coffee tables surrounded a giant TV set and film screen. Off to one side was the 'play area' containing personalized red and yellow slot machines, a rifle range and a large billiards table.' Given that Diana liked her period detail, no matter how faux, it only served to make the place less homely.

Diana hated living in Hollywood. All she did was lie by the pool – it was so boring – but whenever she mentioned moving back, Dawson scoffed. 'Britain's for the birds,' he said. She put it down to the fact that he never really got a break there, so, for him, there were few good memories. Diana remembered nothing but good. The next time she flew to London it was to make a forgettable little comedy called *Allez France* in which she played a film star – in other words, herself. She didn't mind doing that for comedy, it could be most endearing, but anything more serious and she'd have felt quite grotesque. At Shepperton, shooting this two-bit film at midnight in the drizzling rain, the ironies of the situation cannot have escaped her. She was only doing it for the money, but what was that money paying for? The mortgage on a house she didn't want, and the future of two children she loved very much but never saw. 'I have discovered that everything – but everything – in life has to be paid for,' she told set visitor Kenneth Passingham. 'I've paid for it – and I'm still paying.'

In a bid to facilitate the move back to Britain at some yet-to-be-determined date, she took a six-month rental on a house in Elyston Place, Chelsea. In the long term, it was a stepping stone; in the short term, it was a place she could share with Darryl Stewart, who had talked about leaving his wife and joining Diana in London. She had everything planned, but with just a few weeks to go, Stewart wrote to say that the timing was wrong and that he couldn't make it. Diana wrote back with an ultimatum: either he came or they were finished. She took the ensuing silence, which lasted fifteen years, as a no.

To cheer herself up, Diana threw a party. Kim came – and there was plenty to talk about. At the tail end of the fifties he had been living in Tangier, making a living by renting out speedboats to waterskiers and setting up a nightclub, Dandy Kim's, in the Rue San Luca, a fashionable part of town. Bobby McKew had flown over to visit and after ten days he was asked to go to the local police station to sort out his visa. Instead, he was arrested by Interpol detectives under an extradition warrant for his part in the theft from Jack Warner back in 1953. When Kim heard the news he caught the first ferry to Gibraltar and made immediate plans to fly back to Britain. His club was due to open the same week.

Back in London, Kim was arrested on 12 January 1960, and the French government's lengthy bid to extradite him began. Five months later he was boarding a plane that would take him first to a Paris jail, where arrangements would be made to transfer him to Fresnes prison. After serving sixteen months, both Kim's and McKew's sentences were halved under French laws pertaining to first time offenders, and on payment of a sum in the region of £1,000 both were free to go. Kim's star was tarnished, but Diana didn't care too much and she never commented publicly on his situation. She was quite loyal in that respect, and even if she thought Kim was guilty she was just as likely to think that Jack Warner was a careless old soak with more money than sense. She was quite a moral woman, in her way, but she preferred to use her own judgement, not society's.

Kim mingled with Diana's usual show business crowd at the party, where a young, twenty-six-year-old stranger caught her eye. Troy Dante was a musician, the singer with the unknown but groovily titled Troy Dante and the Infernos. Welsh by birth but a Londoner by instinct, Dante (real name Noel Frederickson) was dark-haired, charismatic and funny, leaving Diana in fits with self-deprecating stories of his band's apparent failure. Square-built and stocky, wearing fashionable tight-fitting shirts and drainpipe trousers, Dante looked faintly sinister at the best of times, especially with his shades on. Diana loved the whole mythology of the pop scene and saw in it much the same glamour that she'd seen in forties Hollywood. Her generation was effectively over. 'All that's finished today,' she said. 'Nobody cares any more. It's the age of reality, of the Beatles. And a good thing, too . . . It's great all this pop stuff. *They're* the stars today.'

Within a few weeks, Dante was a fixture at the flat. He was technically married, but Diana accommodated the arrangement, and even told the press she was his manager. What she meant by this was that wherever she could, she would force booking agents to take the Infernos by refusing to appear without them. For the first time in her life, she began drinking more than the odd glass at night, her favourite tipple being Scotch and Coke ('Been drinking it for years,' she told a startled interviewer. 'Now the Beatles drink it. It's *the* drink. You *must* get with it!'). Life with Dante escalated into the social whirl she'd missed so much in Hollywood, bringing a new group of friends, many of them singers, like 'Leapy' Lee Graham, Jess Conrad, Kenny Lynch and, later,

P.J. Proby. Just as the Charm School once took on Hollywood at its own game, so British impresarios like Larry Parnes and Jack Good had recently been cultivating musical talent to take over from New York's famous Tin Pan Alley and Brill Building teams. Everyone seemed 'about' to happen, and though few ever really did, the air was thick with the exciting possibility.

Diana, meanwhile, was still in cabaret and she was shocked when her usual, salubrious round of nightclubs, hotels and restaurants suddenly dipped to take in noisy, overlit working men's clubs. She'd enjoyed it as child, when her audience at the railwaymen's club was so much more generous, but as an adult it was a grim, demeaning affair. Her act — the same half-hour set of songs, with a bit of banter for good measure — was usually well received, but audiences could be unpredictable. Occasionally they'd heckle, sometimes boo, and even the best behaved talked distractingly while she was on. She took it well and didn't condemn them for it, at least not in so many words. 'Ordinary people can identify with me,' she said. 'I mean, they know that with a bit of luck they could be like me. I go down really well with working-class audiences. It's my "touch of the plebs", I suppose.'

And after all, it was money in the bank, and she knew what she was capable of. 'In cabaret, I'm just cashing in on me,' she said, 'not furthering my act at all. People lump me together with Zsa Zsa Gabor and Jayne Mansfield but, without boasting, I can act.' The following October, Diana released a single of her own, 'So Little Time', which she publicized with an appearance on *Thank Your Lucky Stars*, hosted by Pete Murray. The bands on the bill were mostly younger, like The Nashville Teens, but Diana was still an object of curiosity for everybody. Murray asked her to sign a pound note, for old time's sake, and a young girl who followed close behind her as she left couldn't resist furtively touching the back of her immaculately set hair. She was expecting the starched, crispy texture of lacquer on peroxide, but Diana's hair was inexplicably soft. Even then, years after her heyday, there was still something otherworldly about Diana Dors.

As 1964 drew to an end, Diana began to wonder where it was all going. Her marriage was in ruins, her love life a Whitehall farce, her career quickly going down the pan, and the less money she was earning, the more people were queuing up to take it from her. 'I sometimes find myself thinking about the future,' she said in a rare show of morbid introspection. 'But I find it so depressing I avoid it as much as possible.'

Before that season's pantomime began rehearsing, she flew back to LA for a quick pre-Christmas reunion with her children, which she topped up with another visit early in 1965, when she was accompanied by Jess Conrad. Conrad was flying out to publicize his role in *The Amorous Adventures of Moll Flanders*. This was a poorly received attempt to create, in Kim Novak as Moll, a female rival to Tony Richardson's amazingly successful *Tom Jones*. The film proved to be about as lucrative as Conrad's own film career, but Diana was always willing to give a friend a hand, even if it was just a photo opportunity at London Airport and a place to stay.

When she returned to Britain, Diana started work on one of her most important projects of the sixties, which could have completely turned round her troubled fortunes. TV production company, Rediffusion, had approached her late in 1964 with an idea for a long-running series called *The Unusual Miss Mulberry*, and she'd signed a contract in December, allegedly worth £30,000, to make it. Diana would play Kay Mulberry, the daughter of a top-ranking officer at Scotland Yard who starts her own private detective agency with a partner, played by actor William Lucas. Planned as a rival to *The Avengers* – with a suitably kinky undertow provided by the use of handcuffs and batons, and a central dominatrix role in the mould of Honor Blackman's Cathy Gale character – it was Rediffusion's biggest project to date, with thousands spent on sets and chic furnishing for Kay Mulberry's apartment. The prop budget was also huge, splashing out on specially made truncheons which, to this day, appear at auctions as authentic police weaponry.

Diana filmed six hour-long shows, but after eight weeks' shooting the production suddenly closed down. Rediffusion made no comment other than an oblique statement blaming 'legal complications', However, it seems likely that a senior ITV controller was not impressed by the first episodes, possibly because Diana was considered too old for the part. No further episodes were ever filmed and those that had been were never broadcast which, in light of the subsequent success of detective shows over the next thirty years, means either that Rediffusion was incredibly short-sighted or *The Unusual Miss Mulberry* was incredibly bad.

In fact, 1965 was not a good year at all for Diana, and it was mostly spent hawking her act round various nightclubs. She made a brief return to film-making on Michael Bentine's *The Sandwich Man*, a largely silent and not very funny comedy packed with guest appearances from British variety stars and character actors (Diana played a fishwife), but it wasn't much to hold on to. Early the following year she realized she hadn't even been considered as a subject for *This Is Your Life* in a while, which was quite a wake-up call as far as celebrities were concerned. Someone told her that the show's production team thought she was 'too provocative and brittle'.

'If I'm outspoken and controversial it's because I enjoy speaking my mind,' she told *Sunday Express* writer Clive Hirschhorn. 'Apparently, to most people, I come over "too strong". And in 1966 one has to play it cool to be fashionable.

The Julie Christie kooky dolly look is all the rage now. Anything as obvious and fulsome as me – and let's face it, I *am* fulsome – is out!'

And it was true. Her decision to loosen the reins, enjoy her food and the odd night on the Scotch and Coke had started adding pounds where they were all too visible. And though, several years later, she blamed an underactive thyroid gland, a largely mythic ailment that proliferated in the seventies, it seems no accident that her upgrade in size came at a time of great personal crisis. 'But I musn't complain,' she shrugged. 'After all, I've had a bloody good innings – and no doubt glamour will come back.'

It would, but not for many years. In the meantime, she was isolated. It is a well-known truism in modelling circles that once a leading model's period of ultra-fashionability has passed, she can easily accommodate the next wave of style, the next 'look' – it is the wave after that which will deal the killer blow. Diana was finding out the hard way that, having surfed the 'glamorous' naturalism of the early sixties, she was now way out of synch with the authentic naturalism of an increasingly prosperous society that no longer needed escapism. As the economy strengthened, television took hold and transport systems expanded, there was no longer much need for the kind of vicarious lifestyle Diana pioneered in the fifties – it was all becoming affordable.

'The luxury and the glamour that was once part and parcel of being a film star is now passé,' she conceded to Hirschhorn. 'And because, to the man in the street, I so typified what being a film star must be like, this world of tinsel and stardust was automatically associated with me. Now that it's gone, I've been left out in the cold, almost . . . You see, no matter how hard I try, I guess I'll never be able to look like Rita Tushingham.

'I will admit, though,' she added, 'that I did for glamour in the country what the Beatles did for pop music. I've always had a sense of humour and a sense of perspective on things. Let's face it, dear, in this business, if you haven't, you can go to pieces overnight. Just crack up.'

Cracking up would have been a very easy option when the tax man presented her a few months later with a bill for £48,000, but Diana was not about to satisfy her critics. At the time she'd just moved into a rented house known as The Pavilion in Sunninghill, Berkshire, paying 24 guineas a week. She took the place without really knowing how she would pay for it, since there was little work coming in. The year's cinematic masterpiece was to be *Berserk!* (aka *Circus of Blood*), starring sixty-three-year-old Joan Crawford as the owner of a big top blighted by a series of grisly murders. It was a truly disturbing film, if only because of the revealing shorts that its bark-skinned star was required to wear; if Diana thought her own fall from stardom was undignified, God only knows what that said for Crawford – a Hollywood legend since her Oscar-winning role in 1945's *Mildred Pierce*.

There was also a question of property. She wanted to move back to England, but if they sold the house in Angelo Drive, the money would have gone straight to the tax man, leaving her children homeless. She was also warned, incorrectly, that the Inland Revenue had powers of jurisdiction in the States and could legitimately confiscate the house. Over the coming months, she worked out a divorce settlement with Dawson in which she let go of the house and agreed not to contest his petition. Dawson was working steadily now, since his break in the wartime comedy series *Hogan's Heroes* in 1965. Ironically, he was soon to become a household name as host of a quiz show called *Family Feud*.

The Pavilion served as Diana's base for the next few

months, and was the scene of many wild parties; indeed, when she left in August 1966, property owner Captain Walter Stewart (retired) issued a lawsuit to cover unpaid utility bills and damages, including £800 for damage to furniture and fittings plus £66 for re-turfing where the lawns had been disfigured by a helicopter landing. The case was heard and the court upheld Stewart's complaint, awarding him £1,239 2s 11d plus £20 14s 6d. The hard part, however, would actually be getting his hands on it and nearly four months later, he was still unpaid. A credit agency was assigned to find Diana, but every time its representatives turned up at Shepperton studio, where *Berserk!* was filming, they were told they'd 'just missed' her. When they visited the location set, a real circus tent loaned by Billy Smart's company, they were told she'd be 'coming along any minute' – but then she didn't appear. With an unintentional note of pathos, Stewart's lawyer, Robert Clarke, complained, 'It seems remarkable that three or four men from a leading inquiry agency cannot reach such a well-known celebrity.'

It might have been comical if the consequences had not been so severe. Diana's financial problems were now being debated in public, and her attempts to deny them rang cheerfully hollow. 'I'm not down to my last penny yet,' she claimed, but she was only making one movie a year and her cabaret circuit was down to taking in what booking agents witheringly called 'the sharp end' of the venue scale. It was in Wakefield on one such tour that she renewed her acquaintance with Jayne Mansfield, the other movie blonde, who had risen to fame in *The Girl Can't Help It* (1956), a film that Dennis had once turned down on Diana's behalf. Like Diana, Mansfield had peaked in the late fifties and, like Diana, Jayne Mansfield was living on her name, but Diana was amazed to see that she seemed totally oblivious to the reality of the situation, gaily signing autographs with a pink pen, dotting the 'i' in 'Mansfield' with a girlish heart. For the length of the booking, Diana tried to stampede Jayne into frank conversation, but none was forthcoming. When she heard the following year that she was dead – practically decapitated in a gruesome car smash that littered the road with the bodies of her pet chihuahuas – Diana felt sad that she'd never fathomed out what made Jayne Mansfield tick.

'In all the time I knew Jayne, she never let the mask fall once,' she wrote, 'until at the end I finally believed she really did speak and think like a Kewpie Doll.'

In the summer of 1967, after even the usually discreet Harrods had issued a writ for non-payment of a tab worth £581, the Inland Revenue formally sued Diana on 1 July for the sum of £40,208 in back tax, plus surtax and interest. The period covered by the claim went back ten years, before Dennis's death, and the writ ran to two and a half pages of typed manuscript. The publicity was not helped when a Devon club owner joined the bandwagon with a suit claiming she had broken an agreement to appear at his club earlier in the year.

Diana replied that she had had pancreatitis, which was by all accounts true, but the manager was not satisfied and went ahead with legal proceedings. On top of all the headlines that were piling up what happened next, although not the most serious event in the coming months, was perhaps the most damaging. The West End premiere of the sentimental Sidney Poitier vehicle *To Sir With Love* at the Astoria Cinema on Charing Cross Road, took place on 7 September, and as Dante escorted Diana past the waiting photographers, a man rushed forward and pressed something into her hand. He was not a fan, as she initially thought, but a private detective serving a writ on behalf of the club owner, for £1,977 4s 4d. Still smiling, she accepted the papers and handed them to Dante, who pocketed them.

They brazened the evening out, and when someone asked Diana what the commotion was, she replied simply, 'Oh, just someone wanting an autograph.' The laughter stopped the following day, when the press carried the story complete with photographs and headlines such as 'Writ Served At Cinema: Diana Dors Handed £2,000 Claim' and 'Diana Dors Gets A Writ At The Premiere'. Since Dennis first suggested the idea, Diana had often fed the press with fabulous stories about her wealth and earning power, but now the grim reality was being advertised and she knew her market rate would sink accordingly. The woman who was once (self-proclaimed) the second highest-earning actress in Britain, after Vivien Leigh, was in danger of sinking right back down with the others.

Fortunately, she'd already made plans to buy her own property, a large estate in Sunningdale, Berkshire, called Orchard Manor, after persuading her advisors to allow her to use money destined for her sons' trust fund. At first they declined, but Diana persuaded them it would be an investment for their future and they eventually relented. In the last twenty years she had moved almost as many times, and she was desperate for a place in which to settle. Orchard Manor served her purpose, and she never moved again. It was to this address that yet another bill came, this time for £1,500 in unpaid bills and damages from her previous tenancy, a modern, ranch-style house called Gurvjeer in Virginia Water, Surrey. Diana denied responsibility, claiming to have moved out in June 1967, but landlady Lila Kapoor countered that since Dante had taken over the lease, she had seen Diana there on several occasions. Given that Diana had no furniture and was using the money she was getting for *Hammerhead*, one of the two films she made that year, to furnish the house, it seems fairly likely that this was true. In her attempts to undermine Diana's credibility, however, Kapoor was overly dismissive about a 'P. Hayley' who sometimes wrote to her on Dante's behalf. 'So far as I know,' she said, 'there is no such person' – implying that Diana was carrying out a bizarre subterfuge – but Pat Hayley was actually a close friend.

The spiral of debt was offset by cash-in-hand club dates and personal appearances, but finally an interesting film script came her way. It was called *Baby Love*, and she was offered a quirky role playing mother to teenage starlet Linda Hayden, whose initial promise was – like Diana's – ill-served by the British film industry. Just as Diana found herself wasted in low-budget nonsense like *Is Your Honeymoon Really Necessary?* and *Miss Tulip Stays the Night*, so Hayden's CV told a story of its own: *Taste the Blood of Dracula* (1969), *Satan's Skin* (1970), *Something to Hide* (1972), *Confessions of a Window Cleaner* (1974), *Let's Get Laid* (1977). Diana once said her film appearances had 'mostly been in bedrooms, nightclubs or prison', but *Baby Love* was a new departure. She played a tarty cleaning lady who commits suicide, leaving her disturbed, sex-obsessed daughter (Hayden) alone in the world. But aside from a gaudy death scene, she appeared only in flashbacks and dream sequences, with no lines of dialogue. 'I think this will lead the way to the part I want for a big comeback,' she said optimistically.

Even if the right part had come along, it would have been too late to bail Diana out financially. A bankruptcy receiving order was taken out on 31 May 1968, although Diana did not attend the two-minute hearing. This did not mean, however, that she was officially bankrupt just yet and there was more public humiliation to come, starting with a meeting with the Official Receiver. At a further meeting of creditors, held in the Receiver's office on 5 July, Diana was estimated to owe £53,000, including tax, and a resolution was passed, voting to start bankruptcy proceedings. At the time, she had claimed to have just £5 13s at the bank and £197 10s to hand, with a credit limit of £10. Her fate was to be decided at a public enquiry on 3 October. It was an extraordinary fall from grace.

In a touching interview with Clive Hirschhorn of the *Sunday Express*, headlined 'I'm Trouble-Prone Says Diana', she spoke freely about her predicament. 'By rights, I should be dead now,' she said. 'And I mean that, literally. If I didn't have a sense of humour I'd have taken the proverbial overdose long ago. Or I'd have become an alcoholic, or the original bad cookie. All I can say is that I must have a hidden reserve of strength and resilience tucked away somewhere – and thank God for that! Whenever things seem absolutely hopeless – which is about fifty weeks out of fifty-two – I always seem to bounce back again.

'I've earned a million in my time,' she went on, 'or pretty near it, and it's all gone. And not on myself, either. I've always lived well, but to blow a million in ten years is just damn ridiculous! And when I think of the number of people who've sponged off me, I could be sick with anger. It really is terrifying how gullible and naive I was, and still am. I was so unworldly, I fell for hard-luck stories the way boys fall for girls.

'And just to make things worse, I surrounded myself with gangsters and conmen and phoneys. Don't ask me why, I just did. And thanks to them, I squandered away a fortune. Anyway, while it lasted I had a ball. Even in a crisis I had a capacity for enjoying life to the full. And still do. That's one thing about Dors: she knows how to live. I'm the epitome of the swinger.'

Diana arrived at the London Bankruptcy Court in a mini-skirt, facing a forty-five-minute investigation by Senior Official Receiver Wilfred Whitehead. The questioning was thorough, beginning with her first contract as a Rank player in 1947. She claimed, quite truthfully, that her career had reached its peak in the years 1955–56, and produced the relevant figures:

Year (ended 5 April)	Gross	After expenses (net)
1956	£19,165	£ 7,303
1957	£25,344	£15,923
1958	£27,996	£17,801
1959	£15,882	£13,086
1960	£10,717	£ 349

Diana said that in the early sixties she had been advised to start putting money away for future tax bills, but that she never did. Why not, she was asked? 'I was probably very foolish.' It did not look good that during this time, she had taken out three life assurance policies to benefit her sons' trust, paying as much as £999 a year, until 1965. 'Those policies were effected when you knew you were owing a considerable amount of tax?' asked Whitehead. 'Yes,' she replied. 'In June 1967 the policies were surrendered for £23,006. The money went to the solicitors for the trust.' (In actual fact, it most likely went to pay for Orchard Manor.)

The questioning continued, like a bizarre public press conference:

Q: You made no provision for tax, despite the fact, it has been reported, that you were earning up to £90,000 a year?

A: **Yes.**

Q: Would it be true to say you have not paid a penny tax from 1957–8 onwards?

A: **I think some was paid in the early 1960s.**

Q: But that was in respect of earlier years?

A: **No.**

Whitehead seemed incredulous that someone having earned so much could have lost it almost without trace, and accused her of putting her assets beyond the reach of her creditors. She denied it, although she more or less had. 'Are you saying,' he said with no small measure of sarcasm, 'that all this money simply trickled through your fingers?' She nodded. The hearing was adjourned and Diana ordered to return on 5 December, when she would face further questioning. But there were more pressing worries weighing on her mind. She told Hirschhorn: 'It's not the bankruptcy, and the litigations, and the bad publicity, and the scandals and all the things my name has been linked with that fill me with genuine despair but the mess I've made of my emotional life . . . and the failure of my marriage. These are the things that really hurt.

'And what makes me despair even further is the knowledge that it's highly unlikely I'll *ever* have a truly successful love affair. The fact that I'm in show business, which loads the dice against you anyway, and the fact that I've led a pretty hectic life, and that I'm a victim of my own image – oh, and all sorts of other neurotic things – make it almost impossible to think about ever having a successful, happy love life. It's just one of those hard, cold facts you have to face sooner or later. And it makes the future look pretty bleak.'

Chapter Twelve

MADAM TITS AND LIPS MEETS LAKE THE RAKE

THE INQUISITORS **WAS** to be the biggest break of Alan Lake's nine-year career. He was twenty-seven, a gypsy-haired Midlander whose sardonic good looks made him a natural TV villain, but this was his first lead role in a major network series. London Weekend Television had invested an impressive £150,000 in this, their first ever thriller series, and the network was hoping to recoup its costs by trying to siphon off *The Avengers'* cult kudos. Lake was to star with Tony Selby as one of a pair of detectives who used psychology to solve crimes, which was certainly a change from the 'accent parts' he was always being offered. His own accent was now a rich, theatrical boom, although there was still a flavour of his childhood in Stoke-on-Trent, where he was born on 24 November 1940.

Lake was impetuous and headstrong – always one for a dare, the idiot who jumped off the highest wall or railway bridge whenever anyone egged him on. He left school at fifteen, making a half-hearted living on the fringes of the town's famous pottery trade before becoming an actor full-time. When he moved to London in the early sixties, to take up a scholarship at the Royal Academy of Dramatic Arts (RADA), Lake quickly earned a certain notoriety that owed more to his drinking ability than any perceived talent. But that was the culture he came from, where drinking eleven pints a day was considered reasonable, manly behaviour. By the time he arrived in London, Lake could comfortably drink fourteen pints in a session – just lining them up, three at a time – until he threw up. The trouble was, he didn't get a hangover. He claimed he could drink half a bottle of Scotch at lunchtime and feel nothing whatsoever. His drinking exacerbated his moods, and when the mood was right he could be charming and funny, but his temper was famously quick and violent. His friends described him as 'dangerous', and sometimes they even meant it as a compliment.

Diana was asked to make a guest appearance in *The Inquisitors* and she readily agreed. Obviously, she needed the money, but she'd seen Lake before, back in July, when he played the title role in an ITV *Half-Hour Theatre* presentation called 'Thief', and she'd liked what she'd seen. Lake thought quite the opposite, and when the director told him she was to be the guest star he rolled his eyes and drawled, 'Ah, yes, Madam Tits and Lips.' Lake wanted to be part of the new wave, one of the Richard Harrises, the Peter O'Tooles, and Diana Dors seemed so much part of fossilized British history it wasn't even funny.

Diana was to appear in the pilot episode, called 'The Peeling of Sweet P Lawrence', playing a hardboiled stripper called Sweet P who witnesses a crime but refuses to give evidence. Lake arrived for the read-through on the morning of 10 October 1968 expecting to find her – assuming she'd even turned up – in the middle of a tantrum, a hurricane in mink, surrounded by sycophants who were trying to protect her from finding out just how past it she really was. When he arrived at the rehearsal room – a Territorial Army hall, just off Bond Street – he found her perched on a rickety wooden chair, reading quietly, dressed in a low-key woollen twin-set and a red leather coat. 'This is Alan,' said the director, taking him over. 'He calls you Madam Tits and Lips.' Lake was horrified, but Diana just laughed.

He was surprised how down-to-earth and funny she was,

and she, in turn, was equally bowled over. Lake was very easy to get to know – a wonderful, witty storyteller and full of life. It was like being hit by an express train, she said later. They had lunch together and Diana matched him with a Scotch. Lake hadn't been reading the papers and didn't know the first thing about her, so he was surprised when she told him she wasn't married. She didn't tell him about Troy Dante, however, but she'd already decided that Troy was on the way out. Likewise, Lake didn't tell her that he had a daughter from a previous relationship, whom he'd never actually met.

The following day, Lake decided to take her out, and they ended up at the Colony, a famously louche club in the heart of London. Diana didn't know all of Lake's haunts, but she was still quite streetwise, sometimes bumping into Susan Shaw, whose reputation was becoming so bad that by the time she drank herself to death in 1978, even the seedier clubs had started banning her. Diana and Lake sat in the Colony till closing time, when the chairs were stacked noisily and the bar staff turfed them out into the street.

The next day Lake proposed, and a few weeks later, on 29 October 1968, he made the engagement official with an amethyst and silver ring – a Mexican antique handed down to Lake by his uncle. Friends were horrified, but Diana shrugged off the ten-year age difference. 'I have a mental age of 12,' she said. 'Who's counting the difference in years? For me, it was love at first sight.' Her sex-kitten image was well and truly shattered soon after when, on 8 November, the BBC broadcast a one-hour play called *Where Have all the Ghosts Gone?* in which she played a bitter, middle-aged alcoholic who blames her teenage daughter for her husband's death and tries to sabotage the girl's pending marriage.

On 23 November 1968, Diana married Lake in a brisk twelve-minute service at Caxton Hall, where she'd married Dennis all those years before. Swinging with the times, Diana wore a fashionable white lace mini dress and matching lace cape, designed by Eric Darnell, while Lake wore a wide-lapelled black velvet suit and white frill-fronted shirt. The guest list reflected the age difference in more subtle ways – old friends like Lionel Jeffries and Sandra Dorne mingled at the reception with newcomers like John Walker of the Walker Brothers. In time-honoured fashion, Diana was not averse to publicizing her nuptials – that night, she and her new husband appeared on a TV show hosted by former DJ Simon Dee, one of the most dazzling and short-lived success stories of the youth revolution.

Diana was back in the news again, and the wedding stories at least deflected attention away from her money troubles, if only for the moment. The Official Receiver had been reading the news, too, however, and when Diana's bank-ruptcy hearing came up again on 6 December, Wilfred Whitehead seemed very interested in the reception. 'Did you pay for it?' he asked. 'No,' she replied, but the mystery benefactor was not revealed. The next sixty-five minutes were among the most gruelling of her life. Diana knew she'd made mistakes but she was not a woman to dwell on the past, and the whole rigmarole just seemed like a sadistic exercise in ritual humiliation. She was questioned repeatedly about solicitors' letters she had obviously received and apparently never acted on, but she found the manner of her inquisition almost indecent, as though she were being perse-cuted to satisfy some kind of perverted thrill. 'It's my fault,' she finally admitted. 'I never read letters properly. I have been downright irresponsible right down through the years, and that's why I'm in the mess I am today.'

The missing money formed the bulk of the questioning, specifically cash payments being made for club dates. Diana said it was being saved to pay her creditors. The next charge was more serious, however, and she was warned that if she was actually concealing assets or, as they suspected with the house in Angelo Drive, deliberately signing them away, she would be liable to a prison sentence of up to two years. 'It appears,' said Arthur Figgis, representing the creditors, 'that either you are trying to put assets out of the reach of your creditors or that you have no assets because you are giving away your earnings. Which is it?' Diana didn't reply. To make things clearer, Figgis simply asked, 'Do you have any assets hidden away in the names of other people?' Technically, the answer was yes, but her house was not 'hidden away', it was gone forever. She would never set foot in it again, except as a guest, and signing it away had benefited only her husband and their sons. She answered, feeling quite honest, 'No.'

She left the court feeling like a naughty schoolgirl, having promised to keep in touch with the trustee representing her creditors, who would then regulate her payments. Journalists were out in force, and Diana met them with an uncharacteristically heavy heart. She could see their pens at the ready, dipped in vitriol, hoping to write the last chapter in the Diana Dors story. At that moment, she didn't know who was gloating most about her downfall, the tax man or the media. A reporter asked if she was broke. 'Of course I'm not broke,' she replied. 'How can I be with such a fantastic earning potential as I have?' Was she working, someone asked? Actually, she was unemployed, but she had an answer to that, too. 'I'm working at being Mrs Lake,' she said. 'I will never sign on at the Labour Exchange, whatever happens.'

Diana went home to Sunningdale and to Lake, who had really been her backbone throughout the ordeal. She had the feeling that her luck was about to change, and her new husband absorbed much of the stress that the trial had caused her. Unlike Dennis, Lake certainly wasn't after her money; he even had talent. 'I may be earning more than Alan at the moment,' she told a journalist shortly before the wedding, 'but I believe the position will soon be reversed.'

She truly thought so, but the first week of January 1969 proved her wrong – before a single episode was aired, LWT announced that *The Inquisitors* had been scrapped. The network was pleased with the cast, and everyone was paid, but the series wasn't really what its paymasters wanted. 'The idea just didn't pan out,' said a spokesman, unhelpfully.

Diana's friends were wary of her new husband, and their suspicions seemed to be confirmed less than two weeks after the wedding, when Lake was arrested outside a Chinese restaurant in Egham, Surrey. He was suffering from tonsilitis and had decided to stay in the car while Diana and some friends went for a meal. Bundled up in the passenger seat, Lake was woken by a policeman with a flashlight, who asked to see his licence and produce the keys. Lake was not a driver, but his response was clearly so belligerent that a police car was called and he was taken off to the cells, where he spent the night.

When the case came to court, Lake was charged with being drunk and disorderly and using violent behaviour in a police station, but the arrest hinged on a technicality that proved hard to defend in court. Lake was initially picked up as a suspected drink-driver, but he was not the driver of the vehicle, nor was he over the limit, as a breathalyser test showed, so had he not been arrested there would never have been any 'crime'. Lake was not a man to back down and his behaviour probably did warrant a caution, but the police were not willing to risk bad publicity and dropped the case.

Diana's friends were concerned. Was Lake going to be Dennis Hamilton in reverse, splashing her name across the papers for all the wrong reasons? He loved Diana very much, they didn't doubt that, but he was very possessive and jealous, even with old friends like Kim and Lionel Jeffries. At first he used to jump when anyone tried to chat her up, but he soon got used to that and re-drew the line. But if anyone tried to go any further, they'd get panned. 'If Diana ever messed about,' he said much later, 'then there'd be trouble. I'd go mad, I know that. The bloke involved would take a long time to die. He'd be more than happy to go in the end.'

She was pregnant within two months of the wedding, and it was announced in January that she would be having another baby in the autumn of 1969. She took most of the year easy, more out of necessity than choice, but she wasn't ready to become another dowdy mum-to-be. Modelling a range of 'young mother' clothes by Page Boy Maternities – which was a bit optimistic at the age of thirty-seven – she posed for the *People* in a range of above-the-knee, A-line zip-up dresses and trouser suits made from rayon and washable Courtelle. 'I'm just not the twice-a-week-to-the-clinic and flat shoes type,' she conceded. 'I've never rated the maternity bit as a great emotional wonderland. Now, actually holding your baby, that *is* something. But the waiting . . . you can keep it.'

The name 'Caroline Jane' was again on stand-by, but Diana was not too concerned whether the child was a boy or a girl. 'Whatever I have – a son or a daughter – I figure that I won't criticize the life my kids want to lead. And they musn't knock what I do. With my reputation, I think that's quite a bargain. Don't you?' A boy, Jason, was born on 11 September 1969, at a London nursing home, weighing 7 lb 14 oz. 'He's going to be an actor, like his father,' Diana decided.

Early the next year, Lake was sent a script which promised great things. It was a comedy called *Three Months Gone*, by playwright Donald Howarth, which was to be staged at the

Royal Court Theatre in London's Sloane Square. Oddly, Diana was sent a copy, too, and she just couldn't figure it out. It seemed to be about a shy young girl and her wimpy, frustrated boyfriend, but other strange characters came and went, who seemed to be entirely imaginary – just figments of her imagination. She said to the author, 'I must be honest, Donald, I don't get it. Please explain it to me.' He didn't, or wouldn't, so she refused the role she was offered – that of the boyfriend's mother, a sluttish, sex-crazed landlady. But the producers kept on coming back until she finally relented. Lake was playing one of her lodgers, and since they had some good, funny scenes together, she decided to take it.

Three Months Gone opened on 28 January 1970 and was immediately hailed as Diana's comeback. The play itself was considered tricksy and pretentious, but her performance won raves from everybody, including Sir Laurence Olivier, who rushed backstage and made effusive remarks to the effect that people would soon be talking about the Lakes in the same way they talked about the Lunts, a reference to American actor Alfred Lunt and his wife Lynn Fontanne. 'When you've done a lifetime's cheesecake,' said Diana, 'the status you get from a well-done kiss from Olivier is something.'

It also brought a new world of possibilities. 'Being a sex symbol made me and killed me at the same time,' she said. 'It was lovely – but it never led to anything else. Now it's like having a new career. I'm looked on as a theatre actress instead of the sexy joke that I've been for God knows how many years. It's this play that made that possible, and the odd thing is that I wasn't too keen on it at first. I didn't understand it. I'm not really sure I understand it now, but agreeing to be in it was the smartest thing I've ever done.'

The play's success brought a flood of offers. By the time it transferred to the West End's Duchess Theatre, Lake was due to release a pop record ('He's got a bigger voice than Tom Jones,' boasted Diana), a comedy series was being written for them both, and Diana was soon to fly out to West Germany for a movie. She would play a man-hungry matron who tries to seduce one of her young charges in Jerzy Skolimowski's *Starting Out*, later re-titled *Deep End*. For the first time in years her love life and professional life seemed to be running smoothly. In fact, she was so happy, she wasn't bothered about her increase in size, although she claimed to be only 10 lb over her starlet weight. 'Contentment ruins your figure,' she said. 'I suppose I should lose a little weight, but there's really no incentive. I am just so superbly happy being me that I don't get around to it.'

But her happiness was short-lived. Lake's run in the play was suddenly interrupted and an understudy took his place on the night of 13 July. Lake was suffering from bruised knuckles and wounded pride after an altercation at a local pub at the weekend had got out of hand. He'd been down to their local, the Red Lion Hotel, on Saturday, taking Jason with him in his pram. According to Diana, Jason had 'a taste' for champagne, as a comforter. When Lake gave him perry instead, the child wouldn't drink it and they left without paying. The following night, Lake went back there with Diana's old friend Lee Graham, who'd recently had a big hit with 'Little Arrows' – a quirky, catchy pop record that he claimed, 'bridged the gap between "Boiled Beef And Carrots" and the commercially ridiculous.' They'd already been in for a lunchtime session, then gone back for a few drinks at Orchard Manor and then straight back to the Red Lion. They'd been in the pub a couple of hours when the relief manager, Anthony Stack, remembered the perry and asked Lake for three shillings to cover it. Lake refused and an argument broke out – just swearing at first, but when Graham tossed his beer glass at Stack's head, a couple of regulars moved in and a fight broke out. Lake was knocked to the ground and Lee punched his attacker in the face, breaking his nose. The fight moved outside, more glasses were thrown, windows were broken and Graham was hit over the head with a pump handle. Finally, Graham produced a knife – some witnesses claimed Lake had handed it to him, saying, 'Here, use this!' – and lunged at Stack, who darted sideways but the knife slashed his arm, making a long wound that needed eighteen stitches. The police took Lake and Graham in for questioning the following day and then released them. A month later, however, they were formally charged with grievous bodily harm and causing malicious damage costing £23 10s, and a court appearance was set for 2 September.

Despite the bad publicity Lake's court case had attracted (or most likely because he was unaware of it), Dawson allowed their sons, Gary and Mark, to visit Diana. In order to spend more time with them, she arranged a reciprocal trip to the States and, after consultation with the authorities, Lake was given permission to leave the country for three and a half weeks. Diana found the boys happy and in good health, but there was something too grown-up about their set up. Dawson had not yet remarried, and Diana thought they lived more like three bachelors, not father and sons. The slang they used was advanced for their years, and she worried about them falling in with Hollywood's fast track and wasting their young lives. They were also having trouble accepting any new woman who entered their father's life, and Diana blamed their nanny, Amy Brennan, an elderly spinster who had been with the family since 1960, for putting ideas into their heads.

Brennan interpreted this as an assault on her integrity, a suggestion that she saw the boys as her meal ticket and resented any woman who might marry their father and put her out of a job (which wasn't so very far-fetched). Diana and Brennan rarely saw eye to eye, but from this moment on the relationship worsened. In Diana's mind, she was Barbara Stanwyck in *Stella Dallas*, the gallant mother who made great sacrifices for her children; in Brennan's mind, she had abandoned her children and expected them to drop everything when she made her rare flying visits.

Neither was right, and they locked horns continually until Brennan's death in the summer of 1974 – most notably in a long, heartfelt article Diana wrote for *Woman's Own* magazine, without the aid of a ghost writer, published in February that year. Diana poured her heart out, claiming that Brennan had turned the boys against her. 'Why, you may be wondering, did I, Diana Dors, a strong personality and an independent woman, allow this situation to continue?' she mused. 'But I felt sorry for my husband and sympathized with his problems, even though he infuriated me at times and domestic help in Hollywood is so difficult to get that I could not afford to tell Nanny what I thought of her and kick her out.'

She went on to explain her reasons for leaving the boys behind. 'My career, although I had worked all the time, had hit the doldrums,' she admitted. 'I was continually employed in cabaret but films were very scarce. In short, I was a "has-been", trading commercially on my once famous sex-symbol name around all the worst working men's clubs in the country. Was this the life, then, for me to offer my sons? Should I have dragged them around the Northern towns where I worked, living in hotels, and in a cold-weather climate they weren't used to?'

The article ended on a forlorn note: 'One day, perhaps they will grow up and want to get to know me, even love me. Who knows?'

When Lake's case came to court, at Berkshire Assizes, Diana was nervous but quietly confident. Lake didn't have a criminal record and he was pleading guilty, which they thought would help considerably. After hearing all the evidence, however, the presiding magistrate, Mr Justice Eveleigh, was not impressed. Graham was sentenced to three years imprisonment for the wounding of Anthony Stack, plus a separate nine months, to run concurrently, for causing damage to the property. Lake, as an accessory, received a hefty eighteen months, with the same penalty for the damage. 'Crimes of violence are all too prevalent today,' said Justice Eveleigh in his summation. 'It must not be thought that anyone can indulge in this sort of behaviour without being sent to prison.'

Diana was distraught. She had a car waiting to take them to Leeds, where she was to start filming a new Yorkshire TV sitcom – *Queenie's Castle* – written specially for her by Keith Waterhouse and Willis Hall. Lake was to be in it, too, but instead of being chauffeured up north he was already being taken down into the cells. Diana made a miserable figure, wrapped up in a thigh-length white mink that made her look like an ageing gangster's moll. 'I'm absolutely staggered,' she gasped. 'Terribly shocked. It's a very harsh and savage sentence – I can hardly believe it. There will definitely be an appeal.'

An appeal was granted and duly heard several months later. In Lake's absence he was represented by Michael Sherrard QC, who fully accepted the charges on his client's behalf. 'When the hangovers had subsided,' he said, 'it became plain that Lake's hard-built career was in peril ... It [was] a frightful result of ten minutes' violence, ten minutes' loss of temper and ten minutes' befuddled judgment.' Lord Justice Phillimore was not impressed in the least, and his pronouncement was actually worse than the original verdict. 'If there was any criticism to be made,' he announced sternly, 'the sentence on Lake might have been more severe. It was he who handed the knife to Graham and encouraged him to use it.'

Lake was transferred to Oxford prison, Graham to Parkhurst, where the inmates greeted him with amusement.

''Ullo, son,' said one. 'You've really got yer li'l arrers
nah . . .'

Diana soldiered on alone with *Queenie's Castle*. She loved
the role. She played Queenie Shepherd, a plain-speaking
council-flat living harridan who terrifies the residents of a
northern tower block as much as her dysfunctional family –
three sons, a brother-in-law and an AWOL husband. It was
quite cathartic under the circumstances, and the two women
had a lot in common. Like Queenie, Diana was used to
people talking about her behind her back, but Queenie
wouldn't put up with it, as she did – Queenie was fearless,
outspoken and awesomely rude. Through Queenie, Diana
had a release for all her frustrations, and she kept a soft spot
for it long after it was axed, after just a couple of series.
Diana blamed the network, claiming Yorkshire TV thought
her character was just *too* downmarket.

She plied her usual trade for the rest of the year, slotting
cabaret dates alongside TV work and a film role in *Hannie
Calder*, a bizarre, vaguely feminist western shot in Spain and
starring Raquel Welch as a woman taking revenge on the
men who killed her husband. In between, Diana visited Lake
as often as she could, taking in a flask of orange juice laced
with vodka, counting the days until his release. 'There is
nothing more to be done now,' she said philosophically.
'Alan will just have to serve his sentence.'

With good behaviour, Lake's sentence was commuted to
twelve months, and at 7 a.m. on 16 October 1971, he was
picked up from Verne Prison, a semi-open jail in Portland,
Dorset, and taken to a house in nearby Weymouth, where
Diana had laid on a private champagne reception. Posing
with Alan and Jason in white knee-boots and a thigh-length
jersey dress, she was back to her old self, although she did
draw the line at interviews. 'Sorry, boys – no talks,' she told

waiting reporters. 'But you can see that this is *the* day of my life.' Back at Orchard Manor, Diana had arranged a welcoming party of friends, and as a token of her love she presented him with a horse, which they called Sapphire.

Lake's release was quite an event, and Michael Parkinson recorded an interview with the couple less than a week later. The show was due to be broadcast at 11.05 p.m. on 24 October, but the BBC's head of light entertainment, Bill Cotton, pulled the plug. 'We couldn't run the show because he comes over as such a likeable fellow,' he said, and it was thought that running the interview might suggest that the BBC had in some way 'condoned' his behaviour. Instead of the Lakes, viewers were treated to a more innocuous chat with Sarah Miles and Big Chief Red Fox. Curiously, it was not the only programme the BBC pulled that night. Cliff Michelmore's *A Chance To Meet* . . . series was scheduled to include an interview with Richard Neville, editor of psychedelic underground magazine *Oz*. Neville was at that time being tried for obscenity, so Richard Ingram, then editor of *Private Eye*, was brought in as a slightly less risqué replacement.

The court case had brought enough trouble, but Lake's career took another blow in February 1972, while he was out riding Sapphire in Windsor Great Park. Lake crouched to avoid an overhanging branch, but the horse reared at precisely the wrong moment and crushed him against the tree, breaking two vertebrae, his shoulder and a rib; wearing a helmet had spared him a fractured skull. Given morphine to ease the pain, Lake was kept in hospital for three weeks until doctors were satisfied with his condition and he was allowed to go home. He still suffered pain when he walked and he was later readmitted for traction, but that was nothing, thought Diana. He was lucky to be alive, let alone walking.

That year, she worked with Lionel Jeffries again, the first time they'd done so since *Man of the World* in the early fifties.

Jeffries was casting for his new film, a family ghost story called *The Amazing Mr Blunden*. 'Anything in it for me?' she asked him. Jeffries thought he was taking a risk but he asked her anyway. 'Well, yes,' he replied. 'Do you want to play a harridan?' 'I'm there,' she said.

She worked extremely hard to establish her character – the evil Mrs Wickens. It wasn't an easy part – she'd never played such a grotesque character before in her life. When Jeffries insisted she wore a wart on her nose she couldn't *wait* to do it. The more horrific the make-up people could make her, the more she laughed – at last, she'd finally landed a part that didn't trade on her sexuality, past or present, real or imagined.

Diana knew that Jeffries and his wife were Roman Catholics, but the subject was never discussed and the couple were surprised when Diana announced one night that she and Alan were taking religious instruction. Nevertheless, they happily agreed to sponsor the Lakes' conversion, which – given the small matter of Diana's previous divorce – caused a few theological headaches. Finally, after a year of instruction and debate, Diana and her husband were accepted by the church in a small private service at Sunningdale's Church of the Sacred Heart in the spring of 1974. What prompted this, Diana never really made clear. Lake had discovered the church sometime previously, when a housekeeper suggested he might find it calming. He hadn't had much work after the accident and his drinking was getting worse, leaving great black moods of remorse.

For her part, Diana was perhaps looking for something to hold on to through the rough times, which seemed to be coming more and more regularly – almost exactly a year after Alan's accident, she was admitted to a hospital with a broken leg after falling down some steps outside a nightclub in Barnsley. It was an absurd accident: a woman she'd met had been telling Diana about her husband's mistress, and when she pointed to the house where the affair was conducted, Diana craned to see and slipped on her high heels. The injury was serious enough to warrant an operation, leaving her laid up in hospital for two weeks. As if that wasn't enough, Aunt Kit died of cancer later that summer. Diana was left the house in Marlborough Road and she made all the necessary arrangements for the sale. It was her home and it held many memories, but what use was it now? She didn't want to live in the past.

But it's possible there were much more personal reasons, for her conversion – Diana wanted to erase the years of bad publicity and false impressions, answering to nobody but her maker. 'I look back at my life up to now,' she told journalist Ian Woodward, 'and I think, Well, I've been so totally selfish and so totally self-centred and everything has been me, me, me. I mean, I've done marvellously, but there are bigger things in life and also things that can make you, inwardly, a much happier person – not because you're being a goody-goody or being some sort of hypocrite, saying, "I go to church now and that's a good insurance" . . . It's hard to explain it, really, because a lot of people scoff and say, "Oh well, I suppose you'd *have* to, I mean, you didn't turn to drink – something had to happen!" But it isn't that, it isn't that at all. I find great happiness in it.'

Some years earlier, while *Three Months Gone* was in full swing, she said as much to another interviewer – and not for the last time: 'You know, in the films, I was always a bad girl with a heart of gold,' she mused. 'I always repented in the end. You always knew I was all right really. Maybe that's how it will be.'

When *Queenie's Castle* finished its run – 'temporarily', viewers were assured, although the series was axed – Diana made a quick follow-up with *All Our Saturdays*, a less successful variation on the same theme. This time she played a Yorkshire woman, improbably called 'Di Dorkins', who inherits an amateur rugby team. But without Willis' and Waterhouse's keen sense of social satire, it degenerated into sex-war farce – Dorkins renaming the team 'Frilly Things' to promote her clothing company, for example.

But Diana enjoyed doing television and wanted to find her niche – which meant she was absolutely aching to do her own talk show. 'Let's face it, television is the only medium where you can be yourself,' she said to Woodward. 'I mean, you can't sit on a stage, or in a film, and talk as I am to you, now, but with television and the talk shows you can. I've always wanted my own talk show and perhaps they'll finally give me it. But the thing is, I've always done a lot of cabaret – and still do, because it's very lucrative – and I've noticed that the rapport I have with the audience is so much better when I stop singing and doing flip lines. I get the feeling, and I may be wrong, that people are thinking, well, come on, never mind all the singing and putting on the perform-ance – let's hear her talk about when she made such-and-such a film, or what she's got to say, or what makes her tick.

'And I just feel that warmth coming from the audience when I stop performing and start being myself, and this is why I primarily feel that I am a personality first and secondly an actress, because England is a very small island and once you've made it over here, that's it. It's not like America, where you make it one minute and tomorrow you're forgotten. Once they accept you in England, that's it – you're there, for always. That's one of the lovely things about this country.'

Diana's wish was granted that summer with a pilot for a pet chat show, punningly titled *Paws for Dors*, with guest stars Dudley Moore, Zsa Zsa Gabor and the Marquis of Bath. A series did not follow, but her profile was significantly raised the following year, after it was announced in December 1973 that Diana was to appear at the highbrow Chichester festival playing Jocasta in Keith Michell's production of *Oedipus*, Sophocles' classic play. The casting stunned the broadsheet critics, who looked at her with new eyes. Diana could guess what they were thinking. 'If people come expecting *Queenie's Castle*,' she said, 'with Keith Michell parading round like a Greek hero, all dressed in white, saying, "Goodness I'm having intercourse with my mother!" then they'll be disappointed.'

She admitted, however, that she nearly passed on the part. 'I began to feel I'd got past wanting to act,' she said. 'I didn't want to pretend to be someone else. I'd reached the stage where I didn't *want* to be anybody else. I was happy to be me.' These words perhaps came back to haunt her when the play was staged in June 1974, generating lukewarm reviews. 'The best that can be said for her is that she's a game girl,' said *Express* critic Herbert Kretzmer, suggesting in no uncertain terms that she was way out of her depth. Diana took criticism in her stride, and was probably more scathing about flattery, especially when the honours list was mentioned. 'God forbid!' she exclaimed. "Dame Diana" doesn't bear thinking about. It makes me sound like Arthur Askey!'

When *Oedipus* finished its run, Diana extended her gallery of grotesqueries to take the lead role in *Nurse Will Make it Better*, an episode of ATV's gleefully macabre *Thriller* series. Perhaps bowing to her darkest thoughts about Amy Brennan, she jumped at the chance to play an evil nanny who manipulates and destroys a whole family. In the final scenes, 'nurse' reveals herself to be the devil incarnate – which perhaps Diana could relate to. But a part that was intended to be a bit of fun brought nothing but trouble. Filming began in October, at Elstree Studio, and on the drive up, she witnessed a fatal car crash, the set was flooded after a freak rainstorm, and a prop crucifix mysteriously snapped in two. Diana, who had often taken part in séances since her mother died, was not amused. 'I believe in such things as black magic and the force of evil,' she said, 'and there were moments when I wished I had not taken part.'

Worse was to come. A month later, Diana was sitting at home when she began developing headaches and strange body aches. The pain grew so bad she felt as though her head were being split open with a meat cleaver. A doctor was called and Diana was immediately rushed to the National Hospital for Neurological Diseases in London, where meningococcal meningitis was diagnosed. Lake had planned a surprise dinner for her at the White Elephant Club in Curzon Street, but instead she spent much of the evening shaking and sweating in the grip of a fever. When Lake was told she might not last the night, he fainted, bruising himself as he fell. To get a break, he had a quick drink with a journalist in the pub over the road, and as they headed back to the hospital one of the regulars shouted out, 'You go back there and tell her we're all rooting for her. She's one of the all-time great birds!' Lake was worried sick. Even if she lived, what then? Where he came from, in Stoke-on-Trent, meningitis was like the plague. People never recovered – and if they did, they were deaf, dumb, blind . . . or worse. Just before midnight she opened her eyes and asked for him; Lake was elated. The following morning he received a call from a journalist. 'Tell me,' the voice said, 'is Diana dead or hanging on? I can't get any sense from the hospital . . .'

Diana was very much hanging on, and within a few days her room was filled with cards and flowers from well-wishers. Old friends had visited, and even screen legends like Joan Crawford and Myrna Loy had telephoned . . . Diana was touched by their affection but pretended to be bemused. 'They might have known I'd have pulled through,' she said. 'I'm a bit of old Britain – part of the bricks and mortar. And we don't go that easily, do we, love?'

In truth, had Diana's arrival in hospital been delayed by more than two hours, she could easily have died. She was discharged on 3 December 1973 and given so much medication that for the next few months her body clock seemed to be going crazy. The mystery resolved itself early the following year, when tests revealed that she was pregnant again, at the age of forty-two. Believing herself to be past the age when such matters were important, the Lakes hadn't used contraception in quite a while.

The baby was due in October, but Diana wasn't sure if she could go through with it. Her doctor said that, in view of her age, a termination was perhaps the best course of action and that he was prepared to arrange it. She agreed and an appointment was made for her at a clinic in Brighton, but when the day came, she wept at the wheel of her car. She couldn't go through with it. 'Catholic or no Catholic, I would have gone ahead if I genuinely felt there was going to be something wrong with the baby,' she said several months later. 'But I knew that if I did I could no longer walk into a Catholic church.'

The news was made public in May, and Diana was looking forward to being a mother again. She was trying to do right by Jason, and it almost seemed that by having another child she was trying to show that she wasn't a bad mother, to prove that things might have been better with Mark and Gary if the circumstances had been different. 'This wonderful, unexpected pregnancy is the great gift of my tranquil middle age,' she told vintage agony aunt Marjorie Proops, with whom she was quite candid about her memories. 'The past was lurid and rotten. Best forgotten. I truly believe that, for me, life is beginning at 40 – well, nearly 44 to be actual. I'm getting as fat as a house and I don't give a damn. Fat and happy, that's me. Fulfilled at last, I guess. And lucky at last.'

Diana's tranquillity was broken slightly when porn magazine *Cockade* printed a photo of a bare bottom being spanked, claiming it was Diana's and that the picture had been taken on the set of a recent ribald comedy she'd made, called *The*

Amorous Milkman. Diana was outraged and threatened to sue. 'I have never appeared nude in public and I don't intend to start. It's degrading,' she said. 'I know it's not mine. There were a great number of girls slipping naked through the film, and it is one of their bottoms.' The matter was cleared up when twenty-six-year-old actress Jenny Westbrook identified and claimed the mystery buttocks. 'The bottom is mine,' she reportedly said. 'I'd recognize it anywhere.'

This bizarre distraction was nothing beside the awful news coming. Diana hadn't been feeling well for some time and towards the end of the summer her blood pressure became abnormally high. She couldn't feel the baby moving, and when she consulted a doctor he was unable to find a heartbeat. There was a very strong possibility that the baby was dead, but she was advised against a termination in the faint hope that the child was still alive. She was booked into hospital for tests at the beginning of September. When she was rushed into hospital on 28 August, she held out hopes of finally having a little girl. Lake rushed to be with her; he'd heard from his friends what an incredible experience being at the birth was, so he was desperate to be there. What was meant to be one of the happiest days of his life turned out to be one of the most traumatic. Instead of a healthy, living child, he turned to see the surgeon cradling the tiny, 2 lb 3 oz body of their dead son. 'Suddenly,' said Lake, 'I felt everyone was against me. I went against God.' Diana was more philosophical. 'It was ghastly, but it's over now and I must get on with things,' she said. 'I really longed for that baby, but I just have to accept what happened . . . I can't just lie here like the Lady of the Camellias.'

She needed to press on, to occupy her mind. The very next day, she was on the phone to her agent. 'Get me some work,' she said. The following Friday, she appeared on *Celebrity Squares.*

Chapter Thirteen

TWENTIETH-CENTURY BOADICEA

AT FORTY-FOUR, DIANA began thinking of another way to cash in on her fame, a way that didn't involve hawking her body round working men's clubs while leering men spilt their beer on Formica-topped tables and hollered, 'Get yer tits out!' Wolf Rilla, a writer and former film director had approached Diana with a view to writing her biography, and it was an opportunity she relished. She'd thought about it for years, since *Swingin' Dors* was published, but she wasn't sure about the legal ramifications. 'The trouble with me is, being a Scorpio, I want to be there when people read it,' she told Ian Woodward, 'I don't want to be dead and gone.' She spent hours taping conversations with Rilla and looked forward to reading it, but when the manuscript was handed to her – provisonally titled *Dors and Diana* – she didn't like it one little bit. 'I tell you,' she said later, 'I didn't know whose throat to cut first, mine or the writer's. The book was so depressing, so bleak, so *down*, and without any humour or gaiety and fun, that I was thoroughly depressed ... The proof I read was deadly dull. Anyone reading it would have fallen asleep.' She concluded: 'I shall write my own version.'

Some years later she did. Diana's appetite for writing had been whetted by the *Woman's Own* article she'd had printed and she went on to publish several books over the next few years – mostly in an easy-to-edit A-to-Z format, like *For Adults Only* (1978), *Behind Closed Dors* (1979) and *Diana*

Dors' A–Z of Men (1984). The latter was actually written in 1980 and proved too much for publishers W.H. Allen, who dropped it after the company's nervous libel lawyers refused to sign off the manuscript, originally called *Man Born of Woman*. Sometimes, though, she claimed she wasn't sure she was even old enough to write an autobiography. 'I've got at least another 40 years to go,' she told *TV Times*.

Diana was in an especially reflective mood and where she was once self-deprecating about her appearance, she now seemed positively critical. She had seen herself on the Derek Nimmo show a couple of years before and thought how awful she looked, how bawdy – like a dreadful Hogarthian whore – and the view wasn't getting any better. 'When I catch myself at a bad angle in my mirrors – they're all round my bedroom – I tell myself it's not me,' she said. 'When I'm not looking in a mirror I kid myself I'm all right. I never had a pretty face, that's why I still wear all the candyfloss hair to hide it.'

The weight was creeping up on her, but the reality didn't really bother Diana quite as much as the thought. It actually helped her performance as Violet Elizabeth's mother in a TV adaptation of Richmal Crompton's *Just William* books. Diana hadn't, of course, read any – as a girl she sat with her nose in *Picturegoer* – but Alan filled her in and explained the characters. 'Mrs Bott is great fun to play,' she said. 'I can be as vulgar as I like. The Botts are real hypocrites, the sort of terrible people I have always detested.'

The work still wasn't flooding in, but she began taking it easy, spending the time at home with Jason wherever possible. 'I've had 30 years in this business, let's face it, darling,' she said, 'it doesn't hold much enchantment for me.' She was also trying to support Alan, whose career hadn't really taken off in the way either of them had hoped. After good notices for his part in *Charlie Bubbles* (1968), Albert Finney's directorial debut, nothing much had come his way except the odd touring repertory production and more TV villainy. He worked out that in his professional life he had, at one time or another, been poisoned, shot, hanged, stabbed, gassed, driven off a cliff, thrown out of a window, kicked to death, flayed alive and – in one memorable instance – had his toes cut off with a shovel in *Flame* (1974), an unusually downbeat rock movie starring Midlands glam-rock band Slade. His reputation became so extreme that when he guested on the BBC's *Dr Who* series in the early eighties, hundreds of children wrote in to warn the doctor.

His career path, plus the awful memory of his stillborn child, encouraged Lake's worst alcoholic excesses. Ironically, he was paying for the booze with money earnt from a series of lager adverts, where he appeared dressed as Schubert. He was chosen, he thought, because he had the thirstiest voice in the world. 'Wives hate me,' he said. 'Their husbands only have to hear [the words], "Summer's rich madness is spent . . ." and they suddenly disappear to the local.'

Throughout the seventies the British film industry was in decline. Rank was about to cease production altogether in the summer of 1980, and of the films that were being made, many were cheap horrors, TV cash-ins or smutty sex comedies. Diana had more or less collected the set, making *Theatre of Blood* (1973), *Steptoe and Son Ride Again* (1973) and *Adventures of a Taxi Driver* (1975), a grim imitation of the lucrative but equally crass *Confessions of . . .* series. 'I hate what is happening in British cinema today,' she said in 1977. 'I still get sent film scripts but I reject them with alarming regularity. They're nearly all pornographic. They even want *me* to take my clothes off – I've never done that and never will. I know I was a sex symbol, but we knew how to be daring without having to show too much.'

In America, hardcore porn movies like *Deep Throat* (1972) and *The Devil in Miss Jones* (1973) were achieving almost mainstream crossover success in liberal states like New York and California, giving rise to what would later be called 'porno chic'. This was never likely to happen in repressed, censorious Britain, but softcore did attain a certain legitimate status through magazines like Paul Raymond's *Men Only* and media-friendly porn 'artistes' like Raymond's protegée, Fiona Richmond. British sex movies, however, were largely a progression from the saucy postcard era, laced with bathos and juvenile humour, and the first film which really caught the public's attention was George Harrison Marks' *Come Play With Me* (1977), bankrolled by up-and-coming porn millionaire David Sullivan.

Marks had risen to notoriety in the fifties with his nudie-cutie magazine *Kamera*, which featured naked beauties with ample bosoms and coyly airbrushed crotches. Marks' favourite model was Pamela Green – a statuesque blonde who never made it past cult status, despite a good-sized role in Michael Powell's controversial 1960 film, *Peeping Tom* – and featured her in one of his rare excursions into cinema, *Naked as Nature Intended* (1961), a boring, spuriously 'educational' travelogue that rewarded the dirty mac brigade with an all-nude finale. In the years between *Naked* and *Come Play With Me*, Marks' ham-fisted film-making had improved not a jot. Filled with cameos by near-dead celebrities like Irene Handl, Cardew Robinson and Queenie Watts, *Come Play With Me* featured its director and Alfie Bass as two currency forgers hiding out in a remote health farm. The arrival of a rock group and its busty entourage mysteriously transforms the place into a topless massage parlour, but Marks' dismally old-fashioned sensibility – lots of shots of stationary nudes and creaking vaudeville comedy – made this allegedly 'sexy' romp seem positively geriatric. Nevertheless, the film ran in the West End for over four years, a record unbeaten by any British movie since. Admittedly, the venue was Soho's Moulin cinema, which also showed such classics as *Three Into Sex Won't Go* and *Eskimo Nell*.

The reason for this was one of the film's featured stars, Mary Millington, a cheerfully uninhibited, thirty-two-year-old porn model whose rise to fame – or rather notoriety – had been meteoric since she was first discovered while working as a vet's assistant, when she used the money to pay for her terminally ill mother's health care. Millington didn't blanch at hardcore, even though the results were usually censored for her homeland, and her open, artless manner scored a hit with the public. She was born Mary Maxted, in 1945, but after appearing in Sullivan's *Whitehouse* magazine – a two-fingered salute to Christian clean-up campaigner Mary Whitehouse – the proprietor suggested she change her surname to match the magazine's editor, Doreen Millington, to give the impression that they were sisters and maybe spice up their readers' fantasies. Mary wore a special 'MM' pendant, which she rarely removed, partly in tribute to her heroine, Marilyn Monroe.

Millington's success showed just how much Monroe's era had faded in the last twenty years, and just how far Britain's sexuality had evolved in the post-permissive society. Next to Diana's modest, almost tastefully suggestive pin-ups, Millington's porno shoots looked like a gynaecologist's handbook. Tease was out, flesh was in, and Millington catered to these needs by opening her own sex shops in Norbury and Tooting, both in south London, stocking titles like *Weekend Sex* and *White Slave Girls* under the counter. In fact, her personal crusade against censorship brought her to the Old Bailey in November 1977, accused, with two directors of a publishing company called Kelerfern, of possessing obscene publications with intent to circulate them for gain.

Judge Lawton-Scott was not sympathetic and, in his final summation, asked the jury, 'When sex is reduced to the glorification of sex alone, with the absence of love, affection or permanent relationships, may it not then become an instrument of potential harm?' He concluded with a strange, almost surreal, analogy. 'Some of you may have been to the zoo and observed monkeys in their cage,' he droned. 'It sometimes happens that a female monkey is on heat, and the males – with astonishing rapidity and frequency – copulate with that female while she sits unconcernedly eating vegetables . . . It may have occurred to you that [this] perhaps is the kind of behaviour which distinguishes man from animals.'

Unlike her co-defendants, Millington was acquitted. 'I love sex, and I intend to carry on making a living from it,' she announced on the steps of the court. 'I don't consider anything I do to be obscene.'

The first thing Mary Millington went to work on was a follow-up to *Come Play With Me*. The film was called *Playbirds* (1978) – conveniently, also the title of one of producer Sullivan's other magazines – and Alan Lake was set to star as a swinging sex magazine editor whose models are being ritually murdered, one by one. Millington was to play an undercover police officer who poses as a model to lure the killer out of hiding. Tastelessly juggling kinky violence and titillating sex, *Playbirds* was a barometer of its times. Its casual misogyny was hardly considered an issue, and its toe-curling awfulness did not hinder its success at the box office – home video had yet to arrive, and the cinema was still the only place to see naked flesh in motion, however tame it seemed.

Mary Millington was not a gifted actress, to put it kindly, but cinema audiences forgave her terrible, flat squawk and willingly forked out for Sullivan and Millington's next opus, *Confessions from the David Galaxy Affair* (1979). Lake again signed up for what must certainly have been the worst film not only of his own career but of all his co-stars, too, including Derek Griffith, Bernie Winters and Tony Booth, later to become the father-in-law to Labour Prime Minister Tony Blair. Lake played a fraudulent astrologist, David Galaxy, whose crooked past catches up with him, but whatever vestige of dignity he'd retained from *Playbirds* was now entirely gone. Lake's performance was manic and embarrassing, all bulging eyes and dismally unfunny ad-libs; if cocaine was not responsible, someone had found a damn good substitute. Millington was the sex interest, playing a frigid woman called Millie sent to Galaxy to be 'cured'.

To keep an eye on him, Diana took a part as Galaxy's landlady, Jennie Stride and performed the film's breathy, twenties-style theme tune, perhaps its only likeable feature. Lake was supposed to keep his underpants on throughout the sex scenes and when she found out he'd been taking them off, Diana hit the roof. 'Alan was less inhibited when Diana was off the set,' claimed Sullivan. 'We had to have breaks so he could cool down.' However, Diana denied that she was being unduly possessive. 'I wouldn't dream of interfering in his work,' she said. 'It's only a job, you know, and it's no fun to have to pretend to be sexy. He's getting fed up with all these naked bodies.'

Which was not entirely true. 'These sex films are a laugh,' said Lake. 'You have five birds between the sheets and they're all trying to get you excited because it's part of their pride. It's a great feeling, lying back with a line of women all queuing up to throw themselves stark naked at you. But they don't get very far. When it's over I'm Alan Lake again, and then it's back home to the missus.'

Diana liked Mary Millington. There were only two things she hated, hypocrites and liars, and Mary was neither. Her profession left a lot to be desired but Diana admired her honesty and they became quite good friends. Millington, however, was having personal problems that were soon to have terrible consequences. Her mother had died a few years earlier, her shops were regularly being raided, the taxman was demanding a sum in the region of a quarter of a million pounds, and she was dabbling with prostitution, going to bed with politicians and entertainers whose names are still protected by libel laws. Drugs played their part, too, and Millington's insecurity showed itself in the strangest ways. If she slept with a man for pleasure she would first ask him for a pound – not as a fee but as a token, a sign that she had some kind of value – and this quirk blossomed into full-blown kleptomania.

Most of the time she didn't even bother hiding whatever she'd stolen; she wanted to be caught and she frequently was. On 18 August 1979, Millington was caught stealing a bracelet from a jewellery shop in Banstead, Surrey, which would not look good in court after at least two similar offences in the previous year. The following day she took an overdose of prescription tranquillizers, washed down with alcohol, and never recovered consciousness. She left a string of touchingly polite notes, apologising for her actions and asking for her money to go to Battersea Dogs Home, not the taxman. 'I never liked people, only animals,' she wrote.

The funeral was held at St Mary Magdalene Church in Holmwood, Surrey, on 24 August, a day when every porno cinema, mail order firm and sex shop in Britain stopped work as a mark of respect. The Lakes attended – the only celebrities in Millington's sad life who were willing to put their heads above the parapet and pay their last respects. In the pub afterwards, Alan climbed onto his chair, dead drunk, and tried to deliver a passionate speech about censorship and freedom. Almost before the words came out, he toppled backwards into a table filled with empty beermugs, sending them flying. There was more glass in that room than in the Crystal Palace.

Diana, for her part, was in a much more reflective mood. The glamour business had changed a lot since the fifties, but some things stayed depressingly constant. Another unhappy, unfulfilled sex symbol was resting in her grave.

Lake's drinking was hitting crisis point around this time. Diana had persuaded him to enter a clinic early in 1976 and he'd stayed sober for nearly four months, but the news that his mother was seriously ill with cancer caused him to relapse. He'd disappear to the local and didn't always make it back, sleeping off his hangovers in ditches and hedgerows. Landlords accused him of encouraging punch-ups, but he thought that was bullshit. Women giggled and pointed when they saw him, then told their boyfriends he'd been looking at them. Next thing, some bruiser would sidle along and hiss, 'You're looking at my bird, ain't you?' 'That's right,' he'd say. 'I was trying to put a price on her.' He just couldn't walk away from it.

Friends stopped coming round, or made their excuses, and they rarely went out. At parties and premieres, it was always the same, Diana standing in the doorway, ready to go, Lake filling his glass again. Alcohol did not mix with his temper, and when he was especially pissed he deliberately picked fights. 'I don't like you,' he'd goad. 'I don't like your face. I think you're a *cunt*.' In the morning, he couldn't remember a thing. 'Did I have a good time last night?' he'd ask. If he'd behaved particularly badly he'd be horrified but the shame wasn't enough to stop him. Vodka, whisky, brandy . . . he could really sink it. Diana tried to get him into rehab again, but she couldn't get through to him. 'We talked about it from time to time,' said Lake, 'but I never let go. I was roaring round like an eighteenth-century pirate – out of control.'

Gary flew over to stay with Diana in February 1979, but his presence did not temper Lake's drinking. In fact, Lake's problems were made glaringly public when he took the two boys up to see the Blackpool illuminations for Jason's tenth birthday. After being thrown out of the bar at their hotel, the four-star Imperial, for haranguing TUC delegates who were staying there for a conference, Lake drunkenly tried to gain entry to a nearby nightclub. When he was turned away, he produced a knife and waved it at the bouncers, who overpowered him without too much effort. The next day, bruised and remorseful, he was fined £150 for possession of an offensive weapon. 'My wife can do without this sort of publicity,' he sighed. Diana was more sanguine. 'At least he hasn't been leaping into bed with waitresses,' she said.

At 5 feet 11 inches, Lake was not an especially tall man, and his drinking caused him to put on an extra two stone in weight, ballooning up to thirteen stone. His trousers no longer fitted him and he sometimes wore a pair of Diana's green maternity slacks to go drinking down the pub. He just didn't care what he looked like any more, and he didn't care what effect his drinking, and the bad publicity, was having on his son. But then, Jason was pretty bright when it came to dealing with bullies. 'Well, what has your dad done to get in the papers?' he'd sneer. 'When he does, we'll compare the cuttings.'

The spur to give it up came when Lake's mother died in January 1980. He realized there was really no future in it, and that while his drinking had successfully blotted out his own heartache, it caused more for everyone around him. Something in Diana had snapped and she couldn't take any more. He hadn't hurt her yet, but it may only have been a matter of time — his tantrums could be terrifying. She left him, taking Jason with her, and went to stay with friends in Brighton. Lake begged her to return and he looked so sincere she agreed, on condition that he checked into a rehab clinic and faced his problem. She booked him into the same Northampton clinic she'd tried to get him into twice before.

'For two weeks after I dropped the bottle it was misery,'

he admitted. 'After three weeks it was bloody hell. After four weeks it was tempting to become a social drinker, but with me it's got to be all or nothing. I know now I shall never drink again.'

Not to be outdone, Gary claimed some headlines of his own during his brief stay in Britain. On 11 July 1979, the seventeen-year-old appeared at Chertsey magistrates' court charged with driving recklessly, without a licence or insurance, and failing to stop after an accident. He had been driving a Ford Granada bought for him by his mother when he hit a telegraph pole in Egham, Surrey, and clipped a parked Peugeot. He had attempted to drive away, but a passer-by witnessed the accident and reported it. The case was adjourned, and when it finally came to court later that year Diana claimed in Gary's defence that he had an American driving licence, which enabled him to drive at the age of sixteen and which she thought was valid in England. Gary was fined £140, banned for three months and bound over for a year. Lake, charged with aiding and abetting after claiming he'd given the boy permission to drive, was fined £40.

It all seemed fairly straightforward. Gary, however, had not been idle and, in a bid for pop stardom, had recorded his debut single, a double A-side called 'Dreamer'/'I Wanna Be Loved'. When the case was over, Diana put into action a plan formulated by PR advisor Max Clifford. While Gary changed out of his grey suit and put on a white tracksuit with electric blue stripes, a horse box drew up outside the court and a chestnut mare was led out. Gary climbed onto its back and Diana led him down the street, handing out copies of the record to a bemused crowd. 'A publicity stunt?' she exclaimed, wide-eyed. 'Certainly not, dear!'

In the meantime, Diana's wish for a chat show of her own

was finally granted. It was to be called *Open Dors*, and after a half-hour pilot show featuring Mary Whitehouse and comedienne Judy Carne, she was given the go-ahead for seven more, which would only be shown in the Southern TV area. Although her constituency was much, much smaller, Diana saw herself directly in competition with television's chat show heavyweights, Michael Parkinson and Russell Harty. 'I think my personality is stronger than either of theirs,' she said modestly. 'I've got a better background for the job, too. Michael used to be a journalist and Russell Harty was a schoolteacher. I believe that my experience in show business gives me the advantage. Showbiz folk like me hold a mirror to life. My profession contains the most sympathetic people in the world. We are interested in others. We observe. We study. We understand. And another thing – I speak English beautifully, which is more than you can say for Mike and Russell.'

Diana liked to be quite daring with her choice of guests, and tried to avoid blandness whenever possible. She had Lord Montagu debating the future of the monarchy with anti-royalist MP Willie Hamilton, and Lord Longford discussing pornography with Paul Raymond. The series received good reviews and, although it was never networked, it paved the way for a six-part ITV lunchtime 'conversation' series, called simply *The Diana Dors Show*. Again, the shows had a different theme each week – style, fortune-telling, even 'What turns a woman on?' – and she handled the task admirably. It reminded her of a game they used to play at her parties at Orchard Manor years ago, called 'Hot Seat', where one of her guests would sit in a chair and the others would take turns asking probing questions. The victim had to tell the truth and if the others weren't satisfied with his or her answer, a forfeit was introduced. Diana abandoned the game when it became clear it was having an adverse effect on her friends' relationships. She was always amazed by the things people were prepared to say in public.

Diana was looking forward to her fiftieth birthday, it seemed a testament to her resilience that she was still in the business after thirty-five years. She was even appearing on *Top of the Pops*, making a cameo as a shimmering fairy godmother in the faux pantomime video to Adam Ant's 'Prince Charming', which entered the charts at Number One. They'd filmed at Shepperton Studios, where she'd made *Lady Godiva Rides Again* some thirty years before, and the memories came flooding back – Dennis, rushing through the corridor with an armful of flowers – as if no time at all had passed. It was 1981 and punk rock had come and gone, deposing the previous music scene's aristocracy with the same energy and venom that had toppled Diana's generation, but, really, nothing had changed in her world. She liked Adam but didn't think much of his music and she told him so to his face. She still preferred sixties music – the Beatles, the Stones, before they 'went weird' . . . that sort of thing.

Life seemed to be evening out. As part of reformation of the tax laws, new legislation had come in on 1 October 1978, giving an automatic discharge to anyone who had been bankrupt for ten years or more. Diana didn't know how much of the debt had been written off and she didn't like to think about it. She toasted her birthday at a lavish lunch in Kensington, hosted by the publishers of her recently released autobiography, *Dors by Diana*, and happily answered questions about her age. Someone asked how she felt, turning fifty. 'It's like waiting to go to the dentist,' she said. 'Once you get there, it's all right and you feel just the same.' She wasn't one to lie about her age, like some actresses. The way they dropped years, she thought, they must have been in nappies when she worked with them. Accompanied by Alan, Jason and Gary (there was no word from Mark), she moved on to Skindles nightclub in Maidenhead, where she was presented with a heart-shaped cake iced with giant breasts and a giant mouth, a not-so-private joke between her husband and Madam Tits and Lips.

The Lakes still knew how to enjoy themselves and Diana's parties remained the talk of show business. Every so often she threw Orchard Manor open to her friends and for those evenings, it was all systems go. She made sure plenty of single women were free for the night, perhaps even a few professionals, and turned a blind eye while some of her famous friends indulged in a spot of infidelity or perhaps smoked a joint. As she always had done, Diana presided over these nights with almost maternal concern, fetching drinks and food, making her guests feel at home. A lot had happened since the fifties, and Dennis Hamilton's two-way mirror parties had been eclipsed in the early seventies by London brothel-keeper Janie Jones, whose Kensington mansion played host to kinky sex orgies that outclassed even the Profumo set. Diana was no longer the lone trapper on that particular frontier.

She hadn't lost her sense of humour, either. Dennis Gilding, a rather camp young man who handled her cabaret bookings, was surprised to hear his phone ringing at 2 a.m. He answered it and a man's husky voice panted, 'Hello . . . I'm wearing . . . silk . . . stockings . . . and big . . . dangly . . . earrings . . .' 'Listen, I don't mind getting phone calls like that,' yelled Dennis, 'but it's two o'clock in the morning!' Immediately, he heard Diana's hearty, infectious laugh. She'd put Lake up to it and was listening on the extension.

As 1981 drew to a close, Diana began to wonder if the wheel wasn't turning – maybe she was coming back into fashion again. Margaret Thatcher had been in office for the last two years and Britain was in a curious twilight zone, emerging from the discordant, Labour-governed seventies – crippled by strikes, union disputes and inflation – and heading for a short-lived consumer boom, aided by labour reforms, tax cuts and a ruthless privatization drive. 'The people *need* me,' she told the *Sunday Times'* Clive Limpkin. 'In the fifties, when I was Britain's answer to Marilyn Monroe and it was all those tiger skins and waterfalls, I knew it was fake but they lapped it up – austerity days, you see? Now we're going through a depression and they need Diana Dors again. They want a god and I'm their twentieth-century Boadicea, [I] can provide their escapism. I've reached the stage where I'd like to *do* something for people.'

'In politics?' asked Limpkin. No, she said. 'Mind you, the public are fed up with all the parties at the moment. They need a leader, and I like to think I'd make a better prime minister than Margaret Thatcher. I understand the temperature and the climate of the people . . . People can *relate* to me and they can't to her: I'm the girl who came from nowhere. I worry about the advent of nuclear war and germ warfare, and the violence now . . .'

The following year, Diana released a double-A-sided single, a cover version of Peggy Lee's 'Where Did They Go?' and a duet with Gary, on producer Simon Napier-Bell's Nomis label. Napier-Bell had caught her cabaret act the previous year and was thrilled when she included the song in her act – he'd wanted to cover it for years but couldn't find an act so worldly and well-lived to make its sentiments authentic. He even tried to raise £250,000 to mount *This Is Your Life*, a stage musical based on Diana's story, in which dancers and actors would stage key scenes from her life, narrated by Diana herself. 'Diana is a superstar,' said Napier-Bell, 'but for some reason she has not been doing superstar things. I think she's a combination of Boadicea and Liberace. She is Britannia herself.' Diana still wanted her own show and, once again, she advertised herself rather unsubtly through the press, although, fortunately, she stopped short of wearing a sandwich board emblazoned with the words 'CHAT SHOW HOST FOR HIRE'. 'I would love to have a series which combines talking, musical numbers, guests and something which is really ultra-glamorous,' she told *Radio Times*. 'I think we've reached a stage with the recession, the general gloom and the violence and the strikes and everything, when it's a little bit like the days after the war. And, you know, people long for escapism. In fact, they must have escapism in order to carry on. I'd like to provide that, so that people are just transported the way they were in the old days in the cinema, like getting on a magic carpet and just drifting off and forgetting everything.'

But Diana's run of luck was about to change. Gary was becoming frustrated with his singing career and announced that he was flying back to the States at the end of June. Diana was heartbroken but she could see his logic and supported his decision. Hadn't she done the same when she was his age? But, deep down, she was afraid she might lose him, the way she thought she'd lost Mark. Mark never called her, never wrote, and she claimed the only time she ever got to speak to him was when he rang to speak to Gary and she happened to answer the phone. 'Mark doesn't really know me,' she'd told Limpkin, 'and that hurts. It's no good saying you've got the love of two sons out there – to a mother, all her sons are her son. No, that's my biggest regret . . . Mark . . . Not even a card . . .' She still wanted Mark's attention and she wanted him to understand the sacrifice she thought she'd made, but she was running out of ideas. Her last would prove to be the cruellest.

Diana was still working hard to pay the bills. Lake had gone public about his alcoholism many times since the beginning of 1980, in the hope that it would help other sufferers and their families but, ironically, he didn't help himself at all. He did some TV work, a play in Bromley and some voice-overs, but that was about all. 1983 was already an empty book. Diana sometimes thought of herself as a mouse on a treadmill, never taking a holiday, just working, working, working. She was booked to open a hotel on the morning of Thursday 24 June 1982 but arrived feeling rotten. Her stomach was wracked with pains, but she soldiered on, shaking hands and smiling through gritted teeth. Back at home, she collapsed on the stairs and was immediately rushed to the private Princess Margaret Hospital in Windsor.

At the weekend, surgeons operated to remove an ovarian cyst and performed a hysterectomy as a matter of course. This was not routine surgery, however. Afterwards, Lake was taken to one side and told that the operation had revealed cancerous tissue, which had been immediately removed. He kept the news to himself and simply told the press, 'Diana is in great form. She is an incredible woman. She is already itching to get back to work.' A few days later, Diana heard the bad news for herself from a specialist and the words took time to sink in. Cancer? Other people had cancer. Not Diana Dors.

It changed her perspective immediately. She'd been so worried about the mortgage, keeping everything in order, and anxious to get back to work – she was about to start filming *Yellowbeard*, a coarse pirate romp co-written by Monty Python's Graham Chapman. Suddenly, none of that seemed important. She cleared her diary for a few months, breaking her media silence only to fill in for Gloria Hunniford on Radio 2, on condition that she didn't have to 'work all the mechanical things.' She did, however, seriously contemplate a film offer that was still in development. Producer Don Boyd was planning a film biography of the Kray twins and he'd tentatively asked Diana if she would like to play Violet, their mother, who had recently died. Diana had met Mrs Kray while promoting her book and had written a stirring, what's-the-world-coming-to entry about the Krays in *Behind Closed Dors*, which led to a gratefully accepted invitation to visit Reg in prison. 'Violet Kray was a fine, charming woman,' said Diana. 'As a mother, she stood out. Whatever her sons had done, she backed them and fought for them. Every mother could identify with her.'

In May 1983 it had been announced that Diana was joining TVam, a network breakfast TV station set up to take full advantage of the recent deregulation, a measure enthusiastically overseen by Thatcher herself. Regional broadcasters now had to bid for their franchises, a measure that would force rival companies to undercut one another while guaranteeing a certain amount to the Treasury. TVam's launch was troubled and unsuccessful, but its reinvention by producer Greg Dyke was paying dividends largely thanks to the services of a puppeteer and his cult rodent Roland Rat.

Dyke invited Diana onto the show, in a slot that became *Diet with Diana Dors*, every Friday. She wanted to be paid £600 every week, in cash, after each appearance. 'They didn't like it one bit,' she said, 'so I told them, "My way or no way." I'm able to make those kinds of demands, but the small people are the ones who get hurt. I've learnt that there's no sentiment in business, so I'm tough.' She had been trying to lose weight by taking appetite suppressants to keep it down. Now, she could no longer ignore the matter. Throughout the 'fat forties', as she called them, she tried not to look at herself in the mirror. As long as you didn't look, you could kid yourself you were all right. But, finally, she got tired of being called 'plump' and 'buxom' and all the other euphemisms for 'fat'. And she was fed up going into dress shops and knowing there would be nothing in her size. 'I get tired of wearing kaftans that hide a multitude of sins,' she said. 'You yearn to wear something that's skin-tight and shows off a figure you're proud of.'

After taking part in a televised weigh-in on 13 July, Diana's weight was revealed as 14 st 3 lb and her progress was charted each week to see if she was on course to lose her target amount, 52 lb before her fifty-second birthday. She enjoyed her weekly chats and was glad just to be herself. 'To be honest, I'm not really interested in acting any more,' she said. 'I have no great desire to become the best character actress in Britain, or something like that. Someone would have to offer me the most remarkable script before I could get excited.' Nevertheless, she was still open to offers and was considering appearing in a West End stage version of *Whatever Happened to Baby Jane?* with Noele Gordon. On 3 September, however, she was back in Princess Margaret Hospital. In the year since she had first been admitted, Diana had been undergoing treatment, taking tablets and having chemotherapy, which caused hair loss and forced her to use hair pieces. During a routine scan, a trace of cancerous tissue was found and an operation was arranged immediately. The specialist who broke the news told her she was a brave lady – 'I was not,' she said, 'I was scared stiff' – and tried to ease the awkward situation with a good-luck kiss. It didn't help. 'I thought, "God, he wants to be the last man who kissed Diana Dors!"'

Lake was in Greece at the time, filming an episode of the American TV detective series *Hart to Hart*, when Diana called. She didn't want him to worry and told him to stay where he was, but Lake made plans to fly back immediately and was at her bedside before the operation was carried out. She was kept in for eight days and was home in time for Jason's fourteenth birthday, returning to her TV slot after missing just one week's appearance. On 28 October, after a little creative accounting, Diana claimed that she had beaten her target and lost 54 lb. She behaved as if nothing out of the ordinary had happened. 'I don't want to die and I don't think I'm going to,' she told Jean Rook. 'I'll probably see everyone I know out. But maybe this is a test to find out if old Dors, at the end, really does warrant eternal life.'

But the relationship with TVam was turning sour, in particular over the way Diana kept plugging a 'diet calculator' that she claimed had helped her in the past few months. The company withheld over 3,000 fan letters asking for more information about the product and consulted the Independent Broadcasting Authority for advice on the matter. Diana went into a huff and threatened to resign. 'I have no financial interest in the calculator at all,' she said. What she failed to declare was that she was very good friends with the man who did. After a messy, inconclusive court case, Diana was fired by TVam in February 1984, just a few weeks before her contract expired. She also complained that her chauffeur, Vernon Lovejoy, had not been paid for three months, and implied that the company was having severe cashflow problems, but otherwise she showed no visible signs of upset. 'To be perfectly frank,' she said, 'I don't want to be associated with a company which runs rough-shod over small people.'

The following month, Diana started work on what was to be her last film – an adaptation of Nell Dunn's stage play, *Steaming*, about a group of women who meet in a bath house. During shooting, Diana went in for more tests at the the hospital, where it was discovered that 'The Big C', as she called it, was now infecting her lymph glands. She was prescribed a course of tablets, and gave no indication to the film's director, Joseph Losey, that her condition merited any special treatment. Sometimes she didn't even take them, because they made her queasy and affected her performance.

The film had only just wrapped when Diana collapsed,

complaining of stomach pains, and was rushed to hospital on 28 April. Her bowel was blocked, but doctors could not be sure whether the cancer was responsible. Two days later, they operated, removing a large intestinal blockage and draining an abscess that had formed, but it was clear that the cancer had indeed returned and had spread to an inoperable degree. Lake was told she had only a couple of weeks to live, but when he saw her the next day, smiling weakly, he wondered if they were wrong. She'd beaten it twice, couldn't she bounce back again? A priest visited, and they prayed together.

Four days after the operation, it became clear that Diana was not going to make it. Propped up on pillows, wearing her favourite white nightie with green and red polka dots and a treasured gold-letter necklace that spelt out the word DORS, she looked weary and surprisingly serene. It had all happened so fast even some of her closest friends didn't yet know. Lionel Jeffries rang the house and spoke to Jason, who told him that Diana was in hospital. He called the hospital and he was stunned by what he heard. 'I can tell you now,' said Lake, 'I don't think she's got more than a few hours.' 'Right,' said Jeffries, 'we're coming down.' 'No,' said Lake. 'She'll want you to remember her as she was. I *beg* you not to come down.' Instead, he passed the phone to Diana, who sounded exhausted. 'Alan says you'd rather I didn't come down,' said Jeffries. 'No,' she sighed. 'Please . . . It'll be a waste of time.' Jeffries and his wife always wished they'd heard the news sooner.

But Diana was touched by the calls and the cards and asked her husband to thank everyone for their concern. Suddenly, she seemed to focus. 'This isn't the way it was rehearsed,' she said softly. It was a private joke that she and Alan made when things didn't go to plan. That night, she slipped into a coma, and at 9 p.m. on Friday 4 May 1984,

Diana Dors passed away. Lake called Jason at home to break the news, then prepared a short statement for immediate release to the journalists who were gathering in the corridors.

'I lost my wife and a soulmate,' he wrote. 'My teenage son lost a mother, and I think the world lost a legend.'

MORE TROUBLE THAN YOU'LL EVER KNOW

DEATH HAD NOT been an option where Diana was concerned. She'd been through so much, and everyone joked about her invincibility that perhaps she even came to believe it. Lake often said that if the *Titanic* had been named Diana Dors it would never have sunk; Bob Monkhouse quipped that if they dropped the A-bomb on Britain, only Diana and Lord Grade would be left standing. Maybe she truly thought life had thrown its worst at her and she had another thirty years ahead. She sometimes talked about her own death in flippant terms, saying she didn't want to be buried, she'd rather be cremated. 'I'd like to be embalmed, to tell you the truth,' she'd told Ian Woodward, 'and lie around in a glass case – in a museum, with a lot of my old stage dresses and some of my press cuttings – and have people pointing at me, a few hundred years from now, saying "That's what they looked like then . . ."'

For the funeral, which took place a week later at the nearby Church of the Sacred Heart, Diana was suitably dressed, laid out in all her finery, wearing a gold lamé evening dress with matching cape and the gold 'DORS' necklace she was wearing when she died. Lake was wearing the same sober pinstripe suit he'd worn to his court hearing in 1970. After the service was over he intended to burn it.

The little church was filled to bursting with celebrities and friends, like Barbara Windsor, Freddie Starr, Lionel Blair, Danny La Rue and Shirley Bassey, while fans and curious locals gathered outside. Those who didn't, or couldn't attend, sent floral tributes – including the Krays, who sent a wreath with the simple message 'We'll miss you, Diana, from Ronnie & Reggie.' Richard Dawson did not attend and, surprisingly, neither did Gary and Mark, though each son sent a single red rose sprinkled with glitter. Lake thought the boys were on their way and had called them a couple of days before to confirm things; he was deeply upset when they told him they weren't coming. Both, he presumed, were busily pursuing their careers – Mark in television, Gary in music.

For the benefit of those outside, the service was relayed by a public address system, and journalists, photographers and cameramen were permitted to stay during the service. Some of Diana's favourite music was played that day – 'Ave Maria', 'Amazing Grace' and 'Morning Has Broken' – and Patrick Holt, who'd appeared in her film debut, *The Shop at Sly Corner*, back in 1947, delivered a specially prepared tribute. Lionel Jeffries read the lesson from Corinthians, chapter one, and Jim Masters, who had recently been elected mayor of Swindon, also gave a short speech. Masters had invited Diana up to Swindon the previous year and she had been thrilled to accept – he was the only mayor who'd ever asked her. Her visit was short but she promised to come back the following April, 'when the daffs are out', and said she was looking forward to seeing all her old haunts. 'That is,' she said slyly, 'if you've left us any.'

Courteous even at the point of death, Diana had asked one of the priests at the Sacred Heart to ring the mayor and tell him she wouldn't be able to make it just yet. When the coffin was taken outside, Masters was called to the graveside and asked to read his piece again and, as he made his way through the crowd, Shirley Bassey stepped out of his path and bowed gracefully to him. The coffin was lowered into the ground and Lake plucked a single flower from a huge floral cross that lay nearby and dropped it into the open grave. 'I love you,' he murmured.

Although Lake took Diana's death very badly, he managed to hide his misery for a while. It was hard to live in the same house with all her belongings, just as she had left them, and not expect to see her walk in the door or hear her voice. 'To me, she isn't gone,' he said. 'She is still here. I can feel her in every room in this house. And when that feeling gets unbearable I can't help talking to her inside my head. I say, "You can't leave me yet. *You've got to be here.*"'

At first he seemed to cope, but the winter brought so many memories – her birthday, their wedding anniversary, their first meeting – that his troubles just grew harder to bear. Many of his old friends suspected something was wrong, but the first real indications came on 7 October, when Lake was invited to a christening at Freddie Starr's house. He didn't turn up, and rang Starr's publicist the next day to apologize. 'Tell him I'm sorry,' he said. 'I just didn't want to put a damper on things.' That evening Lake visited Starr at his home, looking tired and unusually thin. He sat in Starr's lounge, drinking coffee, trying to put his feelings into words, and left four hours later at 10 p.m.

With Diana gone, Lake had been left with no option other than to sell the house. She had left a trust fund for Jason and Gary, and the rest of the estate to Alan, but in an uncharacteristically vindictive gesture, she actually disinherited Mark. Both Diana's and Alan's wills were filed on the same day in October 1981 – witnessed by their chauffeur and publicity manager – around the time of her fiftieth birthday, which Mark did not attend. It may have been a fit of anger or pique, or maybe it was a sad, last-ditch attempt to get his attention, but wills are flexible and it's likely she thought she'd have plenty of time to change it. Either way, Mark never commented publicly as to whether he knew why she did this.

As Diana had always maintained, Orchard Manor was an expensive place to run and Lake couldn't afford to keep it. It was on the market for £325,000, but losing his home as well as his wife sent him into deep despair. He consulted Father Fontanari at the Church of the Sacred Heart, and the priest was shocked to hear Lake talking in such negative terms. He didn't judge him for his feelings but tried to gently steer him round. 'The way I feel is, "Stop the world – I want to get off,"' said Lake.

At first, 10 October seemed like any other day. Jason had, as Diana always said he would, started working as an actor and he was in rehearsals at the Barbican in a play called *Breaking the Silence*. Lake drove him to the station, where he caught the train to London, then returned to the house where he was expecting prospective buyers to come and inspect the property. His housekeeper Honor Webb noticed that he was restless, wandering from room to room, switching on the lights. 'Don't worry,' she told him. 'Everything will be fine when they get here.' 'No, Honor, it's not that,' he said. There was a pause. 'I am in more trouble than you will ever know.'

At around lunchtime the phone rang; it was columnist Jean Rook, calling to speak to Alan for a few quotes about the sale of the house, but he politely tried to put her off for a few days. 'I'm in a bit of a state,' he admitted. 'It's a bad day today, a very bad day. It's the day I met her.' Softly, he added, 'Everything's going on today. It's bedlam.' At 1.45 p.m., Webb heard a loud bang and ran upstairs to see what the noise was. Opening the door to Jason's bedroom she found Alan Lake lying dead on the floor, a spray of blood on the facing wall. Next to his body lay the shotgun he'd pressed to his head only a few moments earlier. There was no suicide note. The police were informed and Jason was contacted at the Barbican. According to the terms of both parents' wills, Gary was now his legal guardian.

Many of Diana's friends found themselves back in that same church in Sunningdale, a week after Lake's death. Unknown to most of them, his illegitimate daughter Katie attended. She'd contacted Lake three years before and found his family, including Diana, surprisingly welcoming. It was Jason alone, however, who was left to hold everything together. Clasping his Aunt Vilma's hand, he stood expressionless and tearless as they followed the coffin outside. In the churchyard, he laid a single rose in his father's grave. Fellow mourners like Freddie Starr, Kenny Lynch and Anthea Redfern were impressed with the way the fifteen-year-old Jason seemed to be coping. 'I respected Di and I respected Alan,' said Charlie Kray, who proved not the most tactful old cove to invite to a funeral. 'I feel sorry for the boy, but I think he'll survive – he's a strong boy. It's terrible to say, but nobody knows what happens when you're in his position. Your mind goes, and that's it.'

The inquest had shown that Lake was a manic depressive, and that the death of his wife had triggered a psychotic episode. This explained his mood swings, and it seemed likely that Diana was aware of his condition, which would have explained her reluctance to leave him. With Dennis, she was foolish and immature, but Alan's love was so intense that she was prepared to see out the storm – if it ever were to end. In the closing chapters of her final autobiography, *Dors by Diana*, she was curiously cautious on the subject of his rehabilitation, saying, 'I pray to God that Alan remains the wonderful man he has become now that he is cured.' Dr Michael Loxton, the family GP who had treated him for the past fifteen years, revealed that Lake had suffered a serious nervous breakdown earlier in the year. 'During the last few weeks of her life, he hardly left her side,' said Loxton, 'and in the last few days hardly slept. Immediately after her death he was called upon to organize a very public funeral. Due to the physical exhaustion caused by this, his depression returned. He was in this state of weakness and deep despair when he took his own life.'

Lake was buried in the plot next to his wife, and when the soil had subsided, a matching headstone was added. 'Together forever,' ran the inscription.

With Alan gone, it was open season on the Lakes. Newspapers ran spurious accounts of their 'affairs', saying that Diana had planned to run away with her chauffeur and that Lake had been having sex with a sort of vagabond 'maid' nicknamed 'Pixie'. The family linen was duly laundered, and Diana's sad relationship with Mark was blown up into a real-life drama to rival the current vogue for American soaps like *Dynasty* and *Dallas*. There were stories in David Sullivan's tacky *Sunday Sport* newspaper that Diana had had a lesbian affair with Mary Millington, but both women were now conveniently unavailable to comment. Diana made even more headlines from beyond the grave and brought Honor Webb back into the spotlight via frankly ridiculous stories that were told to *Woman's Own*. Webb claimed that Diana's ghost had appeared to her at Orchard Manor, while Lake was still alive, and silently implored her to throw out her wardrobe, which Lake refused to part with. After his death, she said, Lake even made an appearance on the security camera. It was like Piccadilly Circus there.

But when the dust settled, Diana herself was really almost forgotten. By dropping the trappings that made her successful, Diana seemed to epitomize the concept of being famous for being famous – which was cheapened with every passing year by stars and starlets who really hadn't ever done anything to start with. Andy Warhol once said, with a sly ambivalence that went unnoticed, that in the future everyone would be famous for fifteen minutes. Diana Dors was famous for thirty-seven years with scarcely a break, and when she died, she had achieved all her possible ambitions – to be a film star, to be a singer, to be a TV personality. There was only one goal left to tackle: she wanted to be herself. In this she was successful. The ease with which she persuaded the public to accept her as she was, not just as an actress or a performer, made this incredible achievement seem much, much less than it really was. There was no mystery with Diana Dors, her life really *was* an open newspaper, and her refusal to die young, to break under the strain, made her story a peculiar show business tragedy. She was not Judy Garland or Marilyn Monroe – she could cope with pressure and wanted to work right up until the day her body gave out on her. The tragedy was that she had wanted more, and had been prepared to go on.

When she died, Diana was part of the fabric of old England, a cosy, lived-in piece of furniture that everyone was used to, and her death jarred like the passing of a relative. But familiarity breeds indifference, and Diana's ongoing love affair with the public all but wiped out those years of hardship and humiliation. Everyone knew *who* she was, and they all had their opinions about *what* she was, but few on the outside knew how hard, how cruel, that fabulous, glittering life had really been. All the illnesses and accidents aside, she was a survivor in a dog-eat-dog industry, where the path to success was paved with barbiturates and razor blades, selling sex in a country that famously punished the women who dared do so.

Diana Dors epitomized the social upheavals that happened in fifties Britain; the new social mobility which paved the way for the freedoms of the sixties. She had not been hindered by notions of class or gender and simply went out looking for the life she wanted, bending the rules here and there to get it. Diana's idea of 'glamour' was perhaps more in line with the word's archaic roots (an old English word describing the influence of enchantment, or a deceiving charm that makes things seem fairer than they actually are) than any modern concepts of beauty. Like the men of her generation – Teasy-Weasy, or Paul Raymond, or Dandy Kim – Diana was a self-created phenomenon, her own art statement, but she had the inner strength and, above all, sense of humour, to be able to survive. Her relationships left a lot to be desired but she was no candle in the wind. Which, perhaps, was why the British liked her. She was flawed, incomplete, and her efforts to find love in the most misguided places struck a chord with the public. Hers was the voice in 'Come By Sunday' – she wanted warmth in her life, there was a void she needed to fill – which was not the voice of an aloof Hollywood sex queen.

Diana's empire was fake and she knew it, and she was always able to laugh about it. The downside was that she was rarely taken seriously but she was so used to this fact that she never held out any hope of getting any serious work – or at least any serious work that paid well – which would preserve her image for posterity. By the time she died, much of the lifestyle she had pioneered was moving into the public domain. Swimming pools, mansions, flash cars and cream telephones were part of the classless society package that Margaret Thatcher's Conservative party was offering the British public. With the demystification of the stock exchange came the demystification of money, and the idea of making a killing with a paper transaction – by trading shares or selling property – made Diana's work ethic seem really rather quaint and old-fashioned.

Diana had already learned the hard way that she could never really be a movie star – she could only ever be a *British* movie star, and that was not the same thing at all. The film industry in Britain was not special, no one considered it special, and it was not equipped to produce Hollywood stars

– it had the talent but not the budgets or the studio visionaries. Diana Dors failed because Britain's film industry could not compete, and the severity of her reception in Hollywood – over a ducking incident that plainly wasn't of her own making – suggests only that America's movie capital couldn't wait to send the latest pretender packing. Hollywood chose its own stars, putting them through its rigorous studio system – even Monroe was held to her contract at 20th Century Fox – and refused to be impressed by one of Mr Rank's discoveries.

Diana often complained that while Marilyn Monroe was making *How to Marry a Millionaire* in Hollywood, she was up in Manchester making *It's a Grand Life* with the fifties equivalent of Bernard Manning. The comparisons haunted her for the rest of her life, but, really, who won? Marilyn Monroe died with a string of film classics to her name and a tragic reputation as a clinging, neurotic, self-destructive flake. With a few notable exceptions, Diana Dors appeared in some of the worst films ever made, but she never asked for pity and she never made excuses, and the public admired her honesty. Diana knew that, in her case, immortality was not worth dying for.

FILMOGRAPHY

(listed by production date, not release)

Streets Paved with Water (1946,
   unfinished)
The Shop at Sly Corner (1946)
Holiday Camp (1947)
Dancing with Crime (1947)
My Sister and I (1948)
Penny and the Pownall Case
   (1948)
Oliver Twist (1948)
Good Time Girl (1947)
The Calendar (1948)
Here Come the Huggetts (1949)
Vote for Huggett (1949)
It's Not Cricket (1949)
A Boy, a Girl and a Bike (1949)
Diamond City (1949)
Dance Hall (1950)
Lady Godiva Rides Again (1951)
Worm's Eye View (1951)
The Last Page (1952)
My Wife's Lodger (1952)
The Weak and the Wicked
   (1953)
Is Your Honeymoon Really
   Necessary? (1953)
It's a Grand Life (1953)

The Great Game (1953)
The Saint's Return (1954)
Value for Money (1955)
A Kid for Two Farthings (1955)
An Alligator Named Daisy
   (1955)
Miss Tulip Stays the Night
   (1955)
As Long as They're Happy
   (1955)
Yield to the Night/Blonde Sinner
   (1956)
I Married a Woman (1956)
The Unholy Wife (1956)
The Long Haul (1957)
La Ragazza Del Palio/The Girl
   Who Rode In the Palio/The
   Love Specialist (1957)
Tread Softly Stranger (1958)
Passport to Shame/Room 43
   (1959)
On the Double (1960)
Scent of Mystery (1960)
The Big Bankroll/King of the
   Roaring Twenties (1961)
Mrs Gibbons' Boys (1962)

West Eleven (1963)

Allez France (1964)

The Sandwich Man (1966)

Berserk! (1967)

Danger Route (1967)

Hammerhead (1968)

Baby Love (1969)

There's a Girl in my Soup (1970)

Deep End (1970)

Hannie Caulder (1971)

*The Pied Piper/The Pied Piper of
  Hamelin* (1971)

Every Afternoon (1972)

The Amazing Mr Blunden
  (1972)

The Amorous Milkman (1972)

Nothing But the Night (1973)

Theatre of Blood (1973)

Steptoe and Son Ride Again
  (1973)

Craze/The Infernal Doll (1973)

From Beyond the Grave
  (1973)

*Swedish Wildcats/Every
  Afternoon* (1974)

*The Groove Room/What the
  Swedish Butler Saw/The
  Story of . . . a Man and His
  Maid* (1974)

Bedtime With Rosie (1974)

Three for All (1974)

Adventures of a Taxi Driver
  (1975)

Keep it Up Downstairs (1976)

Adventures of a Private Eye
  (1977)

*Confessions from the David
  Galaxy Affair* (1979)

Steaming (1984)

SELECTED TELEVISION
APPEARANCES

Face to Face (BBC, 30 January 1951)
The Bob Hope Show (ITV, 23 May 1956)
Douglas Fairbanks Jnr Presents: The Lovely Place
    (ITV, 11 September 1956)
Armchair Theatre: The Innocent (ITV, 8 May 1960)
A Nice Little Business (ITV, 26 April 1964)
The Unusual Miss Mulberry
    (Untransmitted series, Rediffusion, 1965)
The Inquisitors: The Peeling of Sweet P
    (Untransmitted, LWT, 1968)
Where Have all the Ghosts Gone? (BBC, 8 November 1968)
Queenie's Castle (First series ITV, 5 November 1970)
All Our Saturdays (First series ITV, 22 February 1973)
Thriller: Nurse Will Make It Better (ITV, 11 January 1975)
Sweeney: Messenger of the Gods (ITV, 7 September 1978)
Hammer House of Horror: Children of the Full Moon
    (ITV, 1 November 1980)

DISCOGRAPHY

ALBUMS
Swingin' Dors (Pye, 1960)

SINGLES
'I Feel So Mmm'/'A Kiss And A Cuddle' (label unknown, 1954)
'April Heart'/'Point of No Return' (Pye, 1960)
'So Little Time'/It's Too Late' (Fontana, 1964)
'Security'/Gary' (Polydor, 1966)
'Passing By'/'It's A Small World' (EMI, 1977)
'Where Did They Go?'/'It's You Again' (Nomis, 1982)

BIBLIOGRAPHY

Dors, Diana *Swingin' Dors*, WDL Books, London, 1950
Dors, Diana *For Adults Only*, Star, London, 1978
Dors, Diana *Behind Closed Dors*, Star, London,1979
Dors, Diana *Dors By Diana*, Futura, London, 1981
Dors, Diana *Diana Dors' A–Z of Men,* Futura, London,1984

Selected magazine and newspaper sources
'Intimately Yours', Diana Dors, *Titbits*, October 1953
'Where *Does* Your Money Go?', Ernie Player, *Picturegoer*,
    November 1954
'Diana Dors Ltd', Keith Ellis, *Picturegoer*, February 1955
'Siren From Swindon', Kenneth Tynan, *Picturegoer*, March
    1955
'Are British Films Going Too Far?', John Balfour, *Daily Sketch*,
    13 May 1955
'The Trials of Diana Dors', Robert Muller, *Picturegoer*, June
    1955
'Diana Dors – The Only English Femme Fatale', Eileen
    Winncroft, *Picturegoer*, February 1956
'Diana – Queen of Cannes', Robert Muller, *Picturegoer*, May
    1956
'Why Diana Thinks The World of Miss Dors', Donald Zec,
    Daily Mirror, 21 May 1956
'The Amazing Miss Fluck Pts 1–2', Olga Franklin, *Daily Sketch*,
    9–10 July 1956
'Close That Dors!', Candidus, *Daily Sketch*, 20 July 1956

'The Girl From Swindon Goes Hunting For A House With A Pool And Tennis For Two', Don Iddon, *Daily Mirror*, 30 July 1956

'Hamilton Regrets The End of The Dors Romance', Marshall Pugh, *Daily Mirror*, 3 November 1956

'What Diana Dors Never Knew About Her Ever-Lovin' Hubby', Phillips Chatfield, *Confidential*, September 1957

'I've Been Treated Like A Child', Godfrey Winn, publication unknown, October 1957

'The Dame of the Manor', Donald Zec, *Daily Mirror*, 7 July 1958

'The Far From Shocking News About Diana Dors', Thomas Wiseman, *Evening Standard*, 26 February 1960

'Miss Dors Talks About The Future – As Manager of A Pop Group', publication unknown, August 1964

'I'm Out In The Cold Now, Says Diana Dors', Clive Hirschhorn, *Sunday Express*, 30 January 1966

'I'm Trouble-Prone', Clive Hirschhorn, *Sunday Express*, 15 September 1968

'Plump And Happy, That's Me, Says Diana Dors', Patricia Boxall, *People*, 19 April 1970

'Diana, Freaking Out With Oedipus', Sidney Edwards, *Evening Standard*, date unknown, early 1974

'Where I Went Wrong', Diana Dors, *Woman's Own*, 16 February 1974

'Now That I'm Not Tied Down To Sex And Glamour', Roderick Gilchrist, *Daily Mail*, 20 July 1974

'What Younger Men Tell Diana', Clive Hirschhorn, *Sunday Express*, 15 September 1974

'Men Were My Downfall Says Diana Dors', Clive Hirschhorn, *Sunday Express*, 17 September 1978

'Nobody Knows What I've Been Through', Diana Dors, *Woman*, 21 February 1981

'A Boadicea For The 20th Century', Clive Limpkin, *Sunday Times*, 17 January 1982

Bibliography

'Diana Dors: The Great Survivor', Jean Rook, *Daily Express*, 29
     September 1983
'Alan Lake's A To Z of Diana Dors', As told to Michael Cable,
     Woman, 21 January 1984
'Diana Dors Parts 1–3', Ken Roache, *TV Times*, October 1984

INDEX

A Chance To Meet . . . (TV series), 253

A-Z of Showbusiness (TV show), 154

Adventures of a Taxi Driver, 263

Al Alaam, 106

Aladdin (pantomime), 81

Aldrich, Robert, 141

All Our Saturdays (TV series), 255–6

All-Star Bill (BBC radio show), 73

Allen, Steve, 189, 197, 215

Allez France, 225

Alligator Named Daisy, An, 95

Amazing Mr Blunden, The, 254

Amorous Adventures of Moll Flanders, The, 229

Amorous Milkman, The, 259–60

Anderson, Lindsay, 205

Anderson, PC Roy, 170–1

Andrews, Eamonn, 158, 159

Annakin, Ken, 38–9, 89

Ant, Adam, 273

Any Questions (TV programme), 202

Anzarat, Ray, 72

Arbuckle, Fatty, 138

Armchair Theatre (TV series), 204

As Long as They're Happy, 83

Ashley, John, 208

Ashley, Rosalie, 191

Associated British, 101, 111, 112, 176

Attenborough, Richard, 24

Baby Love, 236

Baker, George, 176–8, 205, 206

Bal Tabarin (restaurant), 209, 212–14

Baldwin, Stanley, 8

Balfour, John, 96–7

Bardot, Brigitte, 90–1

Barnes, Chief Constable Harry, 76

Barraclough, K.J.P., 100

Bart, Lionel, 213

Bass, Alfie, 264

Bassey, Shirley, 283, 284

Bastian, John, 85

Bath, Marquis of, 256

BBC (British Broadcasting Corporation), 114, 129, 158, 253

BBC Radio 2, 277

Beatles, The, 223

Beaumont, Susan, 111
Beauty Queen (Lady Godiva Rides Again), 53
Behind Closed Dors (autobiography), 261, 278
Bentine, Michael, 230
Beresford, Patrick, 43
Bergman, Ingmar, 112
Bernard Delfont Agency, 64
Beserk! (Circus of Blood), 232, 233
Bessone, Jennifer, 138, 146, 191–2
Bessone, Raymond 'Mr Teasy-Weasy', 83, 128–30, 133, 134, 138, 146, 191–2
Big Bankroll, The, 207
Big Money, The, 106
Big Night Out, 224
Black Narcissus, 23
Blackboard Jungle, The, 98–9
Blackman, Honor, 27, 39, 44–5, 230
Blair, Lionel, 283
Blakely, David, 100
Blonde Sinner see *Yield to the Night*
Bloom, Claire, 146
Bogarde, Dirk, 90, 206
Booth, Tony, 267
Boothby, Lord, 224
Borgnine, Ernest, 126
Box, Sydney, 24, 26, 27, 29, 38
Boy, a Girl and a Bike, A, 39
Boyd, Don, 277
Boyer, Jean, 90
Brando, Marlon, 139
Brennan, Amy, 249–50
British Temperance Youth, 156–7

Brook, Peter, 63
Brooke, Henry, 86
Brothers, The, 24–7
Bruce, Lenny, 189–90
Brunel, Isambard Kingdom, 9

Caborn-Waterfield, John, 52
Caborn-Waterfield, Michael (Kim), 5, 42–4, 45–6, 47, 50, 173; arrested, 99–100; in prison, 56–7, 58; and Warner robbery, 78, 226–7
Caborn-Waterfield, Yvonne, 42, 47
Cain, James, MP, 224
Callingham, Clement, 91
Cammell, Donald, 224
Candidus (columnist), 127
Canelli, Georges, 169
Cannes Film Festival, 96, 98–9, 108, 109, 110–12
Carne, Judy, 272
Carpenter, Paul, 191
Carson, Jean, 106
Carstairs, John Paddy, 106
Celebrity Squares (TV show), 260
Chamberlain, Neville, 8
Chaplin, Charlie, 123
Chapman, Graham, 277
Chiari, Walter, 169
Chichester festival, 256–7
Chrisham, Walter, 62
Churchill, Winston, 24
Circus of Blood see *Beserk!*
Clark, Edward, QC, 212
Clark, Leslie, 49

Clark, Petula, 38, 48, 49

Clarke, Robert, 233

Clifford, Max, 271

Clouzot, Henri-Georges, 112

Cockade, 259–60

Cockey, Miss Daisy, 9–10, 16–17

Cockey, Miss Ruth, 9–10

Cogan, Alma, 213

Colleano, Bonar, 48–9, 71, 74, 110, 181–2

Colleano, Rubye, 182

Collins, Joan, 136, 183

Collins, Joe, 182, 183

Collins, Sir William, 91

Come Play With Me, 264

Como, Perry: TV show, 167

Company of Youth (Rank), 26–7, 29–51

Confessions from the David Galaxy Affair, 266–7

Confidential, 144–6, 165–6

Conrad, Jess, 227, 229

Cotton, Bill, 253

Cousteau, Jacques, 112

Cowan, Theo, 32, 33

Crane, Lionel, 136, 190

Crawford, Andrew, 26

Crawford, Joan, 232, 258

Daily Express, 115, 142, 223, 225, 257

Daily Mail, 112, 123, 126

Daily Mirror, 70, 87, 88, 153, 196, 213

Daily Sketch, 17, 93, 127–8

Daily Telegraph, 70

Dalton, Hugh, 29

Dance Hall, 48, 49–50

Dancing with Crime, 24, 25

Dante, Troy, 227, 234–5, 242

Darnell, Eric, 183, 243

Davis, John (JD), 30, 96, 99, 112

Dawson, Gary, 249–50, 259, 269–70, 274; birth, 215–16; and Diana's will, 285, 287; singing career, 271, 275, 276, 284

Dawson, George, 83

Dawson, Mark Richard, 206, 216–17, 249–50, 259; birth, 201–2; disinherited, 285–6; estrangement, 274, 276, 284, 288

Dawson, Richard, 185, 187, 189, 206–7, 284; and children, 208, 209, 225, 249, 250; as comic, 183, 184; divorce, 232; separation, 221–3; wedding, 197–8

Day, Doris, 133

Day, Vera, 191

Dee, Simon, 243

Dent, David, 64, 65

Diador Ltd, 87

Diamond City, 44

Diana Dors' A-Z of Men (book), 261–2

Diana Dors Ltd, 72, 77, 79, 86

Diana Dors Show, The (TV chat show), 272–3

Diana Dors Show, The (variety revue), 182–5, 187

Diana Dors in 3D (book of photographs), 84–5

'Diana Juice', 83

Diet With Diana Dors (TVam slot), 278–9, 280

Dietrich, Marlene, 169

Dior, Christian, 71–2

Docker, Lady Norah, 91–3, 127, 188

Docker, Sir Bernard, 91, 92–3, 127, 188

Doctor at Sea, 99

Dodds, Olive, 30, 31, 31–2, 33–4, 50

Dorne, Sandra, 156, 191, 243

Dors, Arthur, 13

Dors by Diana (autobiography), 6, 140, 161, 175, 273, 287

Dors, Diana (*formerly* Diana Fluck) on acting, 87–8, 100–1, 154, 198–9, 207–8, 228, 257

autobiographies *see Behind Closed Dors*; *Dors by Diana*; *News of the World*, memoirs; *Swinging Dors*

bankruptcy proceedings, 236–9, 243–4

in beauty contest, 19–20

beauty kit venture, 217

birth and childhood, 3–19

birth of Gary, 215–16

birth of Jason, 246

birth of Mark, 201–2

broken leg, 254–5

cancer, 277–8, 279–80, 280–2

car crash, 101–2

career: in America, 59–60, 114–16, 119–50, 189–90, 206–8, 216–17, 225–6; in cabaret/variety, 73–4, 82, 169, 182–5, 187–8, 201, 206–7, 212–13, 216–17, 218, 224, 228, 252; Cannes film festival, 108, 109, 110–12; and censorship, 84–5, 96–8; at Company of Youth (Rank), 26–7, 29–51; at drama college, 20–3; early performances, 11–12, 20, 24–7, 36–9; film contracts *see* Rank Organisation; RKO; films *see individual film titles*; in Las Vegas, 183, 187–8, 201, 206–7; photographic modelling, 19–20, 21, 61, 84–5, 106, 120–1, 246; Showbusiness Personality of the Year, 106; singing, 81, 169, 197, 199–201, 204, 228, 275; stage roles, 22–3, 50, 62–3, 64, 66, 67, 70–1, 246–7, 256–7; TV appearances, 61, 77, 106, 152, 153, 154, 158–9, 167, 168–9, 189, 204, 208, 223–4, 228, 242, 253, 257–8, 260; TV chat shows, 256, 271–3, 276; TV series, 229–30, 251, 252, 255–6, 262, 271–3, 278–9, 280

cinema-going, 9

companies *see* Diador Ltd;
Diana Dors Ltd; Treasure
Productions
cosmetics venture, 198
court appearances, 66, 76–7,
171
death and funeral, 1, 280–2,
283–5
divorce (first), 160–3, 177, 180
divorce (second), 232
driving test, 89, 103
and fashion, 71–2, 112, 119,
183
hair styles, 33–4, 58, 113, 130,
207, 228–9
and Hollywood, 2, 59–60,
113–16, 122–8, 176, 197,
225–6
homes: in America, 132–3,
208, 216, 225; Bray, Berks,
83–4, 105, 143; Dunsfold,
Surrey, 60; Esher, Surrey,
61; in London, 21, 40–1,
45, 47, 52, 79–80, 162,
166–7, 179–80, 226;
Maidenhead, Berks, 105;
'Orchard Manor', Berks,
235, 253, 274; 'Palmers',
Sussex, 168, 180, 198, 199;
'Pavilion, The', Berks,
232–3; Springwoods,
Surrey, 199, 208
image, 1, 81–2, 89–90, 104–5,
153–4, 156–7, 165, 218,
230–2, 275
marriages *see* Dawson, Richard;

Hamilton, Dennis; Lake,
Alan
meningitis, 258–9
as mother, 249–50
and mother's death, 95–6
name change, 23–4
parties, 67–9, 102, 133–7, 220,
232–3, 273–4
pets, 119, 141, 162, 170
piano playing, 14
pregnancies, 48, 61, 101, 199,
209–10, 246, 259, 260
ransom demand, 203–4
relationships: early, 20, 37–8,
39–41, 42–4; with father, 4,
5–6, 7–8, 10–11, 218; with
mother, 8, 9, 10–11, 15–17,
215; *see also* Ashley, John;
Caborn-Waterfield, Michael
(Kim); Dante, Troy;
Newley, Anthony; Steiger,
Rod; Stewart, Darryl;
Yeardye, Tommy
and religion, 254, 255
on retirement, 103, 198
Spencer portrait, 108–9
tax problems, 86–7, 88, 143–4,
232, 234, 236, 238, 273
weight, 37–8, 119, 231, 248,
262, 278–9, 280
will, 285–6
writing, 2, 6, 90, 103–4, 133,
140, 161, 175, 261–2, 273,
278, 287
Dors, Georgina (grandmother),
6–7, 13

Dors, Joe, 13
Dozier, William, 124, 125
Drene shampoo, 21–2, 47
Dunkles, Ernest, 105
Dunn, Nell, 280
Dyke, Greg, 278

Eden, Sir Anthony, 149
Eisenhower, Dwight David, 122
El Dors (club), 160, 162, 165
El Toucan (coffee bar), 98, 103
Elizabeth II, Queen of Great
     Britain, 96
Ellis, Ruth, 100
Elvey, Maurice, 64, 65
English, David, 225
Eveleigh, Mr Justice, 251
Evening Standard, 63, 70–1,
     202–3, 208–9

Farrow, John, 143
Field, Shirley Ann, 147, 180
Figgis, Arthur, 244
Finch, Peter, 108, 111
Finney, Albert, 205, 206, 262
Fisher, Eddie, 133
Flowers, Harry, 224
Fluck, Albert (grandfather), 6
Fluck, Bert (Albert Edward
     Sidney)(father), 5, 11–13,
     17, 45, 57, 119, 201; death,
     218; Diana's birth, 3; and
     Diana's career, 12, 19–20,
     21; health, 3, 4;
     interviewed, 131, 213;
     marriage, 4–5; musical

talents, 3, 4; relationship
     with Diana, 4, 5–6, 7–8,
     10–11, 218; on *This Is Your
     Life*, 158
Fluck, Catherine (*née*
     Carter)(grandmother), 6
Fluck, Mary (Winifred Maud
     Mary)(mother), 25–6, 38,
     45, 57; death, 95; Diana's
     birth, 3–4; and Diana's
     career, 19–21, 34–5; first
     husband, 4, 7; marriage to
     Bert, 4–5; relationship with
     Diana, 8, 9, 10–11, 15–17,
     215
Flynn, Errol, 66
For Adults Only (book), 261
Fowler, Harry, 46–7
Frankie (playboy), 221
Frankie Howerd Show, The (TV
     show), 82
Free Cinema movement, 205
Frewin, Leslie, 102

Gabor, Zsa Zsa, 134, 256
Gainsborough Studios, 21, 24, 26,
     39
Gardiner, Gerald, 127
Gardener, Terry, 25–6, 185, 186
Garson, Greer, 133
Gassman, Vittorio, 163
Gayson, Eunice, 98
George V, King of Great Britain,
     8
Gil (boyfriend), 40, 41
Gilding, Dennis, 274

Girl Who Rode in the Palio, The, 163

Gittins, Stanley, 56

Gobel, George, 113–14, 134

Good, Jack, 228

Goodtime Girl, 37

Gordon, Noele, 279

Goss, Helen, 31

Gracie, Sally, 140, 146

Graham, Billy, 110

Graham, 'Leapy' Lee, 227, 248–9, 251–2

Gray, John, 84–5

Green, Pamela, 264

Gregson, John, 96

Griffith, Derek, 267

Guest, E.R., 173

Guinness, Alec, 30, 41

Gwen, Aunt, 5, 6

Hacker, Bessie, 12

Haigh, Peter, 114

Hall, Willis, 251, 256

Hamilton, Dennis, 55–72, 91, 103, 156, 164; in America, 119–37; boat fire, 173–5; *Confidential* lawsuit, 165–6; death, 190–1, 192, 194–6; as Diana's publicist and manager, 60–2, 65–7, 71–2, 81, 85–6, 89, 93, 96, 110–11, 125–6, 141–2, 147, 149, 150, 151–2, 153–5, 233; divorce proceedings and after, 160–3, 164, 167, 174–5, 177, 180; drunken press conference, 106–8; fights, 99, 135–7, 138–9, 155, 161; ill health, 187, 189; jealousy, 69–70, 157–8; leaves US, 141, 142, 144; marriage to Diana, 57–8; in pantomime, 81; parties, 67–9, 102, 133–7, 220; property investments, 79, 80–1, 83, 98, 105, 126, 132–3, 194–5; and Rachman, 192, 194–5; reconciliation, 154–5, 158, 159; Rogers incident, 75–7; separations, 107–8, 141–55, 160; spending, 93; syphilis claims, 195–6; tax problems, 88

Hamilton, Willie, MP, 272

Hammerhead, 235

Handl, Irene, 264

Hannie Calder, 252

Harbord, Gordon, 23, 24

Harper, Kenneth, 104, 111

Harriman, Averil, 54

Harris, Julie, 31

Harrison, Kathleen, 38

Harrison, Robert, 145

Harty, Russell, 272

Hay, Will H., 138

Hayden, Linda, 236

Hayley, Pat, 235–6

Hayward, Susan, 112

Hearst, William Randolph, 123

Henderson, Dick, Jr, 70

Henley, David, 30

Henry, Joan, 77, 100
Here Come the Huggetts, 38
Hirschhorn, Clive, 230–1, 237, 239
His Majesty O'Keefe, 64
Hitchcock, Alfred, 112
Hoey, John, 160
Holiday Camp, 24
Holt, Patrick, 156, 284
Hope, Bob, 106, 113, 135, 148, 149
Hopper, Hedda, 123, 124, 148–9
House of Commons, 86–7
House of Lords, 127
How Do You View? (TV show), 61
Howarth, Donald, 246–7
Hughes, Howard, 117–18
Hughes, Ken, 207
Huston, John, 84
Hylton, Jack, 67
Hylton, Jane, 26, 38

I Married a Woman, 125
Iddon, Don, 126
In Town Tonight (TV show), 152, 153
Ingrams, Richard, 253
Inquisitors, The, 240, 241, 245
Is Your Honeymoon Really Necessary?, 74, 81
It's a Grand Life, 74

Jacobsson, Ulla, 112
James, Diana, 209
James, Irene, 147
James, Sid, 209

Jean, Ursula, 50
Jeffries, Lionel, 50, 185, 204–5, 243, 253–4, 281, 284
Johns, Glynis, 21
Johnson, Nunnally, 112
Jones, Janie, 274
Jones, Noel Howard, 220
Just William (TV series), 262

Kamera, 264
Kapoor, Lila, 235–6
Kaye, Danny, 113, 207
Kazan, Elia, 139
Keating, 21, 23
Keeler, Christine, 219, 220
Keene, Ralph, 39
Kelly, Grace, 188
Kendall, Kay, 32, 106
Kennedy, John, 209
Kent, Jean, 44
Kid for Two Farthings, A, 82–3, 85, 93, 96
Kim *see* Caborn-Waterfield, Michael (Kim)
King, George, 22, 23
Kit, Aunt, 5–6, 9, 42, 158, 218, 255
Koestler, Arthur, 127
Korda, Alexander, 29, 42
Kray, Charlie, 287
Kray, Reggie, 224, 277–8, 284
Kray, Ronnie, 224, 277–8, 284
Kray, Violet, 277–8
Kretzmer, Herbert, 154, 257

La Rue, Danny, 283
Lack, Gerry, 5–6, 13

Lady Godiva Rides Again (*Beauty Queen*), 53
Lady and the Prowler, The (*Unholy Wife, The*), 126–7, 139, 141, 147, 176, 178
Lake, Alan: acting career, 244–5, 246–8, 262–3, 266–7, 276–7; arrest, 245; assault and conviction, 248–9, 250–1, 252–3; background, 240–1; and Diana's death, 283, 284–5, 286–8; and Diana's illness, 258, 277, 279, 281–2; drinking, 263, 268, 269–71, 276–7; and loss of baby, 260; religious instruction, 254; riding accident, 253; separation, 270; wedding, 242–3
Lake, Jason, 248, 252, 259, 262, 269–70, 274, 279; birth, 246; and Diana's will, 285; father's death, 286–7; mother's death, 281, 282
Lake, Katie, 287
Lancaster, Burt, 64
Landa brothers, 224
Larkin, Philip, 220
Last Page, The, 58
Lawrence, Marjorie, 99
Lean, David, 36
Lee, Belinda, 31, 106, 111, 163
Lee, Christopher, 32
Lee, John, 131
Lee-Thompson, J., 83, 95, 100, 102

Lees, Tamara, 49
Leigh, Vivien, 48, 96
Leon (hairdresser), 130, 152
Lesley, Carole, 84
Liberace, 133, 215
Life with the Lyons (play), 64, 66
Limpkin, Clive, 275, 276
Lippert, Robert, 59–60
Livesey, Roger, 50
London Academy of Music and Art (LAMDA), 20
London Weekend Television, 240
Long Haul, The, 156, 158, 162, 178
Longford, Lord, 272
Losey, Joseph, 280
Lovejoy, Vernon, 280
Loxton, Dr Michael, 287–8
Loy, Myrna, 258
Lucas, Cornell, 32, 116
Lucas, William, 229
Luce, Clare Booth, 98–9
Lupino, Ida, 87
Lynch, Kenny, 227, 287

McCallum, John, 39
MacDonald, David, 44
MacDonald, Ramsey, 8
McKenna, Virginia, 34, 108
McKew, Bobby, 78, 226
Macmillan, Harold, 219, 223
Majdalany (columnist), 112
Man of the World (play), 50
Mankowitz, Wolf, 159
Mansfield, Jayne, 2, 216, 233–4
Markell, Freddie, 75–7

Marks, George Harrison, 264
Marsh, Gary, 24
Martin, Vicky, 54
Mason, James, 215, 222
Mason, Pamela, 215–16, 221, 222
Masters, Jim, 284
Mature, Victor, 156
Maugham, Robin, 87
Mendoza, Joseph, 26, 27
Menjou, Adolphe, 134
Michell, Keith, 257
Michelmore, Cliff, 253
Miles, Vera, 113
Millington, Doreen, 265
Millington, Mary, 265–9, 288
Mink and Millions, 94, 104
Minter, George, 176
Miss Tulip Stays the Night, 82
Mitchelson, Marvin, 222
Mitchum, Robert, 109, 141
Monkhouse, Bob, 68–70, 168,
    169, 283
Monroe, Marilyn, 2, 110, 118,
    134, 198; comparisons with,
    103, 105, 114–16, 121, 291;
    death, 216; and method
    acting, 139–40
Montagu, Lord, 272
Moore, Dudley, 256
Moore, Roger, 190
Morris, Desmond, 17–19, 24–5,
    38
Motion Pictures and Distributors
    Association of America, 138
Mullally, Frederick, 32–3, 128–9
Murray, Pete, 31, 33, 46

My Sister and I, 37
My Wife's Lodger, 64

Naked as Nature Intended, 264
Napier-Bell, Simon, 275
Nasser, Gamal Abdel, 149
National Enquirer, 137
Neville, Richard, 253
New York Times, 156
Newley, Anthony, 39–41, 43, 46
News of the World, 70, 72, 153;
    publishes memoirs, 202–3,
    207, 208–9
Newton, Robert, 86
Nice Little Business, A (TV play),
    223–4
Nimmo, Derek, 262
Novak, Kim, 229

O'Dell, Dennis, 177
Oedipus (play), 256–7
O'Hara, Maureen, 166
Oliver Twist, 36, 39
Olivier, Laurence, 37, 48, 63,
    114, 247
On the Double, 207
On the Waterfront, 139
Onslow, Lewis, 137
Open Dors (TV chat show), 271–2
Oz, 253

Padget, William, 4, 7
Page, Peaches, 210
Page Boy Maternities, 246
Parker, Al, 82
Parkinson, Michael, 253, 272

Parnes, Harry, 228
Parsons, Louella, 123–4, 143
Passingham, Kenneth, 226
Passport to Shame, 178
Pavlow, Muriel, 111
Paws for Dors (TV chat show), 256
Payne, Elijah, 7
Peeping Tom, 264
Penny and the Pownall Case, 37
People, 246
Performance, 224
Pertwee, Jon, 157–8, 191, 195
Philip, Prince, Duke of
    Edinburgh, 96
Phillimore, Lord Justice, 251
Pickles, James, barrister, 85
Picture Parade (TV show), 114
Picture Post, 104–5
Picturegoer, 79, 81–2, 86, 93, 142,
    177, 178
Platz, David, 199
Playbirds, 266
Powell, Michael, 264
Press Council, 202
Price, Henry, MP, 86
Proby, P.J., 228
Profumo, John, 195, 219–21
Proops, Marjorie, 259

Queenie's Castle (TV series), 251,
    252, 255
Quite Contrary (TV show), 129

Racers, The (TV series), 208
Rachman, Perec, 192, 193–5, 219
Radio Times, 276

Rainier III, Prince, of Monaco,
    188
Randle, Frank, 74–5
Rank Charm School *see* Company
    of Youth (Rank)
Rank, J. Arthur, 28–9, 165
Rank, Joe, 28
Rank Organisation, 44, 49, 50–1,
    263; and censorship, 96–8;
    contract offers, 88–9, 96;
    contract with, 26–7, 29–51,
    95, 96, 105–6, 111–12,
    164–5, 168
Raymond (hairdresser) *see*
    Bessone, Raymond 'Mr
    Teasy-Weasy'
Raymond, Jean, 212
Raymond, Paul, 209, 210–14,
    264, 272
Redfern, Anthea, 287
Rediffusion, 229, 230
Reed, Carol, 74, 82–3, 85, 93
Reed, Maxwell, 26
Reisz, Karel, 205
Religious Film Society, 28
Remains to be Seen (play), 67, 70–1
Rendezvous (revue), 62–3, 81
Reynolds, Debbie, 134
Reynolds, Peter, 147
Rice-Davies, Mandy (Marilyn),
    195, 219–20
Richardson, Tony, 205, 229
Richmond, Fiona, 264
Rilla, Wolf, 261
RKO, 113–14, 117, 140, 141,
    156; contract with, 125–6,

138–9, 142–3, 170, 197;
Diana sues, 206
Roberts, Rachel, 205
Robertson, Ker, 127–8
Robinson, Cardew, 264
Robinson, Edward G., 87
Robinson, Robert, 103
Robson, Flora, 30
Roeg, Nicholas, 224
Rogers, Frank, 75–7
Rolfe, Guy, 37
Rook, Jean, 280, 286
Rough and the Smooth, The, 87, 88
Royal Variety Show, 203
Russell, Jane, 118

Sadler, Albert, 183
St John, Earl, 29–30, 96
Sanders, George, 134
Sandwich Man, The, 230
Sapphire (horse), 253
*Saturday Night and Sunday
Morning*, 205
Saturday Spectacular (variety show),
171
Sawyer, Stewart, 135–6, 138, 159
Scent of Mystery, 198
Screen Writers Guild, 118
Selby, Tony, 240
Sellers, Peter, 204
Selznick, David O., 117
Shannon, Johnny, 224
Shaw, Susan, 31, 38–9, 181, 182,
242
Sherrard, Michael, QC, 251

Sholl, Frances (Sholly), 130–1,
149, 162
Shop at Sly Corner, The (play),
22–3, 34
Shoup, Howard, 135
Shrivenham American University
(SAU), 20
Shurr, Louis, 135, 148, 149
Shute, Nevil, 108
Sight and Sound, 113
Sillitoe, Alan, 205
Silva, Simone, 109–10, 124,
171–2
Silver, James, 109
Simmons, Jean, 23
Sinden, Donald, 111
Siodmak, Robert, 37
Size, Mary, 77
Skene, Anthony, 26, 27
Skolimowski, Jerzy, 248
Slocombe, Douglas, 176
Smith, Constance, 31
Smith, Eric L'Epine, 22, 23
Soldier, 19
South Africa, 188–9
Spencer, Stanley, 108–9
Spinetti, Victor, 79–80, 87
Squires, Dorothy, 190
Stack, Anthony, 248–9, 251
Star, The, 70
Starr, Freddie, 283, 285, 287
Steaming, 280
Steel, Anthony, 31, 32, 205
Steiger, Rod, 139–41, 142–3,
144, 146, 147, 150, 167
Steinman, Harry, 197

Steptoe and Son Ride Again, 263

Steve Allen Show, The, 189, 197

Stewart, Darryl, 221, 223, 226

Stewart, Captain Walter, 233

Stocks, Mary, 201–2

Stott, Wally, 199, 201

Strasberg, Lee, 139

Strasberg, Paula, 139–40

Streets Paved with Water, 26, 27

Sullivan, David, 264, 265, 266, 267, 288

Sunday Express, 90, 179, 230, 237

Sunday Night at the London Palladium (TV show), 168–9, 208

Sunday Pictorial, 43, 154; garden party, 32–3

Sunday Sport, 288

Sunday Telegraph, 221

Sunday Times, 275

Swindon, Wilts, 3, 8–9, 23–4, 38, 77–8, 179, 284; during World War II, 13–14, 15

Swindon Scooter Club, 179

Swindon Town Hockey Club, 77–8

Swingin' Dors (album), 199–201, 204

Swinging Dors (autobiography), 2, 161

Taylor, William Desmond, 138

Terraine, Molly, 31–2, 33, 37

Terry-Thomas (comedy actor), 61, 77, 215

Tesler, Brian, 168

Thank Your Lucky Stars (TV show), 228

Thatcher, Margaret, 274, 275

Theatre of Blood, 263

This Is Your Life (idea for musical), 275

This Is Your Life (TV show), 158–9, 230

Three Months Gone By (play), 246–7

Thriller (TV series), 257–8

Times, The, 187

To Sir With Love: premiere, 234–5

Today, 54–5

Todd, Mike, 177

Todd, Richard, 205

Top of the Pops, 273

Town Like Alice, A, 108

Trans-Atlantic Authors, 85

Tread Softly Stranger, 176–8

Treasure Productions, 128, 197, 206

Trinder, Tommy, 106

Turner, Lana, 12, 132, 133

TV Times, 262

TVam (breakfast TV station), 278–9, 280

20th Century Fox, 117, 118

Tynan, Kenneth, 50, 63, 93

Unholy Wife, The see *Lady and the Prowler, The*

Unusual Miss Mulberry, The (TV series), 229–30

Ustinov, Peter, 42, 49

Vadim, Roger, 90
Value for Money, 89, 93, 96, 98
Variety, 206

Walker, Derek, 102
Walker, John, 243
Wallis, Shani, 160
Wanamaker, Sam, 73
Wanger, Walter, 109
Ward, Canon Arthur Evelyn, 53
Ward, Stephen, 53–5, 194, 219, 220
Warner, Barbara, 78
Warner, Jack (actor), 24, 38
Warner, Jack (of Warner Bros), 78, 173, 226, 227
Waterfield, Kim *see* Caborn-Waterfield, Michael (Kim)
Waterhouse, Keith, 251, 256
Watkins, Arthur, 97
Watson, Jack, 19
Watts, Queenie, 264
Wayne, Newton, 70
Weak and the Wicked, The, 77, 78, 81, 81–2
Webb, Honor, 286, 288
Welch, Raquel, 252
Welles, Orson, 117
West 11, 217
Westbrook, Jenny, 260
Weston-Drury, 21
W.H. Allen (publishers), 262

Whatever Happened To Baby Jane? (stage version), 279
Wheeler, Michael, 14–15
Wheeler, Roma, 14
Where Have All the Ghosts Gone? (TV play), 242
Whitehead, Wilfred, 237–9, 243
Whitehouse, Mary, 272
Whitney, Cornelius, 114
Williams, Jean, 35
Wilson, Dennis Main, 73
Windsor, Barbara, 283
Winn, Godfrey, 167
Winncroft, Eileen, 103–4
Winner, Michael, 217
Winter, Thomas, 103
Winters, Bernie, 267
Wiseman, Thomas, 202–3, 221
Wolfit, Sir Donald, 46–7
Woman's Own, 250
Woodward, Ian, 255, 256, 261, 283
Wright, Tony, 111

Yeardye, Tommy, 157, 160, 161, 162, 163–4, 167, 176, 182; arrest, 170–1, 173; as business manager, 185–7
Yellowbeard, 277
Yield to the Night, 1, 100–1, 108, 112, 113, 127, 134, 154; US release (as *Blonde Sinner*), 134, 156

Zec, Donald, 109, 147, 158–9